Bewdley Institute

21-23 Load Street:

a sketch from c1875-c1950

Titles in this series:

1. 'Over agaynst the chappell': 21-23 Load Street, Bewdley - the buildings and occupants from c1632 to c1875
2. Coaching and the Wheatsheaf Inn, 23 Load Street, Bewdley
3. Bewdley Institute, 21-23 Load Street: a sketch from c1875 to c1950
4. Bewdley Institute, 21-23 Load Street: founder Edward Pease (1834-1880) and some of his associates

Dedicated to all my family, especially to my late Mother and maternal Grandmother, who spent many happy holidays in Bewdley throughout their lives and who, with my Father, introduced me to Bewdley. Also to my late maternal Great Grandfather, John Cornforth, a foreman at Tangye Brothers' Cornwall Works, Smethwick, for many years.

Bewdley Institute

21-23 Load Street:

a sketch from *c*1875-*c*1950

by
Sue Brown

Privately published 2003 by
Sue Brown
in association with
History into Print, 56 Alcester Road,
Studley, Warwickshire B80 7LG

www.history-into-print.com

© Sue Brown, 2003

All rights reserved

The author's moral right has been asserted.

British Library Cataloguing in Publication in Data
A catalogue record for this book is available from
The British Library

ISBN 1 85858 302 0

Typeset in Times.
Made and printed in Great Britain by
SupaPrint (Redditch) Ltd.
www.supaprint.com

Edward Pease & Sarah Sturge

(from Benson, R. Seymour: Photographic pedigree of the descendants of Isaac & Rachel Wilson, 1912 - reproduced by courtesy of Darlington Public Libraries)

EDWARD PEASE   SARAH STURGE.

1866

EDWARD PEASE, born at Darlington, 24th June, 1834, died 13th June, 1880, aged 46. Married 26th February, 1862, age 27, Sarah Sturge, daughter of Charles Sturge and his wife Mary Darby Dickinson. She was born at Edgbaston, Birmingham, on 26th February, 1836. Married at 26, and died 14th June, 1877, aged 41.

Issue—One daughter.

(I) Beatrice Mary Pease, born 20th February, 1866. Married at St. Mary Abbot's, Kensington, on the 17th February, 1885, age 19, Viscount Lymington, son of 5th Earl of Portsmouth. He was born in 1856. No issue. Now 6th Earl of Portsmouth.

CONTENTS

Acknowledgements	viii
Abbreviations	viii
Illustrations	ix
Preface	xii
Introduction: *If only he could speak...*	xiii
Frontispiece	xiv

Chapter 1:	Numbers 21-23: Bewdley Institute - The birth	1
	The building	14
Chapter 2:	The long-awaited public room/s	16
	Membership	16
	Some of the Life Members	16
Chapter 3:	Social and recreational facilities	24
Chapter 4:	Educational facilities	32
	The Bewdley & Wribbenhall Working Man's Institute	32
	Kidderminster & District School(s) of Science & Art (Bewdley Branch)	34
Chapter 5:	Library facilities	50
	The Literary & Scientific Institution	50
	The Library and Reading Room	50
	The Institute Library	51
	Miss Eliza Mary Sturge (1842-1905), Librarian	53
	The Wigan Library	54
	The County Library	55
Chapter 6:	Some other occupants of Bewdley Institute premises	57
	The Coffee Tavern	57
	The Museum	62
	The Registrar of Births and Deaths for Bewdley sub-district	62

Chapter 7:	[*If only he could speak ...*] *then what a proud history he could tell!*	63
	The Assembly Room	63
	The Institute	63
Appendix I:	Officers, committee members and members (+ Key to symbols)	69
	Members of the Working Party Committee	69
	Original Committee of Management	69
	Trustees	69
	Managers/Stewards/Custodians	70
	Presidents	70
	Vice-Presidents	71
	Chairmen of Committee	72
	Vice-Chairmen	73
	Hon. Secretaries	73
	Hon. Treasurers	73
	Auditors/Hon. Auditors	74
	Librarians	74
	Members, Friends and/or Subscribers	74
	Class Secretaries	82
	Hon. Secretaries of the Bewdley Branch of the Kidderminster & District School(s) of Science and Art	82
	Representatives on the Executive Committee of the Kidderminster & District School(s) of Science and Art	82
	Representatives on the Council of the Worcs. Union of Clubs & Institutes	83
Appendix II:	Some examination results & free studentships, prizes & certificates gained by students at Bewdley Institute	84
Table 1:	Chief Items from Financial & Administration Accounts plus Membership Numbers	92
Notes and References		113

ACKNOWLEDGEMENTS

I owe a great deal to Mr. David Lloyd, M.B.E., M.A., original tutor of Bewdley Historical Research Group, whose expertise and enthusiasm inspired me, and to all members of the Group, past and present.

I am especially indebted to Mr. Bob Tolley, B.Sc. (Hons.), Dipl.Arch., R.I.B.A. - Bewdley born and bred - for his architectural advice and expertise; to former Stewards Tim, who allowed Bob and me to explore the inside and the back of the Bewdley Institute building, and to Mr. & Mrs. David Carr; to Mr. Bob Gawne (current Steward), Mrs. J. Keane and Mr. Bill Sedgeley for their help; to the Institute Committee for permission to use the cover photograph of the Institute and to reproduce the reduced photocopy of J. M. Gething's Plan, 1877; to Mr. David Edwards for his illustration of a lamplighter; to Mr. & Mrs. W. Bond for an 1870s photograph of the Wheatsheaf; to Mrs. W. Baldwin for an aerial view of Bewdley Town Centre; to Mr. Ken Hobson and to the Proprietor of Victor's Hairdressers for permission to reproduce photographs of Bewdley Institute Dinner at the Red Lion, 1935 and of an old dresser, respectively; to staff of the Reference Library at Kidderminster and Worcester County Record Office; to Mr. Peter White of Darlington Public Library; to the *Kidderminster Shuttle/Times*, the Department of the Environment, Ordnance Survey Maps and to Unilever Plc, for allowing me to reproduce items from their publications; to my husband, David, for his photographs; and last, but not least, to the rest of my family for helping solve computer problems, for checking my typescript and maths. and for putting up with me during the twenty-odd years of research on the complex of buildings which is known today as Bewdley Institute, numbers 21-23 Load Street.

Sue Brown

October 2003

ABBREVIATIONS

B.H.R.G. Bewdley Historical Research Group
C.E.T.S. Church of England Temperance Society
D.N.B. Dictionary of National Biography
I.G.I. International Genealogical Index
KS Kidderminster Shuttle
KT Kidderminster Times
M.C.R. Manor Court Rolls/Records
S.O.E.D. Shorter Oxford English Dictionary
V.C.H. (Salop) Victoria History of the County of Shropshire
V.C.H. (Worcs.) Victoria History of the County of Worcestershire
W.R.O. County Record Office, Worcester

ILLUSTRATIONS and PRESS CUTTINGS

Bewdley Institute today (Photo: David W. Brown, 2003) . . . . Front cover

Edward Pease (from *Pease family album no.5*) . . . . Frontispiece

Edward Pease & Sarah Sturge (from *Pedigree of the descendants of
Isaac & Rachel Wilson*) v

Map of Bewdley town centre, 1884, O.S. sheet XIV-1, Scale: 1: 25 000 xi

Bewdley Town Centre, viewed from a hot air balloon (Photo: Mrs. W. Baldwin) xi

Carved Mask, number 23, 1980s (Photo: David W. Brown) xiii

'The proposed new Institute at Bewdley' (KT, 25th December 1875) 2

The lamplighter outside the old *Wheatsheaf* (Artist's impression: David Edwards,
former student at the Royal Academy of Arts, London) 5

Reduced photocopy of J. M. Gething's Plan, 1877 6

Notice: Task of conversion of *Wheatsheaf* is proceeding (KS, 22nd June 1878) and
Advertisements for the opening of the Institute (KT, 5th & KS 12th October 1878) 7

Opening of Bewdley Institute (KS, 19th October 1878) 8

Numbers 21-23 *c*1870s (Photo: Joseph Humphreys, Bewdley watchmaker) 13

Listed building description of numbers 21-23 (Dept. of the Environment, 1986) 14

First Annual Meeting of Bewdley Institute (KS, 31st January 1880) 18

L/Cpl. Charles Minton who died in the Great War (KT, 18th November 1916) 19

Some fundraising events (KS & KT, various dates) 20

Photocopy of advertisement for Sunlight Soap (Unilever Plc) 23

Institute Dinner at the *Red Lion*, Westbourne Street, 1935 (from Purcell, A. & C. and
Hobson, K: Bewdley's past in pictures, vol. ii, B.H.R.G. 1996) 27

Air Gun League results (KT, March 1907) 28

Bagatelle results (KS, November 1905, January & February 1906) 29

Billiards results (KS, 26th March 1910) 31

'Bewdley and the technical education grant' (KS, 18th April 1891) 35

'Bewdley: Technical education' (KS, 24th October 1891) 36

Dairy instruction (KS 20th August 1892) 37

'Bewdley: The Institute Branch Classes (KS, 10th September 1892) and
'Bewdley Branch Classes: Free studentships' (KS, 17th September 1892) 38

Some lectures which took place in the Institute (KS & KT, various dates) 44

Bewdley Library: Book Issues and Opening Hours, March 1944
& Opening Hours, September 1957(KT & KS) 56

An old dresser belonging to the proprietor of Victor's Hairdressers
(Photograph: David W. Brown, c1980s) 59

Opening of Bewdley Coffee Tavern, October 1879 60

Bewdley Life Boat Lodge, I.O.G.T., February 1881 64

Find by Steward James Geddie leads to 'surprise' centenary for Institute,
February 1976 66

Billhead: James Geddie, 22 Load Street (1970) 68

Distribution of Prizes at Bewdley Institute, October 1879 84

Bewdley Branch Classes: Examination results, September 1893 86

Grants earned by Bewdley Branch Classes, October 1893 87

Bewdley Institute Annual Meeting and distribution of prizes, February 1894 88

Bewdley Branch Classes, Art Division: Examination results, August 1894 90

Bewdley Branch Classes, Art Division: Examination results, August 1897
& July 1898 91

Ordnance Survey Map of Bewdley town centre, 1884 (Sheet XIV-I, Scale: 1:25 000)

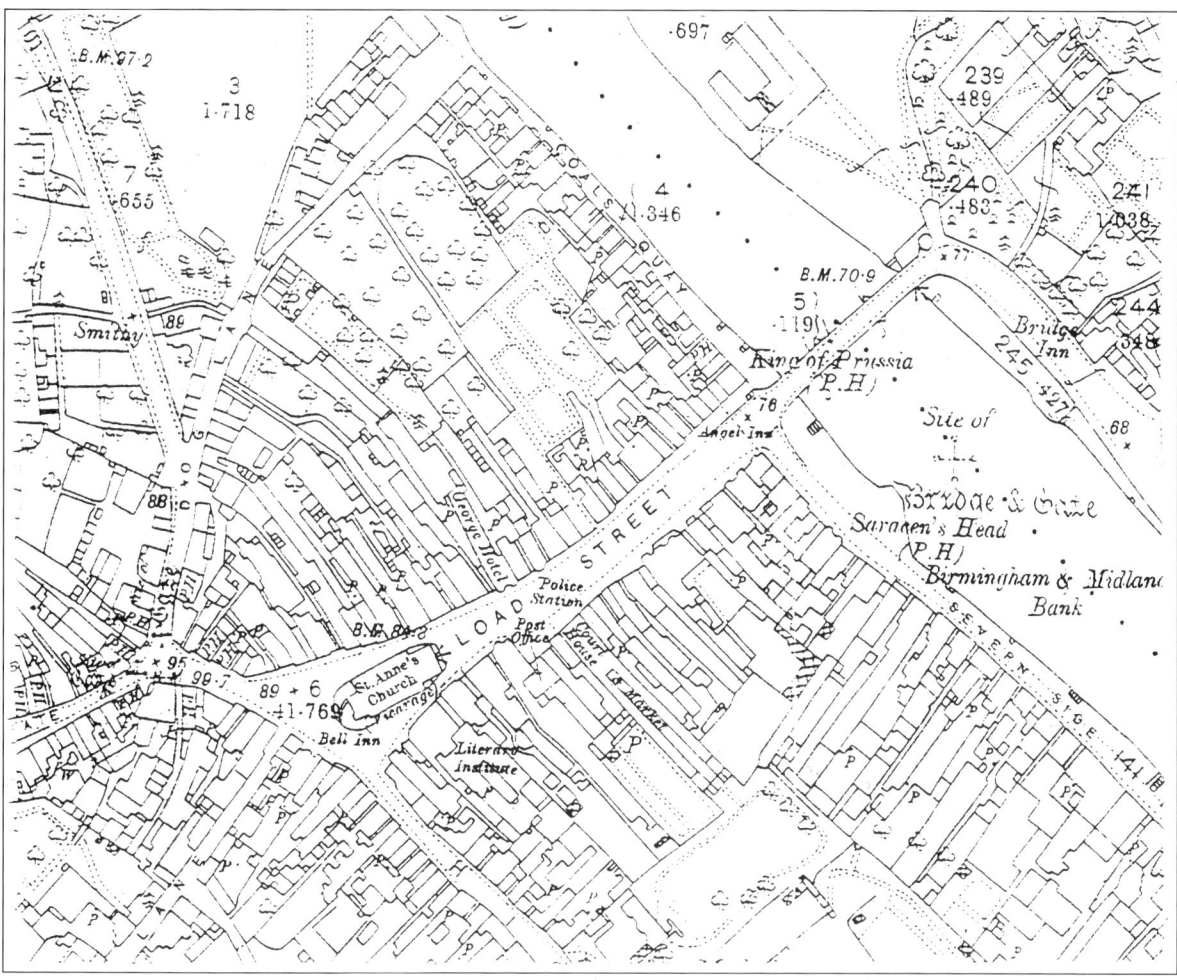

Bewdley Town Centre, viewed from a hot air balloon at about 6.0a.m. one August morning (Photograph reproduced by courtesy of Mrs. W. Baldwin)

Preface

The author is a member of Bewdley Historical Research Group which was founded in 1981 by Mavis Barrett (who suggested the idea), Ken Hobson, Angela and Charles Purcell and Sue Brown and derived from the nucleus of an original Birmingham Extramural Class held in 1971/1972.

All members gather information and, in addition, everyone has a particular area of work or a specific responsibility, with the aim of publishing the results as short, occasional papers. My charge is to co-ordinate data on buildings on the south and west sides of Load Street.

From a wealth of information on Bewdley Institute which has been gathered by all members (including me), I have compiled this and other accounts as preliminary sketches of a building which, perhaps, is under-rated today, but which historic records and architectural evidence show was very important. Although as complete as I can make these studies from the records examined so far (i.e. from c1660-c1950), they are not intended to be definitive histories of either the complex of buildings or its occupants. Neither do they purport to represent anything but my own interpretation. They do not necessarily reflect the opinions of the Research Group. This particular study grew apace - hence the independent venture into print. Any errors and omissions, etc., are entirely my responsibility and I would be grateful for constructive criticism and additional information.

Figures given in brackets after any sums of money quoted in pounds, shillings & pence represent the approximate equivalent in decimal currency (rounded up or down to the nearest penny except where I felt that a more direct comparison was needed) although, of course, a true comparative *value* of money then and now is very difficult to make.

To avoid an excessively long list of references, where none is cited I have taken the information from the Manor Court Rolls (records made when properties of the Lord of the Manor changed hands) or from local Press reports of the Annual Meetings of the Institute.

Although properties in Bewdley were not given street numbers until towards the end of the 19th century, for the sake of simplicity the present-day numbering is used in this text - except where otherwise indicated. So, too, are today's street names.

The Institute Assembly Room, billiards, *Wribbenhall and Bewdley British Schools* and *Kidderminster Schools of Science and Art* are sometimes written in records as singular, sometimes as plural. In this text the form used is that found in the records wherever possible, otherwise brackets have been inserted to reflect both versions.

I have used the capital or lower case forms as found in the records of the social, recreational and educational facilities.

Introduction: If only he could speak ...

A timber-framed building towards the top (west) end of Load Street hides a secret! A secret which, when I discovered it in 1981, inspired me to write this sketch. From the angle formed by the bargeboards of what is nowadays number 23 the carved mask of a man with beard, moustache and curly hair gazes out over a street scene which has changed a great deal since he began his watch in *c*1632!

Today number 23 forms the west end of Bewdley Institute, the address of the whole property being numbers 21-23 Load Street. The middle section of the complex seems to have consisted of two buildings during at least part of the period under review.[1] For convenience, the eastern part of this central section will be referred to as number 22a and the western part as number 22b.

That part of the block at the west end (today's number 23) has been standing since *c*1632, the top storey largely unaltered. By 1788 number 23 was established as the *Wheatsheaf*, one of Bewdley's two principal inns - the other being the *George* on the opposite side of Load Street.[2]

In 1875 Edward Pease, Esq., of Darlington purchased all four properties on the site in this study. Later, he gave the premises to the town as Bewdley Institute, subject to a small chief rent and a small payment to Bewdley Grammar School.[3]

Today the Institute premises house a Club, two shops and a meeting room and, in addition, host regular activities such as Petanque and B.A.T.S. (Bewdley Amateur Theatrical Society) rehearsals. The Wheatsheaf Room (a building in the yard at the rear) is home to a Judo Club and a Weightwatchers' Club.

Pevsner[4] appears to have overlooked the magnificent architectural features of the west end of the building - perhaps because they are difficult to view from the narrow pavement and busy street! This study attempts to trace something of the exciting history of the whole complex after it was adapted to form Bewdley Institute in *c*1875/1877.

Carved Mask, Number 23 Load Street
(Photograph: David W. Brown, 1980s)

Edward Pease, founder of Bewdley Institute
(from *Pease Family Album No. 5* - reproduced by courtesy of Darlington Public Libraries)

Frontispiece

Chapter 1:
Numbers 21-23: Bewdley Institute - The Birth

Towards the end of 1875 Edward Pease offered to give numbers 21-23 Load Street to the town for use as an educational Institute,[5] provided that one thousand pounds could be raised by public subscription to convert the buildings, and that certain other conditions were observed.

A fundraising committee was formed, but 'after some efforts' reported to Mr. Pease that it had proved impossible to raise this amount. Mr. Pease, evidently, was keen that Bewdley and Wribbenhall residents should be able to enjoy the advantages which such an Institute could offer and he generously reiterated his intention to donate the premises, but volunteered to 'reduce his conditions to £500'.

The *Kidderminster Shuttle* of 10th February 1877 reported on a 'crowded and representative meeting' which was held in the Town Hall, Bewdley 'in connection with the proposed Literary Institute at Bewdley', reciting the above and reporting that:

to date, £513 had been promised, 'upwards of £300' being in the bank;[6]

Mr. J. M. Gething, architect of Kidderminster and Stourbridge, had prepared plans showing 'what could be done for £1000, but had also produced a **modified scheme** *'from which it appeared that there would be a good entrance to the buildings, a science room 22 feet by 15* (approx. 6.8 metres by 4.6)*; two class rooms 21 feet by 17* (approx. 6.5 metres by 5.2), *and 27 feet by 16* (approx. 8.3 metres by 4.9); *a reading room 16 feet by 15* (approx. 4.9 metres by 4.6); *a library 16 feet by 11* (approx. 4.9 metres by 3.4); *and apartments for attendants. These would occupy the ground floor. On the second floor there would be a large art room, two committee rooms, a bagatelle room, premises for the attendant and other rooms. The exterior would not be made complete. The tower would not be erected beyond a certain height, and the other portions would be left in an incomplete manner until sufficient funds had been raised to complete the buildings.*

The Committee hoped that the residents would assist them in carrying out the plans in their entirety as soon as possible.'

Having agreed on the importance of the proposed Literary Institute - especially to the young people - the meeting must have moved with alacrity to support the Committee, for a Trust Deed and Plans were approved and signed on 31st December 1877 by the following 15 Trustees of 'Bewdley Institution':

'**Edward Pease**; the **Rev. Edward Henry Winnington Ingram**[7] [Rector of Ribbesford and a relative of Sir Thomas Winnington who had been Lord of the Manor of Bewdley in 1840]; the **Rev. John Fortescue** [Vicar of St. Anne's[8]; the **Rev. John Richard Burton** (Rector of Dowles, 1876-1885[9] and Headmaster of Bewdley Grammar School, 1871/2-1885[10]); **John Gabb** (Surgeon); **Joseph Tangye** (Engineer); **Robert Henry Whitcombe** [snr.] (Solicitor); **John Nicholls, J.P.**; **Richard Hemingway** (Solicitor); **Joseph Tonks** (Chemist [described as Rector at the 1911 Annual Meeting]); **James Parrott** (Ironmonger); and **Thomas Caldwell Dalley** (Stationer): all of Bewdley, and **Jonathan Birtwistle** (Schoolmaster); **Watson Binns** (Agent) and **Thomas Nellist** (Farmer): all of Wribbenhall, near Bewdley; their executors, administrators and assigns.'

Less than twelve months later - on Monday, 14th October 1878[11] - numbers 21-23 opened to both sexes as Bewdley Institute, by which time subscriptions received and the promise of a Government grant of £432-12s-6d. (£432.63) left only £200 to pay!

Proposed New Institute at Bewdley
(press cutting, 25th December 1875 - reproduced by courtesy of the *Kidderminster Shuttle/Times*)

THE PROPOSED NEW INSTITUTE AT BEWDLEY.

SPEECHES BY LORD LYTTELTON AND MR C. HARRISON, M.P.

A public meeting was held in the Town Hall, Bewdley, on Wednesday, "to discuss the desirability of erecting a new institute in Bewdley, on a site which Edward Pease, Esq., has liberally offered to give; and to consider the most feasible mode of raising the necessary funds for the purpose." The attendance was not so large as might be anticipated from the importance of the object in view. Mr. C. Harrison, of the borough took the chair, and amongst those present were Lord Lyttelton, the Rev. J. Fortescue, Rev. R. Gurney, Rev. J. R. Burton, Rev. W. Allen, Messrs. J. Gabb, Whitcombe, Nicholls, R. Hemingway, D. Bury, Morris, DeVit, Dalley, &c.

The CHAIRMAN said the business which brought them together was of very considerable importance to the town and neighbourhood of Bewdley. He had known Bewdley described as a finished town — a place with no further need to be supplied; but he thought those who so described it must have left out of their calculation all those wants which the increased demand for education brought with it. There was nothing on which the mind of the country was so set, as a complete and thorough education of the people, and if the town of Bewdley was able to comply with the Government requirements in primary education, the more primary education progressed and became more efficient — and there could be no doubt that in a very short time the standard of primary education would be raised very considerably — he said it was clear the more primary education was carried on, the more would be the need of secondary education to follow it and supplement it. Now, this secondary education could not be carried on without means and appliances, and the want Bewdley was under, or would be under, would be suitable buildings in which secondary education might be carried on to the advantage of the town. That such a want existed was, he thought, manifest, for in almost all their important towns some provision of the kind had been or was being made. At Birmingham they had the Midland Institute, which was doing very good and efficient work, and no further from them than the neighbouring town of Kidderminster, the late Mayor of the town had presented a very fine site in order that a block of buildings might be erected of a similar character to the Midland Institute at Birmingham, in which the various educational societies of the town might find that accommodation which was absolutely essential. Bewdley had the same wants as regarded education as any of these towns, but, unhappily, it had not the means of supplying them. One difficulty, one great difficulty, was met in a great measure by the offer made to the town by their neighbour Mr. Pease. He had lately purchased the old inn near which they were met, the Wheatsheaf, and was willing to present the site and buildings to the town, on certain conditions, to have the premises converted into an institution which would provide accommodation for various wants in connection with secondary education. He had had no conversation whatever with Mr. Pease on this matter, and was not commissioned in any way to declare his mind, but this much he had understood, that the main condition he laid down with regard to this gift was that never at any time in the future should intoxicating liquors be sold on the premises. This might or might not be a necessary provision to make, but he did not think the place would ever be likely to be used for the sale of such things. That was the one condition. With that exception the building might be used for almost any and every purpose. Mr. Pease thought before making any conveyance of the premises to the town and neighbourhood, that the sum of at least £1,000 should be subscribed. This would be some security in making the conveyance of a valuable property, and in anticipation of the meeting plans had been drawn of what could be done with the present premises by an outlay of £1,000; and he was bound to say after a short examination of the plans that he thought a very considerable amount of accommodation could be offered for the sum of £1,000. The plans were open for the inspection of those interested in the scheme, and the object of their meeting was to lay the matter before the public, and elicit from them a responses as to whether they were willing or not to accept Mr. Pease's offer, and join in a formal effort to provide accommodation, which he ventured to think was wanted in the town. There were some, he had no doubt, who would take exception to any and every plan introduced for furthering the means of education. He had heard some bold enough to declare that education itself, as it was now going on was an unmitigated evil and doing no good whatever. He would not take up time in answering such an objection. (Hear, hear). But there were those in Bewdley who said there was no need for these educational appliances. He thought that objection was hardly a serious one, and if it was it must be held by a small and limited number of persons, and it was entirely contrary to the general feeling of the country at large. They could not go into a town of any size without finding preparations for carrying on the work of secondary education. The want of that education might not be felt so much at the present moment as it would in a few years, but having given primary education they could not stop them. They had the advantage of the presence of Lord Lyttelton, who had always evinced a lively interest in matters connected with education, and evidenced it in that town before now. Some 12 years ago, when the Working Men's Institute was inaugurated, his lordship was present to lend a helping hand, and it was satisfactory to know it had been doing good and effectual work in the town. He must express his own personal conviction that this offer of Mr. Pease, if accepted, would be a very great advantage to the town and neighbourhood. (Cheers.) The offer was made, as he had said, almost untrammelled, with the exception of the prohibition of the sale of intoxicating liquors, and to that prohibition in an institution of the kind he thought there could be no objection made. As to the £1,000, that was a difficulty they could at all events try to meet, and he did not think the town and neighbourhood would be willing to forego the advantage that could be derived from such an institute, and to be the last in the race, instead of emulating the example of neighbouring towns. It was mainly for the benefit of the rising generation of Bewdley that such an institution should be built, and if Bewdley was to keep its head above water, and keep pace with neighbouring towns, the present opportunity should not be lost. He should much regret if there was any reluctance in accepting such an offer. The institute was intended to provide lecture hall, reading rooms, library, science room, art room, elementary education room, museum, and committee room. These would be all highly useful, and might be made of great service. It was only the other day the Government decided to open an art establishment at Dublin, similar to that at South Kensington, and if they once began with Dublin they must go on to other large centres, and include Birmingham, Edinburgh, Glasgow, Liverpool, and Manchester; and so an extensive system must be spread over the country. They must recollect what their universities were doing. They were extending themselves, and taking up what he ventured to think was their proper position as the leading educational institutions of the country. In view of what was going on all around them, they should not let any little matter stand in the way of the acceptance of Mr. Pease's offer.

Lord LYTTELTON moved the first resolution:— "That, having regard to the great efforts which are being made in other places for the advancement of science, art, and literature, it is extremely desirable for the well-being of the inhabitants of Bewdley and its neighbourhood, to accept the generous offer made by Edward Pease, Esq." He said it was an honour to him to be invited to take a prominent part in the day's proceedings. Besides the general connection which he had in virtue of his office with every part of the county, and which at all times he was glad to acknowledge, his especial connection with that place was not very close. It had not hitherto been so close as he could wish it to be with so pleasant and picturesque a place. Neighbourhood in these days was reckoned by time rather than space, and in a short time he should be brought nearer to Bewdley by the railway which was being made. It was not a credit that that railway, which was set on foot 15 years ago, had not yet been brought to a completion, but it soon would be now, and they should then be brought into closer connection. In former times—100 years ago, or more recently—his family had a very particular connection with that borough, and one which, if it were possible, he should be exceedingly glad to renew. Formerly that town of Bewdley was what was called a pocket borough and it was the property of the Lyttelton family. Before the Reform Act the election was in the hands of some half-dozen persons, and the owner of Hagley practically returned the member for Bewdley. They now had household suffrage but if the electors thought proper to depute their privilege to him he should be happy to undertake it. (Laughter). The only other official connection was that of the honourable office of high steward, an office which was hereditary, but during the 39 years he had held it, he had never yet been able to discover that a single duty of any kind was connected with that office. (Laughter) If then he had no special connection, beyond that of neighbourhood, with them, still he did not feel at all out of place, because as they had been reminded, the particular circumstance which gave origin to that meeting was connected with a gentleman who was also not one of the natives of that place, and who, as he understood, only within the last few years had become connected by property with the district. It was to the liberality and philanthrophy of Mr. Pease that they were indebted for the occasion which had brought them together. Mr. Harrison said that town had been called an unfinished town. He confessed he was a little surprised to hear it. He never understood it was very celebrated for the spirit of enterprise. The object in view would, he trusted, constitute an exception to that impression if it did exist, and the very moderate sum of £1,000, which, as he understood, might be taken as the minimum sum, would be procured without difficulty. (Hear, hear.) He had looked at the plans, which seemed very suitable, but he believed they would involve a larger expenditure than had been named. There was very little occasion to dilate on the general subject. Mr. Harrison had very properly described the general object they had in view under the comprehensive term of secondary education, which might be divided into two parts, that dealing with education in grammar and endowed schools, and that carried on in institutions of this kind. In a popular and wide sense, secondary education was a carrying on of one's education during the whole of one's life. He would add one further object to those named by Mr. Harrison for which the institute was purposed—that was the establishment of a working men's club. They all knew that in many parts of the country these clubs had been established and successfully carried on. There was no reason why the several enjoyments which the upper class received from these clubs should not be had by the classes below them. The main object of the clubs was a social one, and for improving the mental qualities of the members. There was one point which he found was not sufficiently thought of in connection with these clubs. If young men did not care to spend their time in lectures, reading, and studying, what was the alternative? They all knew too well that the time not spent in that way was often spent in mischief, dissipation, sin and wickedness. He should therefore be very glad to see a great amount of success attained by that institute. One special reason why he desired to see the success of such institutes especially applied to parliamentary boroughs. Under the recent change in the law householders in boroughs had obtained the franchise, and by that means a great power had been placed in their hands. There was now a claim for the extension of that right of voting to those places at present regarded as the rural districts, but many of which were in reality no more rural than that borough. If they took Balsall Heath, near Birmingham, which was not a parliamentary borough, they found a large and intelligent population, quite as capable of exercising the right of voting intelligently as many residents in that borough, but they were deprived of the privilege which many others possessed. As long as that was the case, those living in boroughs should feel the responsibility and dignity of their position. It was a thing which should be looked upon with great seriousness, to be properly qualified to exercise the power of voting, and how could that qualification be best attained? There was a distinguished member of the House of Commons, formerly member for the neighbouring town of Kidderminster, Mr. Lowe, who said a very sharp and cutting thing, which was not easily forgotten by those who heard it. He was speaking before the late Reform Bill was passed, and spoke as if the working classes would become absolute masters of parliamentary legislation and political power. That was an exaggerated way of putting it, and although a numerical majority, there were many things which influenced them and prevented them all voting the same way. Mr. Lowe said, "I think we should see our masters know their letters." He (Lord Lyttelton) should like to know whether every voter in Bewdley could read and write. It was most desirable it should be so, for the franchise was a great and important power, and persons possessing it, should at least have some amount of education, and some knowledge of English history, and of what was going on in different parts of the world, so that they might exercise their right of voting on intelligent, reasonable, and conscientious grounds. He expressed his satisfaction with the object Mr. Pease had in view ; and in conclusion he urged upon those who might hereafter have the conduct of the institution, not to limit, or attempt to define too closely, the objects they had in view, but to include whatever subject would be for the benefit of the town generally, and come within the scope of the intentions of the liberal donor. (Cheers.)

The Rev. J. FORTESCUE, in seconding the resolution, said there was a line in one of the old poets as to never appealing to the higher powers till they had something worthy of the higher powers to do. They wanted Bewdley to be shown how to raise £1,000. It was all very well to hope to get it, but no one ever got anything by hoping. That institution had not only to be put up, but to be supported, and if efficiently supported it must be by those who used it. He remembered the time when it was proposed to establish a working men's institute in that town, and Lord Lyttelton came to lend them a helping hand. He came, *magna comitante caterva*, and, as he remembered, he (the speaker) could scarcely pack himself into the room. There was, however, a coldness about the present matter which he did not like to see. He could not but think there was a latent suspicion that this was not intended for the object put forth. If that was so, if there was any desire to establish any political dogmas in this institute, the effort would not only fail, but it would deserve to fail. When they came to help the working man they should do it simply and straight-forwardly. They did not want to make him a Conservative or Radical working man. Their business was to give him, as far as they could, a good education, or rather enable him to get that education himself. Their chairman had spoken about secondary education very intelligibly. If a youth did not carry on his education in after life, the chances were, and it was more than chances, that he would forget all he had learnt. If he had not learnt to read what he called comfortably, and did not keep up reading, he would altogether lose the power to read. If these only kept up the power of reading, they did great good. Just let them do what they felt to be right. Let them help their working men, and let them choose their own politics as they chose their own religion. (Hear, hear. Much would depend upon whether working men was sufficiently numerous and desirous of instruction to support an institution like that, and it might very naturally be asked : how about the institute Lord Lyttelton asked them to support 12 or 13 years ago ? It had been supported ever since, and a great number of working men attended it. (Applause.) The property they occupied, and which had been let to them at a low rent, had just passed into other hands, and it seemed a kind of providential arrangement that the present matter should have occurred as it did. If Mr. Pease found out the working men were contributing of their small means to support it, he would not let it drop for want of means. What he had done was, he expected a kind of feeler, as to whether such a place was wanted. No one wanted to put up a pile of building which no one would use after its erection, and what Mr. Pease wanted to find out was whether people would help to put it up and support it. Knowledge was often of pecuniary value to a man, but they should cultivate it not because of pounds, shillings, and pence considerations, but because it would do them good.

The CHAIRMAN said Mr. Fortescue spoke of political objects being at the back of this. He knew of none, and he hoped no one would think there was a political object in view because he took the chair. The idea he should think had not entered Mr. Pease's head, or his own, or anyone else's he should think except Mr. Fortescue's.

The resolution was put and carried.

Mr. GILES SHAW moved 'That a subscription list be now opened, and that the present committee be requested to solicit subscriptions." The committee referred to consists of Messrs. J. Gabb, T. R. Dalley, R. Hemingway, Whitcombe, Newman, Nicholls, Birtwistle, Parrot, Binns, Mellish, Tanuye, Rev. J. Fortescue, and Rev. J. R. Burton. When he first heard of this scheme he expressed disapproval of it, and he feared objectionable subjects might be discussed, and that drinking might be carried on in the institute. When he heard, however, that there would be accommodation for working men to hold their benefit clubs at the institute, it met with his approval. A great deal of drunkenness he was afraid was caused by working men's clubs assembling in public-houses, and the new institute would find them a place of meeting without having to put their hands in their pockets, as at public-houses. He could not himself help the scheme very much, but he would give what he could willingly.

Mr. TANOYE seconded the resolution, and said he saw that the architect had put on the plan of the erection of the proposed institute, the date "1876." He supposed he had in view that a good work could not be done too soon. That was just his own view, and that the Institute would be for the permanent good of Bewdley and the neighbourhood there could be no doubt. They should therefore put their shoulder to the wheel, and each help on the matter. He was not a rich man, but he would offer £50 provided nine or more other gentlemen contribute £50 each. Smaller amounts would he hoped help to make up the £1,000, and secure the object in question.

The resolution was put and adopted.

Mr. GABB said that a resolution had been put into his hands : "That the best thanks of this meeting be given to Edward Pease, Esq., for his generous offer." In the course of his remarks, Mr. Gabb said he did not think the erection of a large room should be included in the scheme. This he thought ought to be left to the Corporation, who had a site for such a room, and invested money which they could use to erect it, and which would by that means yield them six per cent , instead of the three per cent. they were now getting. He was sorry to see so few present, but there were those who would discourage any scheme. Look at the railway. It was said—Who will travel upon it ? But it was brought there, and now see the number of persons who travelled daily. It was the same with these rooms. If provided, it would be found they would be used, notwithstanding what was said by those who had only one idea in their head and no room for another. He hoped Mr. Pease's present of the site would be supplemented by a large donation in money as well.

Mr. NICHOLLS seconded the resolution. He alluded to the fact that out of 16 members of the Corporation only two were present, and complained that members of the Corporation were giving the cold shoulder to the scheme. He himself had been in the Council 20 years, and had been kicked out. (Laughter). He still felt an interest in the town, and should like to see things going on to the advantage of the town. Mr. Pease had made a liberal offer, and he believed it was only the beginning of Mr. Pease's liberality to the town. There was nothing of a political matter in the proposal in any kind of way, but it was made on public grounds to promote the interest and welfare of the working classes of the borough.

The resolution was adopted.

The Rev. R. GURNEY, after pointing out the

advantages of the institute, said he heartily wishes the scheme success. He moved—"That the best thanks of this meeting be given to the Right Hon. Lord Lyttelton, for his great kindness in coming to address this assembly."

Mr. WHITMORE seconded the resolution, and helped to thrash out the notion that politics had anything to do with the matter, by remarking that there were two as good old Tories as any respectable old Tory could wish to see upon the committee, and if anyone imagined that the institute was to be erected for political purposes, they might be satisfied that their interests would be well looked after as long as the present committee was in existence. (Laughter.)

Lord LYTTELTON acknowledged the vote of thanks, and said he hoped no one would be discouraged, because the meeting had not been a large one.

Mr. DALLEY moved, and Mr. PARROTT seconded, a vote of thanks to the Chairman, and the former pointed out some of the advantages of the institute.

Mr. HARRISON responded, and the meeting terminated.

The lamplighter[12] **outside the** *Wheatsheaf* *c*1870 may have looked something like this (artist's impression: David Edwards, 2003) (reproduced by courtesy of the artist, a former student at the Royal Academy of Arts, London)

Note that the entry depicted is roughly on the site of today's Dorian's shop (*cf* the photograph on p.13)

5

J. M. Gething's Plan, 1877
(greatly reduced copy - reproduced by courtesy of Bewdley Institute Committee)

Numbers 21-23: Bewdley Institute - The Birth

Press cuttings regarding the Task of Converting the Old *Wheat Sheaf* & Advertising the Opening of Bewdley Institute, 1878

(reproduced by courtesy of the *Kidderminster Shuttle/Times*)

KS 22-6-1878 p8

BEWDLEY.

THE LITERARY INSTITUTE. — The task of converting the Old Wheat Sheaf premises into a building suitable for a Literary Institute, is being rapidly proceeded with. The builders have reached the second floor of the front building, and the trustees have issued a preliminary notice stating that it is proposed to open the Institute early in September next.

KT 5-10-1878

V.  R.

THE BEWDLEY INSTITUTE

WILL be OPENED on MONDAY, October 14th, with a LOCAL EXHIBITION, BAZAAR, and PUBLIC TEA; and various Entertainments will be give each evening throughout the week.

Classes will be formed at an early date in the following subjects:—

DRAWING, PAINTING, MODELLING, &c.

k469

BEWDLEY.

BEWDLEY INSTITUTE. — This Institute opens on Monday with a bazaar and exhibition, which will be held every day during the week from 11 a.m. till 9 p.m. There will be a tea meeting on Monday and a public meeting at which Charles Harrison, Esq., M.P., will preside. — On Tuesday a lecture by Mr S. Timmins, J.P., of Birmingham. — On Wednesday, dissolving views. — On Thursday, a lecture by Mr Buckmaster; — and on Friday a concert and entertainment.

KS 12-10-1878 p.5

The Opening of Bewdley Institute, 14th October 1878

(report reproduced by courtesy of the *Kidderminster Shuttle/Times*)

THE KIDDERMINSTER SHUTTLE—OCTOBER 19, 1878.

OPENING OF THE BEWDLEY INSTITUTE.

The building committee of the Bewdley Institute are to be heartily congratulated upon the great success, which has attended their unwearied labours in connection with the conversion of the dilapidated buildings known as the Wheat Sheaf Inn into spacious and handsome rooms for educational and scientific purposes. There are many towns in the kingdom of far larger proportions and pretensions (Kidderminster included which cannot boast of such an admirable building, as that which was formally opened to the public on Monday last by Mr J. Gabb, J.P. The history of the progress of the work is a very interesting one. Three years ago an offer was made by Mr E Pease to present to the town of Bewdley, the Wheat Sheaf Inn and two small houses adjoining for a Science and Art Institute, provided the sum of £1000 could be raised to adapt the buildings to the intended purpose. A Town Meeting was called (presided over by the late Lord Lyttleton being the last public meeting which he attended in this neighbourhood), at which it was resolved to accept the generous offer. Mr J. M. Gething was appointed architect, and he prepared plans which received the approval of the Science and Art Department, and have now been carried out. The old inn contained a club room, and several small rooms, which have been utilised; but the only valuable part of the old front was a half-timbered gable, with carved gable boards, and part of the storey beneath it, the tie-beam of which had carved upon it the initials W. M. B., and date 1632. This half-timbered work, of which there are other good specimens, Mr Gething determined to preserve and incorporate with the new front. The design is accordingly Elizabethan in style. The front is 56 feet long, facing North, and has the half-timbered gable referred to at its Eastern end, and the entrance gateway at its Western end. The ground storey is in brick and stone, the room over the gateway being carved up, also in same materials; but the whole of the upper storey is half-timbered. The entrance gateway, entirely of stone, is an elliptical arch flanked by columns, and surmounted by a cornice which breaks forward slightly over trusses, which rest upon the columns. Entering from this gateway we find ourselves in the hall, which has a floor of Mosaic tiles of appropriate pattern and gives access to all the rooms on the ground floor, and, by a handsome staircase of pitch pine, to the landing of first floor. First on the right, we find a Science Class Room, 22 feet by 15 feet, another 21 feet by 17 feet; and on the left a class room 17 feet by 16 feet, and at the end of the hall two rooms of the old inn to be used as library and reading room. The reading room is wainscoted with old oak panelling. Ascending, the staircase opens direct on to the landing of the Elementary Drawing School, 24 feet by 22 feet; painting room, 27 feet by 17 feet, modelling room, 17 feet by 17 feet (the two last being formed out of the old Club room) and ladies' cloak room. Beyond the painting room are the Master's rooms, which formed part of the inn and needed no alteration. In the yard having separate external entrances are chemical laboratory for eight students, and a Workingmen's Club room, 48 feet by 14 feet, divided into two by movable partition. The whole forms an exceedingly commodious and suitable building. The total cost will be about £1200, exclusive of fittings, for which an additional £200 is still required.

The opening ceremony commenced with prayer offered by the Rev. E. H. W. Ingram. Mr Gabb then declared the Institute opened, and expressed the indebtedness of the committee and the town generally to Mr Pease for his generous gift, and the continued assistance he had given to the committee in their labours. He also thanked Mr Tangye for having guaranteed the deficit, and Mr J. Britwistle, the secretary of the building committee, for his untiring energy.

Mr Pease, in a few words, said it must be a source of gratification to the subscribers that they had given their donations before bad trade had come upon them, and expressed the hope that the Institute would be a source of much good to the district.

The visitors, including some of the leading inhabitants of the neighbourhood, then adjourned to the various rooms to inspect the exhibition of articles lent by residents of the district, and which possessed much interest. The list of contributors was a very lengthy one. Mr Pease sent a collection of valuable early-printed books. The "Lyff of the Olde Ancient Holy Fadors Hermites," the first book printed by Wynkin de Worde, was one. De Worde succeeded Caxton, and the book was printed with Caxton's type in 1486. Most of the other nine books were of contemporary date. The Corporation sent two silver maces presented to their predecessors by Queen Anne. The trades of Bewdley were represented by leather from Mr S. Price's tannery, horn goods from Mr G. Humpherson's, and brass articles from Messrs. Smith and Sons. The brass founding business of Bewdley is of ancient date, having been established about the time of the Commonwealth, and is said to be the oldest provincial brass foundry in the kingdom. Now that the railway facilities of Bewdley have been increased a revival of its former commercial activity ought to be aimed at, and the old trades which flourished here extended. At one time Bewdley was the great *entrepot* for the produce of Manchester and the Midlands, which, carried here on packhorses was laden in the barges on the Severn and despatched down the river for subsequent sea transit. Liverpool, then a little fishing village, occupied a very humble position in the world. Among the other exhibits were some splendid ivory carving, lent by Miss Knowles; antique china, Mrs Reynolds; collection of fossils, medallions, and Vallaris ware, Mrs Hemming; a piece of Bath stone sent to be used in the erection of the Wribbenhall Church, containing on one side a large sized crystal, and on the other a quantity of charred wood, two pairs of boots found at Tickenhill, supposed to have belonged to Prince Arthur, a large collection of fossils, gathered in the neighbourhood by Mr Edwin Baugh, brother to Mr T. Baugh, J.P.; collection of valuable shells, Mr

James Humpherson; a case containing a variety of foreign articles, Mr T. M. Tregelles; collection of Welsh, Irish and Swiss oddities, Mr G. Shaw; some splendid embroidery, Miss Baker; top of a worktable, beautifully inlaid with various woods, Mr George Farmers; a 100lbs hydraulic lift, said to have been one of the four lifts used in the erection of Cleopatra's Needle on the Thames Embankment, Messrs. Tangye Bros.; a large number of drawings sent from the Kidderminster School of Art; collection of articles manufactured by George Salter and Co., of West Bromwich, (under the care of J. M. Downing, of Dowles); splendid carved Indian workbox, and model of the sloping tower of Pisa, Mr J. Tangye; a capital bust of Professor Ruskin, given to the Institute by Mr Creswick; large bowl cut out of a solid piece of agate, Mrs E. R. Nicholas; case of stuffed birds, Mrs Cartwright; case of stuffed birds of Paradise, Mrs Clinch. In the room devoted to the bazaar were exhibited on the walls a large number of valuable oil paintings, and water colors, lent by Mrs Marcy, Miss Ransom, Miss Clinch, Mr J. Brinton, Mr Landon, Rev. J. Fortescue, Mr S. Price, and many others. The bazaar was an exceedingly attractive one, some of the articles on view being both valuable and beautiful. At one end of the room was a Good Templar's stall, and during the whole of Monday business was brisk. The ladies who presided at the stalls and superintended the arrangements were Mrs and Miss Harrison, Mrs Burton, Miss Price, Miss Gabb, Miss Flemming, Miss Whitcombe, Miss Owens, Miss Tangye, Miss Ransom, Miss Baker, Miss Rhodes, Miss Molliet, Miss James, Miss Muskin, Miss Jacobs, Miss Sturge, and Miss Crowe.

An Art collection, as it was drolly termed, was held in one of the anti-rooms, and was under the superintendence of Miss Munn.

Tea was provided for the visitors in the Club Room, and in the evening a public meeting was held in the same room, presided over by Mr Charles Harrison, M.P. There was a large attendance including the Revds. E H. W. Ingram, and J. E. Burton, Messrs. E. Pise, C. Sturge, J. S. Wright (Birmingham), J. Tangye, G. Shaw. J. Nicholls, J. Gabb, R. Howling ay, Mrs Harrison, Miss Sturge and others.

The CHAIRMAN said it was with very great pleasure that he acceded to the request made to him that he should preside at the opening of the Institute. At one time he confessed there seemed to him very little prospect that he should ever be called upon to preside at the opening of such a building as they had possessed that day. It might not be known to all how that Institute came to be, and he would describe how it was called into existence. Their excellent friend and neighbour, Mr Pease, became the owner of property in the neighbourhood, and he also became the owner of a well-known hostelry in Bewdley, which was known as the Wheat Sheaf. That was a very old building—almost as old as the borough itself. The house was in a very dilapidated condition, and Mr Pease, being anxious to do something for the good of the place in which he had acquired property, made a proposition that he would make a present of the site and buildings to the people on two conditions—One was that the inhabitants should raise a certain sum within a given time, and the other was that never hereafter should any intoxicating liquors be sold on the premises. The offer was considered by many in Bewdley as a very generous one. Several meetings were held to further the object, and the best mode of raising the necessary funds was fully discussed. He well recollected at one of the meetings being very much annoyed, but disheartened, by a gentleman stating that he should like to see the faces of the collectors on the morning following their attempt to collect subscriptions in the town. The prospect of raising the necessary funds was at low water mark, and a public meeting, over which the present Lord Lyttelton presided, was the means of giving an impetus to the movement. From that time subscriptions began to flow in, and he was correct in saying that now £1000 had been promised towards the Institute, application was made to the Government for support, and by a curious process of calculation the Government determined to contribute the sum of £432 12s 6d. It might seem surprising how the Government came to know the exact amount they should contribute, even to a sixpence, but their subscription to such buildings was always decided upon the amount of cubic space rendered available for the students—so that the residents of the neighbourhood had contributed a little over £600. The committee had tided over their early difficulties, and all who had seen the building must agree with him that a very wonderful transformation had taken place in the appearance of the Wheat Sheaf. The architect had been most successful in preserving the character of the old building, and had given them a very handsome facade which was an ornament to the town. He confessed that when the building was presented to the town by Mr Pease, he was apprehensive lest, in its extremely dilapidated condition it could not be rendered in any way available for the sum proposed; but the skill of the architect and the zeal of those who had assisted him had done wonders, and the rooms were now admirably adapted for the purposes for which they were intended, and all must admit that the best use had been made of everything. He had stated that certain conditions were attached to the handsome gift of Mr Pease. One condition—that relating to the raising of the money—had been complied with. The other—that no intoxicating liquors should be sold on premises—was one against which he had heard some objections. Personally, he must thank Mr Pease for that condition. It would put it out of the reach of any one to be importuned at any future time to introduce the sale of intoxicants—so long at least as that building was maintained in Bewdley as a literary and scientific institution. Some persons had said that every man should be his own judge as to his conduct, but that argument was altogether beside the question. Mr Pease had a perfect right to attach that condition to the gift, and he thought that it would be an additional benefit that for the future the establishment should be a temperance institution. He could not conceive that the least advantage ever could have come from the sale of intoxicants on the premises, and none, he felt persuaded, could say that the Institution would be injured because of the restriction. When the difficulties were at the highest point as to the raising of the money it was suggested that an application should be made to Mr Pease to supplement his generous gift with an additional gift of money; but he was always opposed to such a course; but now that the building was completed he might be pardoned for suggesting that, as a good room was one of the wants of the town, Mr Pease should at some future time be communicated with upon that subject. It was only a hint, and, as Mr Pease was present, he might take it into consideration. The question now arose, having secured that building so admirably adapted for educational, scientific, literary, and artistic purposes, what was Bewdley going to do with it? In towns of any size all over the kingdom institutions of that kind had been established, at which teachers and all appliances necessary for the carrying on of the higher education was provided—an education higher than that provided either by the School Boards or in any of the elementary schools. With foreign countries these kind of institutions had long flourished; and the English nation, feeling the necessity of scientific education commercially and in other ways, saw that if she was to successfully compete with foreign nations—such as France, Germany, Sweden, and even Switzerland—it would be necessary for her to establish such places. Some years ago the Government of that day awoke to that fact, and established the Science and Art Department, and he was old enough to remember the first school of design started in this country in connection with that Department. Since then hundreds of such schools had been established, and the good which had been accomplished could not be over-estimated. He ventured to think that the inhabitants of Bewdley, and particularly the young people, would gladly avail themselves of the means of instruction which would be offered in that Institute. Not only would that be a school of design, but also an Institute for art education, and such an education as would be useful to the students in every department of trade and commerce. There was a room specially provided for the study of chemistry, and he believed there would be classes formed for the study of geology and natural history as well as literature and foreign languages; so that the younger inhabitants of the town having had a fair foundation laid in the elementary schools, would, without having to go any distance have such advantages provided them which would enable them to prosecute their studies to the fullest extent. Mr Harrison mentioned the course of instruction given at the Birmingham Midland Institute during the winter session, and said that that which had for years been given in larger towns had at last come within the reach of the Bewdley youth. The Government of late years had turned its attention to the demands which the people had upon it, for providing education for the masses. They had provided a system of elementary education which already was being duly appreciated by the public, and when he reminded them that already the Government had contributed between £400 and £500 towards that Institute, he should add that they must continue to expect some assistance from Government for proficiency of students, and the Government would keep an eye upon them at their examinations and would be ready to give a helping hand. It was an especial pleasure to him to see that building erected in Bewdley because since he had had the honour of representing that borough he had heard many disparaging remarks about Bewdley, and people had regarded them as a very dead-and-alive sort of people—that it was a "finished" town, that the residents vegetated, very much as cabbages and trees did. He could not remember that any very great effort had been made before to improve the intellectual condition of the population. He did not allude to the establishment of schools, because in that respect he believed the town was amply provided, but he looked upon that movement as a noble effort, and the promise of a great future. It was hardly possible to over-estimate the effects which might be derived from the institution. He could imagine the condition of many of the young men being anxious to attend some such place a few years ago, but absolutely denied any building where they could prosecute their studies, and the only attractions presented to them being of a very questionable character. But now that difficulty would be removed, and it was for the youth to make the best and highest uses of the privileges brought within their reach. He believed that a brighter day was now dawning for the rising generation of the borough and neighbourhood. He could not conclude without alluding to the untiring labours of the committee of management and expressing his great satisfaction at the successful manner in which all the difficulties had been surmounted. He felt sure the committee would be amply rewarded if they saw that the young people of the district were really anxious to avail themselves of the great advantages which that Institution would afford. Several gentlemen had sent apologies for non-attendance. The Vicar of Kidderminster regretted extremely that this being one of the busiest weeks of his busy year, he could not be present. Mr S. Price was out of town, but wished all success to the Institution, and promised to become a supporter. Mr W. Adam, of Kidderminster, was away at Liverpool, but hoped that the Institute would prove a blessing to the town. He felt sure that Lord Lyttelton would have been pleased to be present but for the fact that he was about to take part in a more interesting event during the week. Mr J. Brinton, of Moor Hall, also wished to apologise for non-attendance. In fact it was rather an unfortunate day, as it was the first day of Quarter Sessions. But for that, no doubt the Earl of Dudley, who had been a liberal subscriber to the fund, would have been present on that occasion.

The Rev. E. H. W. INGRAM proposed success to the Bewdley Institute. They could congratulate themselves upon the success which had up to the present attended the efforts to establish that Institute; but they must not suppose that they had succeeded in overcoming all the difficulties. The resolution he proposed involved a certain amount of responsibility. In looking at the progress made by other Institutions, they saw that the one thing they should aim at was to keep clear of any party spirit in connection with the management of the Institute. He did not mean that each one should cease to hold very strong convictions, and that when the proper time arrived they should not give expression to those views, but that they should not unnecessarily bring these views forward, and place themselves into antagonism with those around them. He pointed out the importance of retaining in the Institute the Workmen's Club, as that was one of the means of attracting men to connect themselves with the Institute. There were but few towns in the country where better accommodation was provided for the working-classes than could be found in that Institute and he hoped those advantages would be duly appreciated.

Mr J. GABB seconded the motion. One of the objects of that Institution was to enable the youth of the town to educate themselves after they had been taught how to do so at the elementary schools. The beneficial education of a man's life must take place after he left school, and if the youth of that district made the best use of the opportunities which were now afforded them, there was no reason why Bewdley should long remain behind the rest of the towns in the country. Mr Gabb alluding to the keen competition which existed between England and foreign countries, said that if the English workman would only take the trouble to place himself in an educational sense upon the same level as the workmen of other countries, there was no reason why he

Numbers 21-23: Bewdley Institute -The Birth

should not excel any other people on the face of the globe. He had calculated that if the English race went on increasing at the same rate as it had during the last few years, that in 350 years our race would outnumber the whole of the other races on the face of the earth, and as time went on the struggle would increase, and then those who were best adapted to the circumstances of the times would survive.

Mr J. S. WRIGHT said he supported the motion with very great pleasure. There were many transformations going on in the present day, but he thought the most surprising transformation he had met with was the conversion of the old Wheat Sheaf Inn into the commodious and elegant rooms they had inspected that day. They were in the habit of speaking of Bewdley as a "gone city" with all its glories buried with the past; but there was one thing about Bewdley that whatever might have faded away it was still a very beautiful district. He always came to it with pleasure, and left it with great regret. He was only surprised that there was not a greater influx of persons from the great city—Birmingham—and the neighbourhood, who would add to the material prosperity of the place, and he felt sure would not be backward in lending a helping hand to such works as they were now celebrating the successful completion of. They were greatly indebted to Mr Pease for his initiation of that movement. He had done eminent service to the town. His gift was a noble one, and the residents had subscribed liberally towards the carrying out of that work. He rejoiced at the one condition which Mr Pease had attached to the gift, that it should be a temperance Institute. It was one of the glorious dreams of his life to see the whole population become temperate and anti-tobaccoists. England might glisten in the ray of that beautiful day some time, but whether soon or 350 years hence, when, according to Mr Gabb, our race would predominate, he could not say. Mr Pease had set the machinery in motion, and the question now came what were the people of the town going to do with the Institute. They might as well stick a steam tug in the Severn with no fire under the boiler, as have that Institute in their midst if they did not duly appreciate the advantages which were brought within their reach. He was pleased to learn that it was intended to open the Institute to both sexes, and he would advise the young women of the town to make it a sine qua non that their future husbands should be diligent members of that Institute. While they paid due regard to the recreative feature of the Institute, let them not lose sight of the intellectual improvement of the young, for in proportion as they cultivated the young of the town so would the borough prosper. Every facility was afforded for art study. Not only would good teachers be provided in that Institute; but they were blessed with charming scenery, and they would only have to learn the principles to be prepared to study it practically in the neighbourhood, where nature in its profusion offered every facility for the production of beautiful works of art. There were but few things which could give greater delight and pleasure than the cultivation of that power which was so widely given to all classes of society. It was not the property of the rich only, but of all alike who would apply themselves to the study. He asked his hearers to do what they could to restore the commercial prosperity of that borough, and he knew of few things which would tend to do that more than a constant and warm support given to that Institute,

The resolution was carried.

Mr Giles SHAW moved that the best thanks of the meeting be cordially given to Mr Pease for his generous gift. He said there were some gifts made which were not of much value; others were liberally bestowed, but were not useful, while other gifts valuable in themselves were not appreciated. He thought that the gift of Mr Pease was alike generous, useful, and thoroughly appreciated by the inhabitants. He expressed his unqualified pleasure at the condition attached to the gift by Mr Pease that all intoxicants should be excluded from the building.

Mr J. NICHOLLS, in seconding the motion, said during more than half a century that he had been connected with that borough, no gift so generous and so valuable as that made by Mr Pease had been made. It was true that valuable bequests had been made by persons connected with the district, but that was not a bequest, for Mr Pease was still alive, and long may he enjoy health and much prosperity to see the blessings which he hoped would flow from the establishment of that Institute in their midst.

The resolution was carried amid applause.

Mr PEASE, in reply, said he wished to say a few words as to the why and wherefore of that Institution, and the reasons which weighed with him in endeavouring to bring such an Institute into the town, and first with regard to the restriction as to the sale of intoxicants. He did not look at that altogether in the light of a teetotaler, but rather having in mind the working of two workman's clubs in his own neighbourhood, which were established about the same time. One was started as a temperance workman's club, and in the other intoxicants were sold. The people in charge of the latter place were extremely careful people, of the highest character; but what was the result, that young men who went there each evening with the intention of improving themselves, and he believed had the wish to improve themselves, by degrees were tempted to spend their time in drinking at the club, and eventually became intemperate in their habits, simply from attending the club, and very soon the club had to be closed altogether, while the other club prospered. With such an instance as that before him he felt compelled to make that restriction, although it was painful to differ with so many friends. The better education now given in the elementary schools no doubt prompted the natural craving for knowledge which was the property of almost all young people, and therefore it was their duty to see that craving was satisfied with good and wholesome food. Then there was that other point alluded to, the material objects which that Institution had in view. The amount of competition into which England was brought with foreign nations, had a good deal to do in his decision. In visiting France, Switzerland, and other foreign countries, they found that the communes which corresponded to their boroughs, taking up any of the clever boys as they left the elementary schools and pay for their education at technical schools, where they were taught some of the sciences and trade. In England there was nothing to correspond to that, and what was the result. He was told by one of the most eminent furnace engineers of the day, who had patented processes with regard to furnaces that he had great difficulty in England on account of the ignorance of the foremen of the works in getting his processes carried out. He could send them with the greatest confidence into France, Belgium or Germany, knowing that properly trained foremen would take the work in hand. He was in conversation with a large locomotive builder, and he told him the same story. If they put any delicate mechanism into their engines, they could send the work with confidence to be done on the Continent; but not so in their own country. No doubt his friend Mr. Tangye could tell the same story. He was speaking recently with a dyer of some note, and he told him that the French dyers were far superior to the English. They had a thorough knowledge of Chemistry, and could take up a new recipe and at once carry it out successfully, while English foremen, going altogether by the rule of thumb, spoiled a good deal of material, and were scarcely ever able to obtain the same satisfactory results. No doubt some had read the article recently written by Mr Henderson as to the competition between America and England. He stated that one of the great elements of the greater success of America, was the higher education and the greater sobriety of her workmen. Now what had they to set against all those things. They had first the strength of the Englishman. It seemed to be an admitted fact that Englishmen could turn out more work than any other men in the world. Then there was the perseverance of the Englishman. He was in conversation with a gentleman in France some time ago, and he told him he could not get the same perfection of manual work in France as from the Englishman. The French workpeople were so versatile that they would not keep to the same trade long. He had heard of workmen who were in receipt of good wages, leaving that employment and taking occupation as day laborers, because they would not keep at one occupation long. If Englishmen were properly placed in the race, they had nothing whatever to fear from foreign competition. They found that sterling stuff in the Englishman, partly because of the climate, and partly the result of the race, that was not to be found in any other nature, and he therefore felt that institutions of that kind were the desideratum which had long been looked for. Given the pluck, the energy, and the perseverance of the Englishman, and also the Sabbath, for that he believed had much to do with the success of the English as a working population, and with such educational advantages properly appreciated which were within the reach of most, they need not fear any foreign nation. He trusted that the young people of the town would lay hold of the benefits which that institution was calculated to confer. They could not but believe that if the home became more intelligent, the progress of the nation would be more rapid and durable. He hoped that by bending all their energies of work and play in the hours set apart for recreation and improvement, they would become better citizens and good stewards of all those talents with which they had been entrusted, and be able to look forward to the joy of walking humbly before God, and the rest and blessedness of the hereafter.

Several other speeches were delivered, and the thanks of the meeting were tendered to the subscribers for their liberal donations, and to the Chairman for the great interest he had taken in the progress of the work since its commencement.

Notes relating to some items on display

- a *bust of Professor Ruskin*, (*cf* Wardle, Peter and Quayle, Cedric: Ruskin and Bewdley. Brentham Press for the Guild of St. George, 1989)

- *local fossils* collected by the late Mr. Baugh (*see* Ref. 149)

- a *100lbs hydraulic lift*, sent by the brothers Tangye (*see* Ref. 18)

- *springs*, obtained through Mr. J. M. Downing (*see* Ref. 201)

- The Rev. B. Gibbons (probably the Vicar of Lower Mitton, 1861-1894 (*Source: Worthies of Worcestershire*, p.60) who wrote *Notes and suggestions for a history of Kidderminster*, which was published in 1859 when he lived at Blakebrook)

Photograph of 21-23 Load Street, *c*1870s (taken by Joseph Humphreys, Bewdley photographer & watchmaker - reproduced by courtesy of Mr. & Mrs. W. Bond)

Note dropped kerb to entry between numbers 22b and 23. A Conveyance of numbers 21 and 22a, dated 1807, reserved the entry belonging to the *Wheatsheaf* to the inn's neighbours as 'a right and liberty of a way... including a right of passage for wheelbarrows and also horses but *not coaches or carriages* [my italics] ...'

Thus, although the entry appears to be very narrow, it was evidently wide enough to accommodate coaches and carriages!

Listed Building Description, *c*1986

(reproduced by courtesy of the Dept. of the Environment)

```
SO 7875 SE              BEWDLEY CP           LOAD STREET (south side)

13/145                                       Nos 21, 22 and 23
                                             (The Bewdley Institute)
24.3.70

GV                                           II
```

House, now club and two shops. 1632, partly rebuilt mid-C19 with some late C20 alterations. Timber-frame with rendered infill, rebuilt in brick with planted framing and ashlar dressings, machine tile roof, stacks in ridge. Two storeys with attics lit by casements in the two gables to left and right, central gablet above a roof light; gables have C17 carved bargeboards and finials; four windows: 3-light casement and three 5-light casements, that to right under jettied C17 gable; ground floor: brick, carriage entrance to left with segmental head and engaged stone columns, three windows: 5-light casement to left, then two 3-light casements, all with stone dressings, entrance to shop to right of centre has a 2-pane overlight and glazed door, entrance to other shop is to left of right window with overlight and half-glazed door. Framing: in front only survives to right gable, which is close-studded. On the lower of two collars the date 1632 and on the tie-beam "M/ WB".

The building

When the Institute opened in 1878 the eastern part of the complex had been 'pulled down or converted', the architect employed having been Mr. J. M. Gething. It was probably at this time (1875-1878) that the entry depicted in Joseph Humphreys' photograph (previous page) disappeared.

It seems that Mr. Gething's *modified scheme* for the Institute was not used, for the measurements therein do not quite agree with those in the 1877 Plan approved by the *Trustees* or with the descriptions given in the local Press and Littlebury's 1879 Directory (*see* pp.1, 8 & 63). Perhaps he upgraded his modified scheme, for the total cost of conversion, including fittings, amounted to almost £1,500. Or maybe inflation was rife then, as now!

The *Kidderminster Times*, 19th October 1878, describes the building thus:
'The old inn contained a club room, and several small rooms, which have been utilized; but the only valuable part of the old front was a half-timbered gable, with carved gable boards, and part of the storey beneath it, the tie-beam of which had carved upon it the initials W. M. B., and date 1632. This half-timbered work, of which there are other good specimens, Mr. Gething determined to preserve and incorporate with the new front. The design is accordingly Elizabethan in style. The front is *56 feet long (17.2 metres)*, facing North, and has the half-timbered gable referred to at its Eastern end, and the entrance gateway at its Western end. (sic) The ground storey is in brick and stone, the room over the gateway being carved up also in [the] same materials; but the whole of the upper storey is half-timbered. The entrance gateway, entirely of stone, is an elliptical arch flanked by columns, and surmounted by a cornice which breaks forward slightly over trusses, which rest upon the columns. Entering from this gateway we find ourselves in the hall, which has a floor of Mosaic tiles of appropriate pattern and gives access to all the rooms on the ground floor, and, by a handsome staircase of pitch pine, the landing of [the] first floor. First on the right, we find a **Science Class Room**, *22 feet by 15 feet (approx. 6.8 metres by 4.6)*, **another** *21 feet by 17 feet (approx. 6.5 metres by 5.2)*; and on the left a class room *17 feet by 16 feet (5.2 metres by approx. 4.9)*,[113] and at the end of the hall two rooms of the old inn to be used as **library** and **reading room**. The reading room is wainscoted with old oak panelling. Ascending, the staircase opens direct on to the landing of the **Elementary Drawing School**, *24 feet by 22 feet (approx. 7.4 metres by approx.*

6.8); **painting room**, *27 feet by 17 feet (approx. 8.3 metres by 5.2);* **modelling room,** *17 feet by 17 feet (5.2 metres square)* (the two former being formed out of the old club room) and **ladies' cloak room.** Beyond the painting room are **the Master's rooms**, which formed part of the inn and needed no alteration. In the yard having separate external entrances are [a] **chemical laboratory** for eight students,[14] and a **Working-men's Club room**, *48 feet by 14 feet (approx. 14.8 metres by 4.3 metres),* divided into two by a movable partition. The whole forms an exceedingly commodious and suitable building...'

Littlebury's Directory for **1879** notes that, during the restoration, '... several relics have been found; among the notable are coins of the reigns of James I, Charles I, Charles II and William and Mary, which are in the possession of the Rev. J. R. Burton, and are in a very good state of preservation.' Presumably, these coins are now in the County Museum at Hartlebury or in Worcester City Museum.

Littlebury's Directory continues:
'The subscription for honorary members is 10s-6d. (53p), and ordinary members 5s (25p) per annum.[15] **Refreshments** are supplied by the steward at a moderate charge. There is a **social room** and a **spacious yard for recreative amusements** consisting of skittles, quoits, gymnastics, &c.'

Opening hours were from 7.0a.m. until 11.0p.m. that year. The *President* was the **Right Hon. Lord Lyttelton,** while *Vice-Presidents* were **Charles Harrison, Esq., M.P.,**[16] the **Rev. E. H. Winnington-Ingram**, M.A. and **Samuel Price, Esq.**, the last-named being the Alderman of 1876 and Mayor of 1884[17] and probably the *tanner* of Severn Side. **John Gabb, Esq.**, of number 6 Load Street, was *Chairman of a Committee of 21 members.*

The *Treasurer* was **Joseph Tangye, Esq.** (1826-1902[18]), an Alderman of Bewdley in at least 1884 and 1896.[19] This Birmingham entrepreneur had purchased the freehold of Tickenhill in *c*1873 and was to build Herne's Nest House in *c*1886.[20] He was 'the most prominent technician connected with Bewdley Gas Works';[21] Mr. Jonathan Birtwistle, Master, British School - for boys, girls and infants - Wribbenhall was *Hon. Secretary*;[22]

The *Art Master* was **Mr. W. Tucker**, assisted by **Messrs. J. Birtwistle, A. Longbottom**[23] and **W. H. Vickrage.**[24]

Other staff included:
Lecturer on Practical Chemistry **Rev. J. R. Burton, B.A., F.G.S.;**
Professor of Modern Languages **Monsieur Wuillemin, B.L.;** and
Steward **Mr. H. Sherwin.**

The Rev. E. H. Winnington-Ingram, John Gabb, Joseph Tangye, Jonathan Birtwistle and the Rev. J. R. Burton were all original *Trustees* of Bewdley Institute.

Chapter 2:
The Long-awaited Public Room/s

The need of a Public Room had been felt for some time.[25] Initially, however, there was some suspicion that the Institute would be used for sectarian or political purposes, despite Mr. Pease's stipulations to the contrary. Perhaps these doubts arose because:

• it is natural to be wary of the unknown - and the whole concept of having *their own Institute* would have been entirely new to residents;

• people must have been uncertain of the motives behind unselfish actions of Quakers in general and of Edward Pease in particular. A rich man, he was not a native of the town, so that few members of the local community would have felt that they really knew him; and

• some of his relatives were active in Parliament.

As will be seen, such misgivings were soon proved unfounded.

Membership[26]

At the public meeting on 22nd December **1875** regarding the formation of Bewdley Institute there had been **72** signatories to a subscription list. These can be regarded as the very first members. One hundred years later, membership stood at **200**.[27] Table 1 includes a summary of numbers and changes of rules during the intervening years.

Approximately 38% of members (67 people) joined the Forces during **World War I**, 8 of whom made the supreme sacrifice.

In **1919** £10 from Club funds opened a subscription list for a **War Memorial**, the cost of which was expected to be about £30. When unveiling the Memorial at the **1921** Annual Meeting, Dr. U. W. N. Miles said that, as he read the names thereon, he remembered about 12 years earlier when eight or nine small boys had banded together to form the 1st Company or Troop of Boy Scouts in Bewdley. "The first two names on that List were Frank Tolley and Bert Coldrick. Those boys were among the number then who, with uplifted hand, bound themselves to do their duty to God and the King. The Memorial tablet bore witness to how worthily they had carried out that promise." The inscription on the tablet, which was of oak and bronze, with lettering of hard fired cream enamel, read as follows:

'To the glory of God and in sacred memory of those connected with Bewdley Institute who made that great sacrifice in the Great European War, 1914-1918

Private Thomas Bentley,
 Worcester[shire] Regiment[28]
Lieutenant Thomas Coldrick,
 Worcester[shire] Regiment[29]
Private Herbert Coldrick,
 R[oyal] War[wickshire] Regiment[30]
Private Arthur J. Ewins,
 Worcester[shire] Regiment[31]
Private Reginald E. Heath,
 R[oyal] War[wickshire] Regiment[32]
Lance-Corporal Cha[rle]s E. Minton,
 R[oyal] War[wickshire] Regiment[33]
Lieutenant J[ohn] A[ubrey] Moore,
 South Staffordshire Regiment[34]
Lance-Corporal Frank Tolley,
 Worcester[shire] Regiment.[35]

During World War II at least 20 members joined the Forces.

At the A.G.M. in **1947** it was agreed that a **memorial plaque** be erected in honour of those who had fallen in action between 1939 and 1945.

Some of the Life Members

In 1937 Mr. Edward **Southan** ('Uncle Ted') - 'one of the few remaining original members of the Committee and Steward for several years' - was elected a Life Member in recognition of past services.

1939 saw the election to Life Membership of Mr. Tom **Hobbs**, 'one of only two inaugural members still surviving (the other being Mr. [R. H.] **Whitcombe**, the first Life Member appointed'.[36] Mr. Hobbs, a member for 60 years, recalled that he had been on the site before the Institute was built and confessed to having been "one of the noisy youths who hindered the gentlemen from reading the newspapers in the Reading Room!"

Mr. E. C. **Hemingway** was elected to Life Membership in 1940.

When elected a Life Member in 1944 Mr. E. P. **Shepherd** had been connected with the Institute for 48 years and had been in office for 44, having been *Chairman, Treasurer* and *Secretary* at various times!

At the Annual Meeting in April 1946 a special committee was formed and a fund opened for a presentation to Mr. Plevey, who had recently retired as *Steward* after 17 years. It was proposed to elect him a Life Member but in order to do so formal notice had to be given prior to the Annual Meeting. Mr. A. G. Humpherson therefore gave notice that he would move the proposition at the next Annual Meeting.

For continued good services to the club over a long period, Life Membership was voted to Messrs. W. **Gardner**, B. **Plevey**, A. **Watkins** and T. **Wall** in 1947. The Annual Meeting records that before these elections there were only 3 surviving Life Members, suggesting that Mr. Hobbs was still living. By this time he would have been in his 80s.

Finance and administration

Although it was important to keep a balance between the social and educational aspects of the Institute, it is clear from the Annual Meetings that the social activities brought in much-needed funding towards the upkeep and maintenance of the property. Many were the times when the Institute struggled financially, but members always rallied to its support. A summary of the financial situation can be seen in Table 1.

First Annual Meeting of Bewdley Institute, 1880

(report reproduced by courtesy of the *Kidderminster Shuttle/Times*)

KS 31-1-1880

ANNUAL MEETING OF THE BEWDLEY INSTITUTE.

The annual meeting of the Bewdley Institute was held on Thursday evening, at the Institute, under the presidency of Mr. Charles Harrison, M.P. There was a moderate attendance of members and friends, including Miss Sturge, the Revs. E. H. W. Ingram and O. Parker Ford, Messrs. Gabb, Tangye, C. Sturge, Downing, Dalley, Birtwistle, Peach (hon. sec.), etc.

The Chairman at once called upon the Rev. E. H. W. Ingram to read the first annual report of the committee, which showed the number of members to be 101, an increase during the year. The committee reviewed the work of the institute in the past with feelings of satisfaction. They regretted its present financial position, but hoped the debt would soon be cleared off. On the building fund account there was still a deficit of about £100. The greater portion of this debt was caused by the non-payment of Government grant on the building, which had been anticipated. The annual balance sheet showed receipts amounting to £131 9s. 4d., and the expenditure up to December 31st left a balance in hand of £1 5s. 11d.; but there were now outstanding liabilities which left a deficit of £17 6s. 1d. The course of lectures and entertainments organised by the committee had been well patronised. The educational results of the year had been, on the whole, very satisfactory. Ample provision had been made for enabling young people who had left school to carry on their higher education, and much attention was paid to the imparting of elementary education. The evening classes had been well attended, and some very useful work had been done, many valuable prizes having been gained.

The Rev. Mr. Ford moved the adoption of the report, and expressed the hope that the residents of the borough would come forward and clear off the debt upon the building. Alluding to the question of education, he said it was utterly useless that Acts of Parliament should be passed to compel children to attend school, if no provision were made for them after school life was over; and that need was met by institutes like their own.

Mr. C. Sturge seconded the motion, and

Mr. Harrison, in supporting it, regretted the absence of the president of the institute, Lord Lyttelton. He (the speaker) had taken great interest in the progress of the institution, and, when asked to preside that evening, he felt that for two reasons he could not refuse—first, because he had closely identified himself with the institute; and secondly because, as the Parliamentary representative of the borough, it was his duty to take part in any movements which were for the benefit of the borough. The two great objects of the institute were to provide reasonable and proper recreation but the greater object was for educational purposes. It was extremely satisfactory to see the attention paid in the report to the educational work done during the year: not only were the number of students attending the science classes large, but many of them had greatly distinguished themselves. He thought that there ought to be more members connected with the Institute; but that 60 members out of a total of 100 should attend the School of Art showed how thoroughly art was appreciated. The black feature in the report was the heavy debt upon the building. Still it should be distinctly understood that that was in a great measure owing to the fact that the Government had not as yet fulfilled its promise, made under certain conditions, to give a grant towards the building, and he was convinced that when that grant was received and a special effort made, no difficulty would be found in clearing off the whole of the debt.

The report was adopted

Lord Lyttelton was re-elected President, and the other annual appointments were made.

The Chairman said Mrs. Fortescue had kindly presented to the Institute that day a very handsome graphascope and photographs accompanied, with the following letter addressed to the members of the Institute:—"This graphascope with the accompanying photographs are presented by the widow of their late President and friend, the Rev. John Fortescue (the then Vicar) as a memorial of his interest in, and sympathy for the Institution for which he worked so long and so earnestly. Now, perhaps, that his own day's work is closed, they may recall his anxious and continued efforts to do what would seem to further the well-being and prosperity of the working man himself having lived and died a working man in the Master's Vineyard.

The thanks of the meeting were tendered to Mr. Harrison for his attendance, and similar compliments were also conveyed to the officers for their labours in the past.

Photograph of L/Cpl. Charles Minton
(reproduced by courtesy of the *Kidderminster Shuttle/Times*)

KT 18-11-1916

LANCE-CORPORAL CHARLES MINTON

Birmingham Battalion, son of Mr. W. Minton, Load Street, Bewdley, was reported on September 21 as having been wounded in action. Over a month later, however, he was posted as missing, and his parents have now received official notification that he was killed in action on Sept. 3rd.

Some Fundraising Events[37]
(reproduced by courtesy of the *Kidderminster Shuttle/Times*)

Kidderminster Shuttle, 8th January **1881**
'CAROL CONCERT. - On Monday evening a very successful carol concert was given in the Town Hall, the proceeds of which will be applied to the Lending Library. Among the performers were Mrs. Gabb, Mrs. E. H. W. Ingram, Miss Price, Miss Fleming, Miss B. Fisher, Miss A. Baker, Rev. J. L. Cheshire (sic) and Mr. J. A. Anstice.'

Kidderminster Shuttle, 22nd January **1881**

> CONCERT AT THE TOWN HALL.—A concert was given in the Town Hall on Friday last, the proceeds of which were devoted towards the reduction of the debt on the Bewdley Literary Institute. There was a large and appreciative audience, and the following programme was most efficiently rendered. Miss Fisher's singing of "Bid me discourse" and "Pretty Polly Oliver" was exceedingly good, and Mr. E. Southan's "Bay of Biscay," and "The Gipsy Countess" duett by Miss Fisher and Mr. Harry Whitcombe, were also worthy of being specially mentioned:—
>
> Duet (Pianoforte and Harmonium) ...... Marche aux Flambeaux....Miss M. Fleming and Rev. W. Dunn
> Song..The Message .... Mr. Harry Whitcombe
> Glee..Stars of the summer night....................
> Song..Bid me discourse .... Miss Fisher
> Pianoforte Solo..Gavotte .... Mrs. E. H. W. Ingram
> Song..The blacksmith's son.......... Mr. T. L. Hall
> Violin Solo..Oberon.............. Mr. Horace Fisher
> Song..Turnham Toll .... Miss B. Fisher
> Quartette..Breathe my harp.... Mr. E. Southan, Mr. H. Whitcombe, Rev. W. Dunn, and Mr. T. L. Hall
> Pianoforte Duet...... Sleigh Bells (Reminiscences of Canada...... Miss Fisher and Miss Price
> Song..Pretty Polly Oliver .... Miss Fisher
> Song..Bay of Biscay................. Mr. E. Southan
> Duet..The gipsy countess...... Miss Fisher and Mr. Harry Whitcombe
> Song..A hunting we will go.......... Mr. T. L. Hall
> Trio (Piano and Harmonium)..The crown diamonds.. Miss M. Fleming, Miss Price, and Rev. W. Dunn
> Song..The Mariner................... Rev. W. Dunn
> Glee..Hurrah for merry England ....

The chief event of **1884** was a combined **Sale of Work and Exhibition**, held for two days in November. Opened by the Mayor (Alderman S. Price), the event raised £36 towards a debt of £63. 'Five stalls were erected round the room and in the centre was a boat rigged up with the title "H.M.S. Victory" under the care of two juvenile sailors. In an adjoining room one evening was a most instructive exhibition of scientific instruments and other objects under the superintendence of Mr. Russell, the demonstrator of the Midland Institute. On the next evening members of the Birmingham Microscopical Society revealed the wonders of pond life and various hidden forms of Nature. Mr. Charles Pumphrey of Birmingham was present on two evenings to illustrate by lime-light photographs taken by himself whilst travelling in America, with members of the British Association during its recent visit to Canada.' Thanks were extended to the Committee of the Midland Institute and to members of the Birmingham Microscopic and Scientific Societies for their kind attendance with microscopes and instruments. On the evening of the last day over 100 visitors sat down to a generous 'Yorkshire Tea' provided by Mrs. and Miss Nellist.'

Kidderminster Sun, 17th January **1885**

> **WRIBBENHALL** *Kidderminster Sun 17-1-1885*
>
> CONCERT AT THE BRITISH SCHOOLS.—A concert was given at the British Schools on Friday evening last for the benefit of the Bewdley Institute. There was a large and appreciative audience. Mrs Miller Corbet gave a couple of recitations in her own inimitable style. Miss Maud Pearse played a couple of violin solos very cleverly. In the second one a string snapped, but another was quickly substituted, and the performance resumed. A similar accident happened to the Rev. T. L. Claughton whilst playing at the Town Hall on Monday night. Miss Pearse also sang "Tell me, my heart," and in response to an enthusiastic re-demand, "The Midshipmite." Miss Thomas's "Dolly's Revenge" was also encored, and the whole of the performers were applauded. Programme:—
>
> | | |
> |---|---|
> | Pianoforte Solo...Gavotte | Miss Tangye |
> | Song...The Owl | Mr J. L. Robinson |
> | Song...The Better Land | Miss Emilie H. Thomas |
> | Recitation | Mrs Miller Corbet |
> | Song...Killarny | Miss Maud Pease |
> | Song...I am Waiting | Mr T. Lawley |
> | Recitation | Mr F. Perkins |
> | Song...No Surrender | Mr D. Mackay |
> | Song...The Arab's Farewell | Mr E. Southan |
> | Pianoforte Solo...Gigue and Gavotte | Miss Tangye |
> | Song...The Old Brigade | Mr J. L. Robinson |
> | Recitation | Mrs Miller Corbet |
> | Song...In the Heart of London Town | Mr D. Mackay |
> | Violin Solo...Air Varie | Miss Maud Pearse |
> | Song...Dolly's Revenge | Miss Emilie H. Thomas |
> | Recitation | Mr F. Perrins |
> | Song...Tell me, my heart | Miss Maud Pearse |
> | Song...Ruby | Mr T. Lawley |

A very successful **concert** was held in the Institute **Lecture Room** in October **1885** with Mr. Box, organist of St. John's, Worcester providing the programme.

In January **1886** entertainment organised by Mr. Birtwistle took place in the **British School** because the Lecture Room at the Institute did not accommodate a large audience. Mrs. Miller Corbet [38] and several ladies had helped at the occasion. Admission charge was small, but so many people attended that £3-17s-8d. (£3.88) was realised.

In April **1887** the writers of *Church Monthly* appealed: 'We hope that our readers will extend their kindly sympathy and, still more, their practical support, to the grand Bazaar, which is to be held upon the premises of the Bewdley Institute on Thursday, Friday, and Saturday, April 21st, 22nd and 23rd, for the purpose of raising £100 or more in order to put the Institute upon a really satisfactory footing with regard to its finances.

Now that the **Coffee Tavern** (*q.v.*) is amalgamated with it, an increasing prospect of usefulness is by degrees opening out before it in the hiring of rooms for meetings of different kinds, and in the attracting of young men to the social room &c... The eight years and more that have passed since it was first opened have entirely belied the suspicion (in which we ourselves never shared) that it was intended to be used for religious or political propagandism of a party character, and it would be a most desirable thing if all parties in the town would combine to make it more and more a centre of united work for the social and moral welfare of the inhabitants. We understand that with the Bazaar there will be combined many novel features, including Tableaux Vivants, a Toy Symphony, and Entertainments of different kinds. Lady Lyttelton has very kindly promised, if possible, to come and open it and a number of ladies are cordially interesting themselves in furnishing the stalls.'

The success of the Bazaar was recorded *in Church Monthly*, May **1887**:

'We are glad to learn that the Institute Bazaar held on April 21st, 22nd and 23rd, has quite fulfilled the expectations of its promoters. Lady Lyttelton was, unfortunately, at the last moment unable to come, but her place was most kindly taken by Mrs. W. Brinckman [of Ribbesford House]. The receipts from the various stalls on the first day are said to have amounted to £39-10s-0d. (£39.50), on the second to £20-2s-0d. (£20.10) and on the third to £36-1s-5½d. (£36.07)... We hear that this has been brought up to over £100 by subsequent sales, and that the Entertainments have, in addition, produced a sum of about £25, making £125 in all. Of course, the expenses will have to be taken out of this, but we think we may well congratulate all concerned on a very successful issue of their endeavours.'

The *Kidderminster Shuttle* for 24th March **1888** noted: 'An attractive **concert** was held at the Institute on Saturday evening under the presidency of Mr. G. L. Webster. The programme included songs by Mrs. Purdey and recitations by Mrs. Miller Corbet of Kidderminster.'

The Committee were not able to arrange as many Saturday evening **entertainments** as they would have liked during **1891**. 'On the whole they had been successful, but there had been so many concerts in Bewdley at about that time that attendance at each had suffered. There was a fair attendance on 7th December, when an attractive programme of songs and recitals had been provided by Mr. Mackay, Miss Mildred Mackay and others. In November Mr. Birtwistle had arranged a Magic Lantern display of *Views of Pompeii*, with accompanying readings by the Rev. H. Wilson. Sadly, only a small audience was present.'

Concerts in aid of the Building Fund were planned and in May **1900** a successful two-day Bazaar raised £106-14s-6d. (£106.73) for this and for some modern books for the Library. The Countess of Portsmouth opened Day 1 and Viscountess Cobham Day 2...[39] One of the highlights was an amusing **Washing Competition**:

The *Kidderminster Shuttle* of 9th June 1900 reported: 'Messrs. Lever Bros., of Sunlight Soap fame, gave the prizes. The gentlemen had first turn, and six of them were provided with empty buckets, dirty towels, pieces of soap, and clothes pegs. At a given signal they raced out to the pump to fill their buckets, scattering the spectators, and nearly knocking down the doorkeeper. Then back to their places, and to work on the towels. The next few minutes were most exciting, and the washermen, stimulated by the cheers and chaff of their friends, scrubbed their hardest. The towels were then pegged out on a line, and Mrs. Edward Smith, of the Heath, decided on the most successful attempt. Mr. R. D. Hemingway received as first prize an armful of soap and pegs; and Mr. Bawdon, who came in second, carried off enough soap to supply a regiment for a fortnight. The ladies' competition followed minus the water scramble. They were allowed five minutes to wash and hang out their towels, and it was a period of laughter and activity. Miss Hughes' towel was judged the best, and she received the first prize, a guinea (£1-1s-0d./£1.05) set of teaspoons and a sugar tong. The second prize, more soap. was won by Miss Mildred Mackay.'

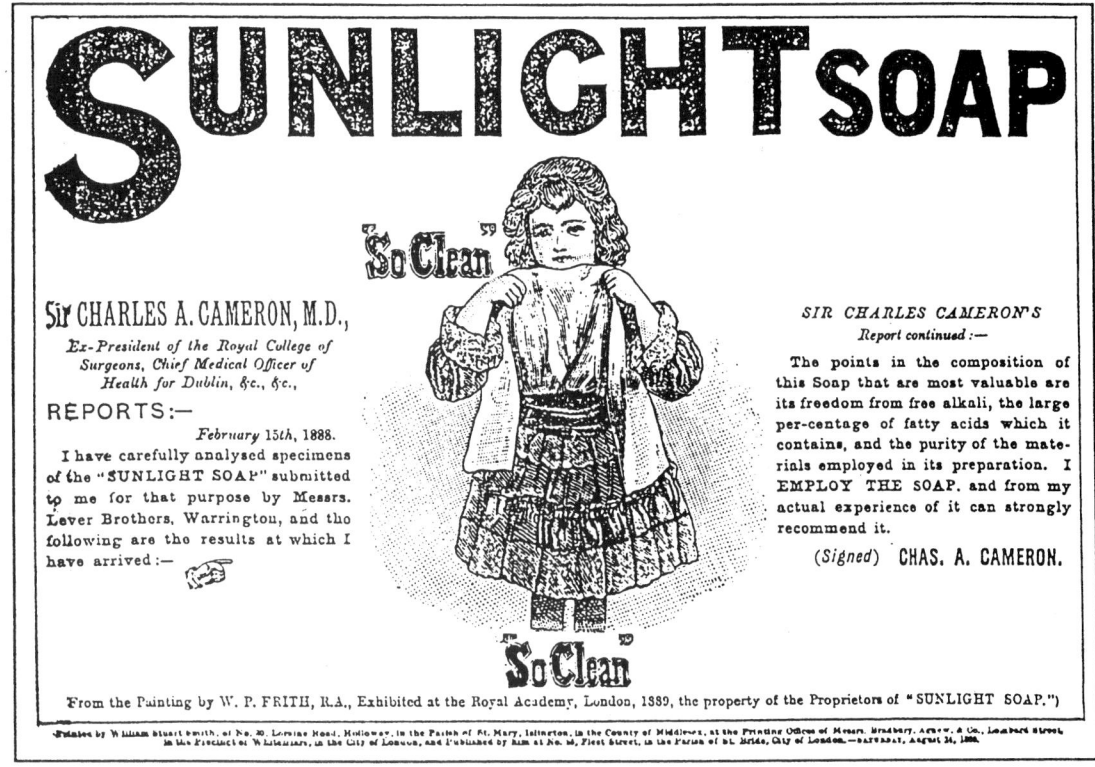

Sunlight Soap advertisement reproduced with kind permission of Unilever Plc

Kidderminster Shuttle, 2nd March **1929**
'A whist drive and dance in aid of funds for the Bewdley Institute will be held at the Town Hall on Monday next.'

Chapter 3:
Social and Recreational Facilities

At the Annual Meeting in **1891** the *President* remarked that there were many places with a much larger population than Bewdley where nothing like the same activity was shown. That this was so from the beginning (for the men, if not always for the womenfolk) can be gleaned from the brief outline which follows.

Parallel bars for gymnastic exercise were installed in the **Social Room** in **1884** and a **cricket club**, established in connection with the Social Room that same year, was allowed free use of a field by the executors of the late Edward Pease, Esq. During **1885**, however, although the **cricket club**[40] continued, the **parallel bar** did not seem to be used and it was thought that the Room itself might have to be closed if it did not receive more support. Thirty-five years were to elapse before the suggestion of having a **Gymnasium** was considered again, chiefly as a way of providing newly-returned Servicemen with the opportunity of keeping up the physical training they had received during the War. At the **1920** Annual Meeting it was decided to start the gymnasium in a small way by obtaining some **parallel bars** and two pairs of **boxing gloves**: the initial expense would be little and the benefits large. Mr. Davies offered to supply the parallel bars and Dr. Miles the boxing gloves if members showed interest.

In **1890** funds were so low that purchasing a **piano** 'for the moderate sum of £7-10s-0d.' (£7.50) was not possible, unless members were prepared to subscribe towards it. Located in the **Lecture Room**, the piano in question was the property of a Committee member who had allowed members free use in return for its safe keeping, but who now offered the Institute first refusal. This piano was purchased, for the commitment and dedication of committee members and friends was always such that the various fund-raising initiatives proved successful.

Whether a second instrument replaced or supplemented the original over 40 years later is unclear, but the intention was that the piano which was purchased in **1934** and overhauled for £14-7s-0d. (£14.35) would prove a useful asset to the **Assembly Room** and to the Sports Committee.

Billiards and snooker

An original member, Mr. T. D. Potter, remembered that facilities for playing **billiards** had been among the first at the Institute when it opened in **1878** and that the first billiard table was purchased in **1883** for £36.[41] What happened to the original table is not clear, but by **1890** the financial situation was such that members could only consider procuring a **billiard table** through subscriptions. The money raised to purchase it had all been repaid by the time of the Annual Meeting in 1891 and, although in need of **repairs** [42] costing about £14, several contributions had been made towards this sum.

The *Church Monthly*, March **1892**, reports: '... the **Billiard Table**, which was established a year or two ago with the object of enabling those who liked a game to have one without all the associations of a public house, has now been paid for, and the proceeds of the table will in future go to swell the funds of the Institute.'

Maybe the building's friendly ghost[43] originates from this period! He does like to move things and he evidently enjoys playing billiards, for the 'clack, clack' of action is often heard at night, although rarely is anything but his vague shadow seen. A little shy, perhaps...

A **new Billiards Room**, built by Mr. James Oakes and measuring 54 by 24 feet (approx. 16.62 by 7.39 metres), was established at the Institute by May **1900**. The debt recorded as remaining on it in March 1905 was £103-0s-4d. (£103.02), but this sum had been reduced to £51-15s-2d. (£51.76) when the Institute's Annual Meeting took place in March 1906. The Room had been well-used during 1905, the takings of £48-11s-0d. (£48.55) representing a slight increase over those of the previous year. To encourage even more use of the Room, the

Committee had decided to reduce the charge per game to 2d. (approx. 0.83p) for 50 and 4d. (approx. 1.66p) for 100 (sic).

Billiards remained among the most popular activities at the Institute for many years. In **1902**, however, ping-pong competed with billiards for supremacy, but the latter soon vanquished the threat.

During **1904 billiard handicaps** and **tournaments** were held and matches were played against Stourport Institute.

Under the Captaincy of Mr. T. Wall, Bewdley Institute **Billiard Team** won the championship of the **Kidderminster and District Billiard League** in the first year of its existence (**1911**), the **"A" Team** repeating the success in **1913-1914**. The Team occupied a fair position in the **League** tables during **1920** and in **1921** won the **League (Division II)** championship. A Team played in the **District Billiard League** in **1927** and again in **1928-1929**, when a Team was also entered in the newly-formed **Kidderminster and District Snooker League.**

Billiards competitions were held in **1912**, prizes being voted by the Committee. Cues were won by Messrs. T. Coldrick ('A' Team) and E. Hunt ('B' Team).

At the **1913** Annual Meeting thanks were expressed to Mr. H. Stonehouse for a **billiard prize** for competition between members aged 40-plus. Once again, the Committee had offered a cue and case to the members in each team who won the highest number of games in League matches - an offer it repeated two years later, when cue and case were valued at 10s-6d. (53p).

A **billiards** competition raised £2-2s-0d.(£2.10) in **1920** and the following year a **billiards and snooker competition** raised £1-10s-0d. (£1.50p) for St. Dunstan's, who provided certificates for the winners (Messrs. R. A. Harcombe and B. Plevey, respectively).

Several **billiards** and **snooker handicaps** were held during **1921**.

1922 saw good entries for **competitions** in **billiards, snooker, cribbage,** etc. Special Christmas prizes were donated for these by Messrs. F. W. Davies and F. P. Brettell in **1922** and again the following year.

In **1923** a **prize**, value 10s-6d. (53p), was shared between Mr. J. R. Homfray and Mr. J. Taylor. Mr. W. Bishop of Kidderminster played in an **exhibition billiards** match at the Institute in March **1932**.

During **1933 handicaps** and **competitions** were held, teams were entered in the **Snooker League** and 'a further effort in the Royal Cripples' Hospital competition was launched'.

Two teams were entered in the **Kidderminster and District Snooker League** during **1934**. The Club also competed for the Birmingham Hospital Shield, but failed at the first fence to Lea Hall Allotment Institute. The **annual handicaps** were well supported.

In **1935** teams were entered in both divisions of the **Snooker League**, winning in **Division I** and only losing in **Division II** by one point. The following year the **Institute Second Team** won the championship of **Division II** of the **Kidderminster and District Snooker League.**

During **1937 Teams were entered in the local Leagues**, upholding the tradition of the Club.

At the **1940** Annual Meeting it was announced that annual competitions for both **Billiards** and **Snooker Cups** were to be held under handicap rules. The *Secretary* was thanked for his gift of a **Cup** for **snooker** competitions. Mrs. Sturt had sent £1 towards prizes for a **freak billiards competition** which was to be held.

Bagatelle

Mr. Gething's *modified scheme* had included provision for a **bagatelle** room on the second floor. Whether it was ever built is unclear,[44] but bagatelle was certainly played before **1905**. In summer that year, with the agreement of the Horticultural Society, a **new Bagatelle Room** was established in a room formerly used by that Society. £18-15s-0d. (£18.75) was spent on purchasing a new bagatelle table and £7-15s-0d. (£7.75) for [repairing] the *old* table at the time. These investments evidently were well worthwhile, for the bagatelle room proved very popular and just over £19-0s-0d. (£19.00) was taken for use thereof during its first nine months of existence.[45]

During the season **1905-1906** members joined the **Kidderminster and District Bagatelle League**. The names and results of the **Institute Team** who played in some of the early matches are recorded in issues of the *Kidderminster Shuttle* (*see* pages following this Chapter).

The silver challenge cup and prize in the **Bagatelle Tournament** in **1910** were presented to the winner, Mr. W. Coldrick.

Competitions were held in **bagatelle** in **1912**, prizes being voted by the Committee.

The **Bagatelle Team** won the championship of the **Kidderminster and District Bagatelle League** in **1913** and were runners-up in **1914**. Winners again in the **1914-1915** season, they repeated the feat in **1918 and 1919**. The Challenge Cup was presented to Mr. E. Coles at the 1920 A.G.M., together with a prize for being the individual who won the highest number of games (27 out of the 34 he had played). Runner-up Mr. A. J. Millington received a prize for winning 19 out of 29 games.

The **Team** occupied a fair position in the **League** tables during **1920** and played in the **District League** in **1921** and **1927**, in which year Mr. J. Taylor won the Godsall[46] Cup as the best bagatelle player in the League.

The **bagatelle table** was re-covered in **1931** but was little-used during the following 3 years and, after careful consideration, the Committee sold it for £7-14s-6d. (£7.73) before its value depreciated further.

Chess and draughts

Facilities for **chess** and **draughts** were among the attractions at the Institute from at least **1894** to **1906**. It seems likely that a **Chess Club**, in existence in 1900, became more active as membership of the Institute increased.

Airgun shooting

A popular national sport at the time, **airgun shooting** was introduced to the Institute in **1906**.

Mr. Edward Smith presented the Club with two new airguns and members joined the **Institute Airgun League** that season, playing with varying success. About twelve months later Mr. S. Hemingway and the Mayor (Mr. J. Green) offered to provide a **silver medal** and half the cost of a **silver challenge cup**, respectively, for competition among the **Airgun Club** members

In **1907** both medal and cup were won by Mr. Frank Barnfield. In addition to individual prizes, the Institute **Airgun Team** won a challenge shield and medals in open competition at the Annual Meeting of Clubs and Institutes which was held at Overbury Court.

Airgun shooting receipts were satisfactory during **1907**, but in **1908** were decidedly less than those of the two previous years and by **1910** interest had faded. Although the sport was revived during **1915**, it seems to have been short-lived - perhaps because those members who might have taken it up had volunteered for War Service. At the Annual Meeting in **1917** Mr. Barnfield (who had joined the Forces before March 1915) observed rather tellingly that if local Clubs had been able to continue **airgun shooting** matches, then efficiency with a rifle would already have been gained by any members who joined the Army. Training time within the Forces was so short that many men were compelled to go into the firing line before thoroughly understanding the use of the rifle.

Cards

Although **cards** had been played at the Institute since at least **1905**, a new attraction in the form of a **Card table** was introduced in **1918**. This proved popular and a valuable source of income. At the **1920** Annual Meeting the possibility of having a **Card Room** was considered, the question being principally one of obtaining coal[47] for the fires.
Cards evidently continued popular, receipts in **1937** being nearly £11 compared with just over £7 in **1936**.

Whist drives were a regular and successful feature at the Institute for many years and in 1922 the Institute Committee decided to hold 'A further series of four whist drives, the first and last to include a dance. The first gathering [was] at the Town Hall, when there was a fair attendance.'[48]

Some whist drives took place in the Institute Billiard Room: e.g. one on 2nd April 1930.[49]

Sports prizes

Institute members were always generous with their time and money. Among donors of sports prizes were Messrs. F. P. Brettell and W. S. Harcombe (1924) and Messrs. F. W. Davies and R. A. Harcombe (1924 and 1927). At the 1931 Annual Meeting Mr. Stanley Hemingway offered a prize to the value of one guinea (£1.05) for competition.

Social activities

About twenty-five people from the **Conservative Club** (no address given) **visited** Bewdley Institute in March **1930** 'where they had an enjoyable evening playing **billiards, snooker, bagatelle, cards, etc.**'[50]

A dinner was held in **1935** (see photograph, below), but in **1936/1937** a proposal to have an **Annual Dinner** was left in abeyance because some thought the cost too high. For similar reasons, the suggestion of having an **Annual Outing** had not been pursued although, evidently, there had been a successful **summer outing** to Blackpool in **1930**.

The provision and layout of a proposed **bowling green** was discussed informally at the close of the **1941 Annual Meeting**. After further consideration, the Meeting 12 months later heard that, disappointingly, the idea could not be carried out, although the Secretary was convinced that the project was well worth borrowing money to set up.

Visits were **exchanged** with **Wribbenhall Social Club** during **1942** and it was hoped to foster the spirit of friendship further.

Bewdley Institute Dinner at the Red Lion, Westbourne Street, 1935
(from Purcell, A. & C. and Hobson, K: Bewdley's past in pictures, Vol. ii. Bewdley Historical Research Group, 1996 - reproduced by courtesy of Kenneth Hobson)

Bewdley Institute's Air Gun League Results, March 1907
(reproduced by courtesy of the *Kidderminster Shuttle/Times*)

KT 16-3-1907

INSTITUTES AIR GUN LEAGUE.

Considerable surprise has been caused by the downfall of Wribbenhall in their match with Stourport, after making such a good display the previous week. Stourport put on 222, thus winning the match by a couple of points. St. John's and the Artillery was another exciting affair, the last Artilleryman to shoot requiring 23 to win, which proved three too many for him. Some interesting shooting was witnessed at the Workmen's Club, where the Duke of York made a plucky bid for victory. Possibles were made by W. M. Hughes and R. A. Ovens for the Workmen's Club, and A. Snape for Stourport.

Workmen's.		Duke of York.	
H. Longmore	22	J. Simmonds	24
A. Winbury	19	F. Barth	21
G. Longmore	22	R. C. Bridges	21
T. Cull	23	F. Madeley	21
L. Humphries	24	H. Lench	21
M. Smith	24	C. Collins	22
A. W. Brown	23	W. Bennett	20
R. E. Grove	22	A. Bird	24
W. M. Hughes	25	F. Bell	19
R. A. Ovens	25	A. Taylor	23
	229		217

Wribbenhall.		Stourport.	
E. Bishop	24	W. Lee	23
H. Moles	17	A. Jones	20
W. Ife	24	C. Walker	22
E. Page	22	C. Bourne	23
Reg. Southan	22	H. Long	19
B. Plevey	23	H. Massey	23
G. Gillam	21	A. Snape	25
C. H. Farmer	22	H. Payne	20
E. Southan	23	L. Richards	24
G. Wallis	22	R. Jones	23
	220		222

Wolverley.		Bewdley.	
A. Pinnegar	23	R. Bowdler	22
C. Woodberry	22	J. H. Taylor	20
A. Wyer	22	R. Harcombe	22
G. Webb	22	J. Bennett	21
J. Potter	23	F. Barnfield	23
H. Lea	21	S. Pritchard	18
C. Pitt	22	G. A. Moore	22
W. Smith	21	E. Page	20
A. Bennett	21	F. Harris	22
W. Potter	21	T. Wall	21
	218		211

Bewdley Institute's Bagatelle Results, November 1905

(reproduced by courtesy of the *Kidderminster Shuttle/Times*)

KS 11-11-1905

BAGATELLE.

Kidderminster Bagatelle League.

BEWDLEY INSTITUTE v. KIDDERMINSTER WORKMEN'S CLUB.—Played at Bewdley on Saturday and resulted in a win for the home team by 8 games to 1.

BEWDLEY.		WORKMEN'S CLUB.	
F. Barnfield	121	H. Bickerton	88
F. Bowdler	99	C. Pannel	121
E. Page	121	J. Oaskie	90
T. Wall	121	A. Penny	110
B. Hunt	121	J. Crane	32
G. Cope	121	T. Williams	82
J. Lewis	121	A. King	69
O. Wall	121	T. Salter	66
W. Gardner	121	J. Skerratt	80

ST. JOHN'S v. ST. MARY'S.—This match was played at St. Mary's Brotherhood on Saturday and ended in a victory for St. John's by 5 games to 4. Scores:—

ST. JOHN'S.		ST. MARY'S.	
J. Taylor	121	C. Rollings	98
W. Houghton	121	A. Sheldon	74
W. Cole	121	D. Powell	86
W. Hepwood	121	W. Price	69
E. Andrews	88	F. Tyler	121
W. H. Taylor	8	G. Youngjohns	121
W. Webb	84	A. Morris	121
A. Walters	113	B. Beddowes	121
S. Newey	121	F. Barker	105

STOURPORT INSTITUTE v. WRIBBENHALL WORKMEN'S CLUB.—Played at Stourport on Saturday. After the match an enjoyable evening was spent. Scores:—

STOURPORT.		WRIBBENHALL.	
B. Starr	52	G. Wallis	121
V. Starr	67	H. Cuthbert	121
F. Nott	47	E. Jay	121
W. Horton	121	H. Mole	64
J. W. Knape	103	J. Homfray	121
A. Lloyd	118	J. Taylor	121
A. Davies	100	E. Page	121
G. Gittens	121	G. Morris	86
A. Piper	82	A. Southan	121

KS 25-11-1905

BAGATELLE.

Kidderminster Bagatelle League.

ST. JOHN'S v. STOURPORT INSTITUTE.—This match was played at St. John's Institute on Saturday and ended in a victory for St. John's by 7 games to 2. Scores:—

ST. JOHN'S.		STOURPORT.	
W. H. Taylor	121	H. G. Southall	77
W. Hepwood	121	F. Nott	96
W. Webb	38	V. E. Starr	121
J. Taylor	121	W. J. Knape	85
W. Cole	121	A. Piper	108
E. Andrews	121	G. W. Gittens	86
J. Wakefield	121	W. Horton	119
W. Houghton	29	B. Starr	121
A. Walters	121	F. Starr	55

BEWDLEY INSTITUTE v. BEWDLEY AND WRIBBENHALL WORKMEN'S CLUB.—Played at Wribbenhall on Saturday and resulted in a win for the home team by 6 games to 3.

WRIBBENHALL.		BEWDLEY.	
H. Southan	77	E. Page	121
E. Jay	81	W. Gardner	121
G. Morris	121	F. Bowdler	9
H. Cuthbert	121	G. Cope	68
J. Taylor	121	B. Hunt	43
H. Moule	115	F. Barnfield	121
A. Southan	121	O. Wall	90
J. Homfray	121	J. Lewis	42
G. Wallis	121	T. Wall	108

WORKMENS' CLUB v. ST. MARY'S BROTHERHOOD.—Played at the Workmen's Club on Saturday and ended in a win for the home team by nine games.

WORKMEN'S CLUB.		ST. MARY'S.	
H. Bickerton	121	Youngjohns	41
A. Cole	121	Price	116
A. Tandy	121	Barker	74
C. Pannell	121	Tyler	86
A. Penny	121	Sheldon	98
J. Oaskie	121	Beddoes	87
J. Skerratt	121	Morris	72
T. Salter	121	Powell	20
T. H. Williams	121	Cooper	8

Bagatelle Results, January 1906

(reproduced by courtesy of the *Kidderminster Shuttle/Times*)

KS 20-1-1906

BAGATELLE.

Kidderminster Bagatelle League.

ST. MARY'S v. STOURPORT.—Result: St. Mary's five games, Stourport four.

ST. MARY'S.		STOURPORT.	
A. Sheldon	78	V. E. Starr	121
C. Rollings	18	W. J. Knape	121
T. Moule	121	A. Davies	13
A. Morris	121	F. Starr	79
F. Tyler	62	B. Starr	121
W. Parker	121	F. Nott	0
W. Price	121	A. W. Piper	100
B. Beddoes	62	L. J. Rathbone	121
G. Youngjohns	121	G. W. Gittens	77

BEWDLEY INSTITUTE v. KIDDERMINSTER WORKMAN'S CLUB.—Played at the Workmen's Club on Saturday and resulted in a win for the home team by 7 games to 2.

BEWDLEY.		WORKMEN'S CLUB.	
G. Cope	11	E. Pannell	121
H. Barnfield	48	H. Bickerton	121
W. Gardner	51	A. Penny	121
T. Gardner	29	W. Priest	121
J. Lewis	43	J. Caskie	121
C. Wall	101	J. Skerrett	121
B. Page	42	T. Gill	121
E. Hunt	121	A. Tandy	101
T. Wall	121	J. Smith	91

WRIBBENHALL v STOURPORT INSTITUTE.—Played at Wribbenhall on Saturday, the home team winning by seven games to two. Scores:—

WRIBBENHALL.		STOURPORT.	
G. Morris	26	G. Gittins	121
H. Cuthbert	121	E. Starr	90
H. Moule	121	A. Piper	82
J. Homfray	121	A. Davis	68
J. Taylor	121	F. Nott	70
A. Southan	74	W. Horton	121
H. Southan	121	W. J. Knape	116
G. Wallace	121	V. E. Starr	65
E. Jay	121	L. Rathbone	25

KIDDERMINSTER BAGATELLE LEAGUE TABLE.

		Played	Won	Lost	Games Won	Games Lost	Points
1	Wribbenhall	6	5	1	25	19	35
2	Bewdley Institute	5	3	2	25	20	25
3	Kidder. Workmen's Club	5	2	3	23	22	23
4	St. Mary's	5	2	3	18	27	18
5	St. John's	4	2	2	17	19	17
6	Stourport	5	1	4	17	28	17

Bagatelle Results, February 1906
(reproduced by courtesy of the *Kidderminster Shuttle/Times*)

KS 10-2-1906

BAGATELLE.

ST. MARY'S v. BEWDLEY INSTITUTE.—Played at Kidderminster on Saturday, the visitors winning by 5 games to 4.

ST. MARY'S.		BEWDLEY.	
C. Rollings	121	J. Lewis	67
W. Parker	121	T. Gardner	78
B. Beddoes	121	C. Wall	118
W. Price	60	T. Wall	121
T. Moule	108	E. Shepherd	121
F. Tyler	48	W. Gardner	121
G. Youngjohns	106	E. Page	121
C. Cooper	121	G. Cope	70
A. Morris	85	F. Barnfield	121

Billiards Results, March 1910
(reproduced by courtesy of the *Kidderminster Shuttle/Times*)

KS 26-3-1910

BILLIARDS.

BEWDLEY INSTITUTE v. ST. JOHN'S.—This match was played at Bewdley on Saturday, and resulted in a win for the home team by 67 points. Scores:—

BEWDLEY.		ST. JOHN'S.	
T. Wall	50	W. Tew	100
A. J. Stephenson	100	E. Tyler	95
P. Bristow	100	W. Hepwood	91
F. Hunt	26	A. Walters	100
T. Coldrick	100	R. Phipps	57
F. Dunn	100	W. Cooke	26
R. Southan	100	C. Johnson	65
E. C. Hemingway	100	W. Wright	75
Total	676	Total	609

ST. JOHN'S v. BEWDLEY INSTITUTE.—The return match was played at St. John's Institute on Wednesday evening, resulting in a win for the home team by 6 points. Scores:—

ST. JOHN'S.		BEWDLEY.	
E. Tyler	100	T. Wall	72
W. Cooke	42	R. A. Harcombe	100
W. Hepwood	100	A. J. Stephenson	37
A. Walters	100	P. Bristow	38
J. Walters	78	F. Dunn	100
C. Johnson	90	T. Coldrick	100
W. Wright	74	F. Hunt	100
E. Andrews	100	E. C. Hemingway	96
W. Randall	65	R. Southan	100
Total	749	Total	743

ST. JOHN'S II. v. BEWDLEY INSTITUTE II.—This match was played at St. John's Institute on Saturday, and resulted in a win for the visitors by 10 points. Scores:—

ST. JOHN'S.		BEWDLEY.	
D. Newey	100	C. Allcock	79
A. Youngjohns	91	P. F. Mountford	100
F. Walters	95	L. Lawley	100
A. Cook	100	W. Coldrick	74
F. Godsall	60	W. Gardner	100
W. Cooke	100	T. Gardner	95
A. Preston	78	B. Plevey	100
C. Allen	96	R. A. Andrews	100
W. Randall	100	E. Hunt	82
Total	820	Total	830

The return match will be played at Bewdley on Saturday, March 26th.

Chapter 4:
Educational Facilities

The Bewdley and Wribbenhall Working Man's Institute

Established in Bewdley in the early 1860s[51] (or in 1859, as Mr. Birtwistle recalled[52]), the popular *Bewdley and Wribbenhall Working Man's Institute* met in Severn Side by 1873.[53] By 1877 there was an average attendance of 50 at the classes held there.[54] The organization was merged with Bewdley Institute when it opened in 1878.[55]

An indication of the growing popularity of the movement, by 1884 there was another, separate Club in Wribbenhall. Known as the *Bewdley and Wribbenhall Working Man's Club*, Alfred Longbottom, schoolmaster of Wribbenhall National School, was Secretary - as he was in 1892 and 1893.[56] Interestingly, Mr. Longbottom was an original Assistant Art Master at **Bewdley Institute** in 1879 and a member there for many years.

The following reports appeared in *Church Monthly*, September and October 1887, respectively:

'On Tuesday September 20th the Annual Meeting of the Worcestershire Union of Workmen's Clubs and Institutes will be held in Bewdley. There will be a Conference in the afternoon at 3 o'clock open only to members of Clubs in Union [sic]; but in the evening there will be a Public Meeting at the Bewdley Institute at 7.15, which will be addressed by Lord Lyttelton, Sir H. F. Vernon, Bart., Rev. Canon Creighton,[57] and J. Brinton, Esq. The Union has now nearly 60 clubs and institutes associated with it, including the two in Bewdley and Wribbenhall, and others at the Far Forest, Rock, and Arley. It is the first time the Annual Meeting has been held in Bewdley, and we trust that all will combine to make it a success.'

'The Annual Meeting of the Worcestershire Union of Workmen's Clubs and Institutes, held at the Bewdley Institute on Sept. 20th, was very well attended, though there were not so many members of the local clubs present as we should like to have seen. Unfortunately the meeting was disappointed of two of its speakers, Sir H. F. Vernon having to leave early to catch a train, and Mr. Brinton finding himself at the last minute unable to come. Lord Lyttelton and Canon Creighton, however, gave two very excellent and practical addresses, full of point and interest, and the audience seemed to be well-pleased. There were a good number at the Conference in the afternoon, but the discussion was somewhat desultory.'

There was still a separate Working Men's Club in Wribbenhall in 1906, as indicated at the Annual Meeting of Bewdley Institute Members that year. Nevertheless, the range of educational, as well as social, facilities at the Institute gradually expanded - as the far-sighted Mr. Pease had anticipated.

The provision of **educational facilities** was, of course, one of the prime reasons for the creation of Bewdley Institute. Its rooms had been constructed to meet the requirements of the Science and Art Department, South Kensington, and the original hope was that Bewdley might have become a centre for technical teaching with its own School of Art. This, however, had proved impractical for various reasons, not least the fact that Bewdley's population was not sufficiently numerous to qualify for a realistic grant. Another factor was the proximity of Kidderminster, which had greater attractions for students.

Nonetheless, Committee and other members not only worked hard to organize classes and lectures but evidently influenced some of their young relatives to become students (see Appendix II). Some also attended themselves, e.g. teachers W[illiam] H[enry] Vickrage, (aged about 30 - see Ref. 24); Jonathan Birtwistle, (aged about 43 - see Appendix I, *Trustees*); and Alfred Longbottom, (aged about 27 - see Ref. 23) were among the first students in the Advanced Chemistry Class in 1879.[58] Among **successful students** over the years were A. J. Millington (*see* Appendix I, *Members*) and Miss Ethel M. Elgood of the Yew Trees, Bewdley, who was one of the successful candidates in the 1895 Higher Local Examination, University of Cambridge.[59]

The 1st Annual Report and Accounts of the Institute Committee, presented at their Annual General Meeting in **January 1880**, recorded: 'The course of **lectures and entertainments** organized by the committee had been well patronised. **Educational results** of the year had been, on the whole, very satisfactory. Ample provision had been made for enabling young people who had left school to carry on their **higher education**, and much attention was paid to the imparting of **elementary education**. The **evening classes**[60] had been well attended, and some very useful work had been done, many valuable prizes having been gained. Rev. Mr. Ford ... alluding to the question of education, said it was utterly useless that Acts of Parliament should be passed to compel children to attend school, if no provision were made for them **after school life was over, and that need was met by institutes like their own**... Mr. Harrison said: "... **the two great objects of the Institute** were to provide reasonable and proper **recreation**, but the greater object was for **educational purposes**... Not only were the **number of students attending the science classeslarge, but many of them had greatly distinguished themselves**... There ought to bemore members connected with the Institute; but that **60 members out of a total of 100 should attend the School of Art showed how thoroughly art was appreciated**..."

Classes held during **1884**[61] were:
(1) the Rev. J. R. Burton in **Theoretical Chemistry** with 13 students (6 passed the South Kensington examination, one being in the advanced stage);
(2) the Rev. J. R. Burton in **Practical Chemistry** with 8 students (6 passed, 2 of them being first class);
(3) Mr. J. Tucker in **Drawing** with 15 pupils during the summer (5 sat for the examination, 2 passed - 1 in free-hand drawing and 1 in model drawing);
(4) Mr. Birtwistle in Pitman's Phonetic System of **Shorthand**. This class was discontinued in March, when those students who had attended regularly were sufficiently advanced to proceed with the subject by private study and practice.
Mr. Birtwistle had donated the fees of his Shorthand Class to the Institute, these amounting to £1-18s-3d. (£1.91).

At the May examinations the Science Committee of the Institute also superintended the examination of pupils at the Grammar School. Since the opening of the Institute the students had gained the following successes at the Government examinations:

Theoretical Chemistry	53
Practical Chemistry	22
Mathematics	34
Sound, Light and Heat	28
Agriculture	23
Physiography	16
Building Construction	4
Freehand Drawing	15
Model Drawing	7
	202

In distributing prizes in October, Lord Lyttelton spoke very highly of the advantages possessed by such an Institute as Bewdley's and the Committee invited more students to join their ranks.

Lectures had been given on *George Herbert* (by blind lecturer, the Rev. Mr. Marston); *Old English Customs, with notices concerning the tenure of land* (by Mr. Joseph Sturge[62]); *Profitable Management of Small Dairy Farms* (by Mr. F. Impey, who had illustrated a simple and accurate mode of testing the quality of milk); and, the last of the series, Miss M. D. Allright's *Travels in India* 'with numerous photographic views, kindly exhibited by Mr. Charles Pumphrey with his oxy-hydrogen lantern'.

Except in bad weather, attendance was good at **Lectures** held at the Institute during **1885**. Subjects included *Nineveh* (two illustrated lectures by Mr. Thomas Sharp); *Three hundred years ago* (by the Rev. J. R. Burton); and *Electricity, including a variety of interesting experiments* (by Dr. Masterman of Stourport). Messrs. Sharp, Burton and Masterman had kindly given their talks free. Arrangements for autumn lectures had been delayed because of the General Election, but Mr. E. A. Mason of Worcester was due to speak soon. The Committee hoped that **Classes** would be formed again at the Institute. They had lost their much esteemed teacher of science when the Rev. J. R. Burton moved to Kidderminster; and outbreaks of scarlet fever in the town had discouraged arrangements for elementary classes.

The Committee regretted that no arrangements could be made for **Lectures** during **1888**. The **Educational Classes** had not been well supported despite best efforts to make them attractive and useful. The **Drawing Class** was the only one which had done any successful work. Some of the students in the **Wood Turning** and **Carving Classes** were unable to make progress because they had no knowledge of drawing.

Again in **1889** the Committee was unable to organize any **Lectures**, but was planning for several to be given during 1890. **Cookery Classes:** Mr. and Mrs. Tangye had arranged for Miss E. Dods from the Birmingham School of Cookery to give 10 lessons to a ladies' class at the Institute in the mornings and to teach cottage cookery in the afternoons. The ladies each paid a fee of 10s-0d. (50p) for the whole course and a special rate of 2d. (1p) per time was charged for cottage cookery to make these 10 lessons affordable 'to those for whom they were intended'. The Committee recognized that the expense would not be met by receipts, but felt that the response to its efforts had been very gratifying and that the classes had been much appreciated.

Mr. Tucker reported that although 7 students had been included in the **Drawing Class**, the average attendance had not exceeded 4. Two sat for the examination in May, one of whom succeeded in gaining a pass in the Second Class.

During **1890** the number of students attending the Bewdley Institute **Drawing Class** was just 8, with an average attendance of 5.

The **Shorthand Class**, taught by Mr. Birtwistle, numbered 10 students, 'some of whom made decided progress'.

In **1891**, however, fresh impetus was given to the work of the Institute by classes organized under the Technical Education Scheme promoted by the County Council.[63] A Bewdley District Committee was formed in September and, by October, a branch of the <u>**Kidderminster and District Schools of Science and Art**</u> was located in the Institute - as it was until c1913.

Lessons in a variety of subjects began and the number of students was described as *very large* in the new branch at Bewdley. The *Church Monthly* for **October 1891** reports:

'The Worcestershire Union of Working Men's Clubs and Institutes have taken a step which may prove one of great usefulness to many in these parishes. Having received a grant of £100 from the County Council for the furtherance of **Technical Instruction**, they have made use of it to secure the services of a skilled gardener, who shall hold himself at the service of occupiers of **cottage gardens and allotments**, and shall be willing without charge to give practical advice as to the management of such gardens, the best rotation of crops, the best way to get rid of blight, disease, &c. He will be willing to visit personally the garden of any one willing to receive him and consult on the spot as to how it may be turned to best advantage. The gentleman appointed is **Mr. James Udale** [*see* Ref. 63], and arrangements are being made with him to visit Bewdley shortly. It is hoped also to draft a scheme whereby others, not cottagers, or allotment holders, may obtain the benefit of his services on payment of a small fee to the Union. Meantime the Local Committee in connection with the Kidderminster centre has not been idle. A **Drawing Class** has already been started on Monday Evenings at the Institute, and in course of formation there are also classes in **Chemistry, Agriculture, Cookery,** and **Languages**. Particulars may be obtained from **Mr. R. H. Whitcombe, Junr., Local Secretary**.'

There was much interest in these classes and also in **Lectures** given during the year by Dr. Swete and Alderman Ernest Day.

In the Session **1891-1892** the following **classes** were held:

	Number of students
Drawing, Freehand and Model	
Afternoon Class	32
Evening Class	50
Chemistry (Theoretical)	15
(Practical)	10
Principles of Agriculture	15
Foreign Languages (French and German)	17
Cookery	
Total number of class entries, excluding cookery	---- 139 ----

'Attendance at the **Cookery Class** was very large, being on some evenings between 50 and 60.'

Bewdley & the Technical Education Grant, April 1891

(reproduced by courtesy of the *Kidderminster Shuttle/Times*)

THE KIDDERMINSTER SHUTTLE—APRIL 18, 1891.

BEWDLEY AND THE TECHNICAL EDUCATION GRANT.

On Thursday evening a public meeting convened by the Mayor was held in the Town Hall, Bewdley, to consider a letter from Viscount Cobham, the representative of the borough on the County Council, with regard to the grant for technical education. Only the residents of Bewdley were invited to the meeting, but the inhabitants of Dowles and Wribbenhall were present and took part in the proceedings and, as will be seen, this fact led to some difficulty and disturbance during the progress of the meeting. The Mayor (Mr. Langley Kitching) presided; and among those present were the Rev. H. Wilson (Rector of Dowles), Alderman Tangye, Councillors Blight and Christopher Pountney, Messrs. A. Hodgson, M.A., (Head Master of the Bewdley Grammar School), R. Hemingway, Birtwistle, Longbottom, Vickrage, Teague, W. Stone, Denison, Miss Sturge, and others. The attendance was not very large.

Before the Mayor had an opportunity of explaining the object of the meeting, Mr. Blight asked if it would not have been more consistent if the letter from Lord Cobham had been printed on the notice calling the meeting, and then it could have been considered and no one would have been taken at a disadvantage. A mine would not have been sprung under their feet.

The Mayor failed to see how any one could be taken at a disadvantage. Everyone knew the object of the meeting.

Mr. Blight again interfered with the question: Is not Lord Cobham the Chairman of the Bewdley Grammar School?

The Mayor answered in the affirmative, but failed to see what that had to do with the object of the meeting. His Worship then read the letter which he had received from Viscount Cobham, who is Chairman of the sub-committee on the Technical Grant question. The application from Kidderminster and district, including Bewdley and other localities, for a share in that grant had been considered on Saturday, and was provisionally approved. It was not, however, intended that that scheme should be carried out against the wishes of the inhabitants of the district, and therefore Bewdley could, if so minded, stand out of the proposed scheme and take its own grant separately, which would be based upon population and would not exceed £50. He did not think any separate grant would be made to the Grammar School. He had not received any intimation of the feelings of the inhabitants on that subject, and therefore wrote for guidance in the matter as the sub-committee would meet again on Saturday, and it would then be decided whether Bewdley should be included or excluded in the Kidderminster scheme. The Mayor also read a lengthy letter from Alderman Grosvenor, Chairman of the Kidderminster School of Science and Art, in which he assured the Mayor that the committee had no selfish view in initiating the proposal to combine all the district, but simply desired to extend the usefulness of the schools. Such subjects would be taught in the district as the people of each district desired, and if Bewdley united in the scheme the borough would have its proper proportion of representatives on the committee and its share in the responsibilities of the control of the school and scheme.

Ald. Tangye was called upon to move the first resolution, but Mr. Vickrage intervened with a definition of what he conceived to be technical education. It was the teaching of the use of tools in such handicrafts as wood and iron, and was not that teaching of science and art which was carried on at the school at Kidderminster. They wanted to make men better workmen. They would begin at the wrong end if they began dabbling with Science.

Mr. Blight protested against Ald. Tangye being asked to move the first resolution. He had selfish interest in doing so. His son had derived benefit from science education, but what they wanted was something which would benefit all the lads of Bewdley. He objected to centralisation; and if they joined Kidderminster they would be literally snuffed out. It was rot and rubbish to talk about obtaining benefits from Kidderminster. Let them have the grant themselves and spend it for the benefit of the town.

Ald. Tangye then moved a resolution in favour of joining with Kidderminster on the basis of the letters from Viscount Cobham and Mr. Grosvenor. He strongly advocated the teaching of cookery, declaring that it would mean a saving for a working man of at least 2s 6d per week.

A working man remarked that what they wanted was the means to get something to cook.

Mr. W. Stone said if they joined Kidderminster cookery would be one of the subjects taught.

The Rev. H. Wilson seconded the motion, and asked of what benefit would £50 be to them. They could not engage a teacher with such a sum, and the money would be frittered away.

Mr. Vickrage said it would materially assist in teaching practical knowledge to the boys.

Mr. Birtwistle supported the motion, and said what Bewdley needed was not a low kind of teaching, but the very best which could be obtained, so that Bewdley boys, when they went out into the world, would be able to compete with those who had had advantages of the larger towns.

Mr. Hemingway said it was unfortunate that technical education should be mixed up with science and art teaching. The desire was to give to the English youth better inventive knowledge, because it was admitted that foreigners were better in handicraft and inventive genius. He felt sure that greater benefits would be derived from amalgamation with Kidderminster, but they would have to insist upon a fair representation on the Board of Management.

Mr. Blight moved as an amendment, "That inasmuch as Bewdley is allotted a sum of say £50, it be allowed to control the fund, the management to be arranged at a future meeting." He entered a strong and emphatic protest against the system of centralisation.

Mr. Christopher Pountner seconded the amendment, which upon being put was lost, 9 voting in its favour and 10 against. The motion was declared to be carried by 12 votes to 9, some in the room not voting.

Then some disorder and merriment arose. Attention was called to the fact that, although only the residents of Bewdley were invited to the meeting, others outside that district had voted upon the motion.

Mr. Blight rose in haste, and, raising a point of order, demanded to be heard. The Mayor told him that his point of order was one of disorder, and he could not be heard. Mr. Blight, however, was pertinacious, and insisted on being heard. He declared the whole proceedings illegal, and called upon the Mayor to put his amendment and the resolution again to the meeting.

The Mayor said the motion had been carried, and the question could not be reopened.

Mr. Blight said he was determined that the question should be reopened, and asked that the Town Clerk should give a ruling on the matter.

A good deal of commotion followed, and Mr. Hemingway said it was quite true that that was a question which affected Bewdley alone, and ought to be determined by the Bewdley residents only. Outsiders were not interested in what their County Council representative had to say to them. The people of Wribbenhall objected to be incorporated with Bewdley, and so share the burdens, but they wanted to share in all the benefits which Bewdley could give them. If he had been a resident of Wribbenhall, he should certainly not have voted on that question.

Mr. Blight said, after that clear expression of opinion, he asked the Mayor to take the vote again.

The Mayor said he should be ruled entirely by the Town Clerk in the matter.

Mr. Hemingway said if the objection had been raised before the motion was put it would have been in order. It was a question affecting Bewdley alone. He understood the Mayor to hold that the resolution was carried by a majority of Bewdley residents.

Miss Sturge said where the interests were so closely identified it was difficult to discriminate.

During the course of further discussion, Mr. Hemingway said he hoped the Bewdley people would not allow themselves to be swamped by Kidderminster. Still he was in favour of amalgamation in that case, as he believed they would get greater advantages by joining than they would by remaining isolated. If Wribbenhall wanted to share in those advantages, let them also share in the responsibilities.

Mr. Blight again insisted upon the vote being retaken; but the Mayor was obdurate, and the incident ended.

The Rev. H. Wilson moved that three representatives should be appointed from Bewdley on the board of management of the Kidderminster School, one representing the Grammar School, one elected by the trustees and committee of the Institute, and one representative of the Bewdley Corporation. All interests in the town would then be properly represented.

Mr. Teague seconded the motion.

Mr. Blight: Are we so moribund that we cannot act for ourselves? Are we such a poor, worn out, deserted lot of folk that we cannot manage our own affairs, and have to go to Kidderminster to get our work done for us?

The motion was carried by a small majority and the proceedings, which had been inordinately prolonged, and were at times somewhat turbulent, closed with a vote of thanks to the Mayor for convening and presiding over the meeting.

Technical Education, Bewdley, October 1891
(reproduced by courtesy of the *Kidderminster Shuttle/Times*)

KS 24-10-1891 BEWDLEY

TECHNICAL EDUCATION.— A branch of the Kidderminster School of Science and Art has been established at Bewdley, under the management of a local committee. The session was not formally opened by a public meeting, presided over by a Duke, or a Bishop, or even a local magnate, as in many places, but the committee set quietly to work, and the results so far are most gratifying. The various classes are now well started, and the attendance of students is very satisfactory and far exceeds the most sanguine expectations. Drawing, as usual, is the favourite subject, and there are already nearly 80 names on the register. The lectures in Cookery are also very popular, the number attending the class last Wednesday being close on 50. There is a large class in Foreign Languages, and so many students have joined the classes in Theoretical and Practical Chemistry that it has been found necessary to hold a second class in the latter subject. There is also a class in the Principles of Agriculture, which, when the fact becomes wider known, it is hoped will be largely attended, and be of great benefit to the neighbourhood. The Technical Education grant enables the School of Science and Art to provide good teachers for the working classes at almost nominal fees. The charge at the Cookery Class is only one penny per lesson; for Drawing, 2s. 6d. for 16 lessons; Agriculture and Theoretical Chemistry, 2s. 6d. per course of 30 lessons; and the other classes in proportion. There was keen competition for the Free Studentships open to scholars at the Bewdley and Wribbenhall elementary schools, and the result of the examination showed not only most careful and thorough work on the part of the teachers, but excellent abilities on the part of the scholars. Two of the competitors obtained 260 marks out of a maximum of 320. Four studentships were open to each school, and were awarded to the following in order of merit:—

		Marks
1	Mabel Payne, British Schools (Full marks in Arithmetic and Composition)	260
1	Mary Wrather, British Schools (Full marks in Arithmetic and Composition)	260
3	Charlotte Bishop, Wribbenhall National School	229
4	Arthur Payne, Bewdley National School	222
5	Edmund J. Aust, British Schools	187
6	David J. Potter, Bewdley National School	187
7	Edwin Payne, British School	177
8	Annie Ricketts, Wribbenhall National School	176
9	Charles Maylett, Wribbenhall National School	170
10	Maggie Hunt, Bewdley National School (Full marks in Arithmetic)	163
11	Thomas Barnett, Wribbenhall National School	150
12	Ernest Hunt, Bewdley National School	117

Examinations in those subjects which were comprised in the syllabus of the Science and Art Department were held in **May 1892**. Results:

	1st Class	2nd Class
Drawing, Freehand	5	13
Drawing, Model	1	5
Chemistry (Theoretical)	-	2
Chemistry (Practical)	-	1
Agriculture	1	6

Total numbers of certificates, 34: grant earned, £24-0s-0d. (£24.00). A list of the names of the successful students appears in Appendix II.

Lectures were also given and **classes** held in **1892**, under the management of the Bewdley District Committee, as a local committee of the Worcestershire Chamber of Agriculture: by Mr. Duncan Munro, in *the Principles of Agriculture*; and Mr. Cecil Hooper, in *Fruit Growing and Insect Pests*. The attendance at these lectures and classes 'was not as large as could have been wished in a neighbourhood so essentially agricultural as the Bewdley district'. An examination was held at the conclusion of the courses and prizes were awarded. A list of the winners appears in Appendix II.

The Bewdley District Committee was also constituted a local committee to co-operate with the Dairy School sub-committee of the Worcestershire County Council, in the management of a **class in dairy instruction and butter-making.**

Lectures and practical instruction were given by Miss Boycott of the British **Dairy** Institute, Aylesbury to a large class, numbering 19. A **competition in butter-making** was subsequently held at the Shire Hall, Worcester, when 10 competitors from Bewdley attended and prizes and certificates were awarded. A list of the winners appears in Appendix II.

Dairy Instruction, August 1892
(reproduced by courtesy of the *Kidderminster Shuttle/Times*)

DAIRY INSTRUCTION.—The County Council of Worcester have arranged for the holding of classes in various centres in the County for dairy instruction and have engaged Miss M. A. Boycott, of the British Dairy Institution, near Aylesbury, to give the lectures and demonstrations in butter making. The Mayor of Bewdley, Mr. Langley Kitchen, opened a centre in the social room at the Bewdley Institute on Monday morning and the classes have been held each day during the week. Among those present were the Mayoress, Mrs. Geo. Baker, Beau Castle; Mrs. Tangye, Miss Mauby, Mrs. Moxon, Tickenhill, Miss Hartland, Mrs. Rhodes, Netherton, Miss Woodward, Arley Castle, Miss Brazier Summerdyne Miss Mansell, Mrs. Cornish, Miss Booth, Mrs. Hollington, together with Mr. Oliver J. L. Bird, manager of the County dairy school, Mr. Mason, the organising secretary for the county and Mr. R H. Whitcomb, junr., hon. sec. to the centre. The Mayor remarked that these were times of great advancement and there was still much to be done. Every year thousands of tons of butter were imported into this country which he believed might be produced here if our people were better educated on the subject of dairy-farming. The Worcestershire County Council were doing what they could to remedy the defect. The highest ladies in the land were now lending their influence in that direction and from the Princess of Wales downwards they entered the dairies to study the art of butter making. Practice with science was the remedy for all defects and he commended that motto to all. In connection with the classes to be held during the week his worship remarked that the County Council would offer prizes to be competed for at Worcester in butter making, and all pupils of the classes would be eligible to compete. Miss Boycott then delivered an interesting address explanatory of the work to be taken up in the classes as well as upon the general question of dairy farming and the best method which ought to be adopted. After the address the classes were formed and the practical demonstrations given. The most approved dairy appliances were provided for the use of the students, and the cream separator was at work.

Bewdley Branch Classes & Free Studentships, September 1892
(reproduced by courtesy of the *Kidderminster Shuttle/Times*)

District News.

BEWDLEY. KS 10-9-1892

THE INSTITUTE.—Branch classes of the Kidderminster and District School of Science and Art begin at the Institute on Monday. There will be afternoon classes in Drawing, Chemistry, and Cookery and evening classes in Agriculture, Mathematics, Drawing, Hygiene, and Physiology. The lectures have been successful during the past session, and will doubtless be well attended. Mr. R. H. Whitcombe, Junr., who is acting as district secretary, will give all information that may be required by intending students.

District News.

BEWDLEY. KS 17-9-1892

KIDDERMINSTER AND DISTRICT SCHOOL OF SCIENCE AND ART.—FREE STUDENTSHIPS.—The examination of pupils from the elementary schools of Bewdley and Wribbenhall, to fill eight vacancies, was held at the Bewdley Institute on September 9, by Mr. H. E. Hadley, B.Sc., Head Master of the Science Department at the Central School; and Scholarships have been awarded to the following, in order of merit:—

		Marks.
1	William John Heydon, British Schools	246
2	Elizabeth Bambridge, "	232
3	Emily C. Lawley, Wribbenhall Nat. School	185
4	Florence Emma Stone, British Schools	180
4	Arthur James Payne, Bewdley Nat. School	180
6	Annie Elizabeth Newell, " "	167
7	Fanny May Clarke, " "	160
8	Charles J. Salter, Wribbenhall Nat. School	158
9	Sybil Emily Poole, "	150
10	George O. Postins, "	140

Maximum marks, 300. There was only one vacancy at the British Schools, and this is filled up by the election of William J. Heydon; but Elizabeth Bambridge and Florence Emma Stone, from the same school, having both done exceptionally well, the Examiner recommended that extra scholarships should be awarded to them. The following are re-elected Free Students on account of their industry and regular attendance last year:—Mary Wrather, Edmund J. Aust, and Edwin Payne, British Schools; and Maggie Hunt, Bewdley National Schools.

The A.G.M. in February 1893 reported that the Session **1892-1893** began favourably, with the following **classes**:

On the whole, attendance was well-maintained, but it was regretted that the class in agriculture did not seem to be appreciated.

	Number of students
Drawing (Afternoon), Freehand, Model and Shading from Models	37
Drawing (Evening), Freehand, Model, Outline from the Cast, Shading from the Cast, & **Geometry**	39
Chemistry (Theoretical)	8
Chemistry (Practical)	7
Principles of Agriculture	8
Cookery	-
Mathematics	9
Hygiene	27
Physiology	24
Total number of class entries, excluding cookery,	159

The Annual Report continued: 'Considerable improvements had been made to the **Chemistry Laboratory** at a cost of over £20 and accommodation was now provided for students. £40 had also been spent on apparatus. Twelve **free studentships** were awarded in 1891 to scholars at the Elementary Schools and four were renewed for the current session. A competitive examination was held in September 1892, on the results of which 10 **free studentships** were awarded. Under the new regulations the **pupil teachers and monitors**[64] of the Elementary Schools [had] also **free admission to all science and art classes**. The Committee were pleased that, to a considerable extent, advantage was taken of this privilege.' Thanks were extended to all the teachers 'for the zealous and able way in which they fulfilled their duties and for their earnest efforts to further the welfare of the School'.

'The Education Committee were grateful to the Institute Committee for charging only a **moderate rent** for the admirable Lecture Rooms of the Bewdley Institute. It would not have been possible to organize the School without the grant for Technical Education, but it had been intimated that such grant would only be continued in those districts where it was supported by local assistance. No call had yet been made on local rates or private generosity, but the Committee now thought that they were not only justified but that it was their duty to try to raise by subscriptions a sum at least sufficient to pay the rent of the Lecture Rooms, so that the whole of the grant could be expended in salaries of teachers, apparatus, etc. It would also be an additional encouragement to the students if a Prize Fund were established. The Committee felt it fair to say that the School had now been established on a firm basis; that good, practical and useful work was being done; and that they were confident of continued improvements and further development.'

In summing up at the end of the Annual Meeting, the Mayor (Mr. Langley Kitching) commented that he would be very glad if the Bewdley Town Council would vote a rate in support of the educational classes and for the establishment of a Free Library - a suggestion which was met with hearty applause.

At their Annual Meeting in **February 1894**, the Institute Committee reported that educational work continued to show progress. **Classes** had been held each evening except Saturday during 1893. Most were well-attended. Edward Pease's view of promoting secondary and higher education when he gave the Institute to the town was now being realized and was much appreciated.

The 2nd Annual Report of the Bewdley Branch of the **Kidderminster and District Schools of Science and Art** was presented at this meeting. It showed that the local school continued to improve and indicated signs of further development:

'28 Certificates had been secured in the examinations last May and the grant earned[65] was £24. The Committee had tried to arrange a class in Dairy Work and Butter Making, but the number of students was not sufficient. Classes held during the year were: **Drawing**; Practical and Theoretical **Chemistry**; Principles of **Agriculture**; **Cookery**; **Mathematics**; and **Physiology**, elementary and advanced. The total number of students, exclusive of those attending the cookery classes, was 132. Attendance at most of the classes had been good and regular. The Committee regretted that the class in agriculture had failed to draw the number of students which it ought[66] and unless attendance at the chemistry classes was increased, the classes would either have to be discontinued or reconstructed on new lines. Of the 14 **free studentships** granted last year, 10 were renewed and 6 other free studentships were presented.

The Committee expressed satisfaction that a considerable number of pupil teachers and **monitors** of the elementary schools took advantage of the free admissions to the science classes. The teachers of the classes had fulfilled their duties in a zealous and able way. The work of the School could not be carried on without the aid of a grant made by the County Council, and that grant would only be continued on condition that it was supplemented by local subscriptions. They ought to raise from £15 to £20 to pay the rent of the lecture room and establish a prize fund. The School was appreciated and was doing good work and therefore the Committee appealed to private generosity to support the Institute...'

A popular suggestion by Mr. Kitching was that of forming a Naturalist Field Club or a Natural History Society in connection with the Institute. Mr. J. Birtwistle, regarded as the pioneer of the art and science classes in Bewdley, regretted that more of the youths of the town did not take greater advantage of the Institute, remarking, "At present the ladies seemed to have everything their own way." 'He strongly advocated the establishment of **continuation schools**, where the boys and girls leaving the elementary schools could learn the elementary sciences, and then they would be ready to take advantage of those classes.' Art was taught in the elementary schools, but science was not. It seemed that the youths of the town would rather play football than study! Mr. G. W. Grosvenor, D.L., Chairman of the County Council Technical Education Committee, who presided at this meeting, afterwards presented prizes and certificates to the students.

Classes run by the local branch of the **Kidderminster and District School of Science and Art** during **1894** progressed well and examination results were satisfactory (*see* Appendix II).

Lectures during the year included: a hugely successful course of 6 free lectures to women, organized under the auspices of the **Worcestershire Health Society**. Attendance at the opening lecture was 194 and the average attendance at the course was about 150. The cost of printing and other incidental expenses was paid by some of the ladies who attended the lectures. The Ladies Local Committee *Secretaries* were **Mrs. Spencer** and **Miss Whitcombe**. Mr. **Udale** (*see* Ref. 63) gave 3 very interesting and instructive **lectures**: *Fruit Growing*; *Window Plants*; and *Green Crops*. Institute *Chairman* Mr. John **Gabb**'s very able and useful lecture on *Poultry* was well attended.

During **1897** a special committee was formed to consider how to make the Institute more attractive to 'the man in the street'. Among suggestions were those of having a Debating Society[67] and of holding a course of popular and scientific lectures. No decision had been made about either of these plans by the time of the Annual Meeting in **1898**, but **Continuation Classes** *had* been established - although, sadly, these were running at a loss. Lord Cobham suggested that, 'where possible lady teachers should be secured: they had proved most successful in many districts'.

Classes held by the **Kidderminster Schools of Science and Art** at Bewdley Institute during **1898** were well attended and the students produced very satisfactory examination results. There were about 90 students in the Art classes, these being the best **Art** Classes in the district - with the exception, of course, of those at Kidderminster! There appeared to be a misunderstanding over whether or not the Kidderminster Schools... should pay rent to the Institute for the use of rooms for the science and art classes held there - a misunderstanding perhaps exacerbated by the fact that for some time past there had been no representative of Bewdley Institute on the Kidderminster Executive Committee.[68] Members at the current meeting (1899) elected **Mr. Birtwistle** to fill this role and it was suggested that Lord Cobham, as representative of the Borough on the County Council and as President of Bewdley Institute, be asked to make enquiries into the matter at the County Council. Mr. **Lancashire** was appointed the delegate on the Committee of the [Worcestershire] Union [of Workmen's Clubs and Institutes].

A sum of over £50-0s-0d. (£50.00) - which had been shown in the assets of former years as being due from the Kidderminster and District Schools of Science and Art for rent of rooms - was written off during **1899**.

The report presented at the Annual General Meeting of the Institute, held in March **1900**, showed that **classes** in connection with the **Kidderminster and District Schools of Science and Ar**t had been continued during **1899**. It was agreed to print results of classes at the end of Bewdley Institute's Annual Reports provided it was clearly stated that classes were held there by permission of the Institute and that the Institute received no rent for the use of their rooms. Mr. J. **Birtwistle** was re-appointed representative of Bewdley Institute on the Committee of Kidderminster and District Schools of Science and Art and was voted delegate on the Council of the Worcestershire Union of Clubs and Institutes.

Mr. S. Hemingway, Town Clerk and *Chairman* of the Management Committee of the Institute, was "very sorry to see that the educational side of the Institute made such a poor appearance in the Annual Report for the year **1900**. It must be remembered, however, that the principle that all children should receive elementary education was not recognized by law until 1876 - just two years before the Institute opened - and that school attendance until the age of 10 was only made compulsory in 1880. At first, the majority of the population did not realize the value of education. Consequently, they were slow to take advantage of the opportunities which an Institute like theirs offered of supplying the deficiencies in education which existed at that time." Since then, Mr. Hemingway "suspected that most people thought the education which their children received in the State-aided schools was sufficient, but doubtless the time was coming when there would be a demand for classes such as could be held at the Institute. The Bewdley Committee had done its best to carry out the wishes of the founder..." and he felt sure that Mr. Birtwistle would tell them that some successes had been achieved.

Mr. Birtwistle said, "The Institute had its origin in the desire of the founder to provide for the education of the young people of the place. It arose out of night school work, the founder hoping it would be a centre for the continuation of the education of children after leaving school. At that time, 22 years ago, it was an easy matter to get together a number of young men who felt their education needed supplementing, but since compulsory education came into operation, young people fancied they had completed their education when they had passed through the standards... That was a great fallacy, of course, but it would take time for that to be realized by the community at large. At present, apart from the **art classes** held at the Institute, there was no opportunity in Bewdley for young people improving their education. Public men of all parties were continually referring to the national need for supplementing elementary education, for if people were not educated then the country would fall behind other nations." Mr. Birtwistle's view was that 'the Institute was born before its time and that before long it would be used for educational work again. Classes could very easily be arranged if young people were encouraged to request and attend them. Teachers would be sent from the Kidderminster School of Science if 8 persons could be got together to form a class in any science subject. He did not know whether people were sufficiently aware of that fact. Last October certain classes were advertised, but only 2/3 would-be students presented themselves. The Institute was very well equipped on its social and recreational sides and he hoped in time educational work would be developed. A **Horticultural Society** now met within their walls and if that Society really meant business, then the very first thing it would do would be to have classes in botany. If a class were formed, then there would be no difficulty in getting a teacher.'

Dr. Gabb and Mr. Leacock suggested that some popular lectures might be arranged which would be the preliminary step to forming classes on scientific subjects. Examination results for 1900 appear in Appendix II.

Art and other **Classes** did extremely well in **1902** and the awards secured by the students compared very favourably with those gained at other local Institutes. **Mr. Leacock** called attention to the new Education Act and advised officials to seek a revision in the financial relations with both the Kidderminster School of Science and Art and the Technical Committee of the County Council.

Lectures in **1903** included four on **poultry-keeping for profit**.[69]

At the Institute's 1904 A.G.M. Mr. J. Birtwistle, the local *Hon. Secretary,* reported that **Art Classes** had been held regularly and successfully during **1903** and the examinations in connection with the Board of Education were very satisfactory. Mr. R. B. Dawson, Head Master of the **Kidderminster School of Art**, had arranged an exhibition of the Bewdley and Kidderminster students' work. Held at Bewdley Institute, it had proved both popular and interesting. On the same evening, Alderman P. Adam, President of the *Kidderminster Schools...,* had presented the prizes. (*see* Appendix II)

All the students at the **Shorthand Classes** had passed the examinations and, as well as receiving Certificates from the Midland Counties Association of Institutes, some had won local prizes. (*see* Appendix II)

Twelve **Free Scholarships** had been awarded, i.e. four from each of the elementary schools. 'French and German Classes were abandoned when the teacher, Monsieur Fredreichs, left the town to return to his native country. County 'E' **Scholarships** were awarded to R. E. Lowe and B. J. Oakes for **Building Construction**.' It was important that people should know that the Central Committee offered 'E' Scholarships to anyone who wished to study a subject for which there was no provision at the Institute. Mr. **Birtwistle** was re-appointed representative of the Institute on the Union of Workmen's Clubs and Institutes and also on the Committee of Management of the Kidderminster and District Schools of Science and Art.

In his Report to the Annual Meeting of Institute Members, **1906**, **Mr. Leacock**, *Hon. Secretary* of the Bewdley Branch of the **Kidderminster & District School of Science and Art,** said:

"... Despite the falling off in the number of attendances, good careful work had been done during **1904-1905**; particularly good results were obtained. The two Students who entered a Board of Education Examination had both obtained First Class Certificates. Considering the fact that so many of the students [were] children at school, the general level of work accomplished was good. Students had been encouraged to draw plant-forms from Nature, in addition to the ordinary work done at the school from casts, models, etc."

There were 48 students on the register in July 1905, although - as Mr. Birtwistle pointed out - at present there were only 3 or 4 in regular attendance. Dr. Pennington, presiding, thought this was because local **pupil-teachers** - who formerly attended the Institute classes - now had to attend the centre at Kidderminster instead. There had formerly been a separate Education Committee at the Institute, but currently the classes were under the control of the Kidderminster Committee. Dr. Gabb noted that they could no longer even send pupil-teachers to Bewdley Grammar School. Mr. Birtwistle observed that there did not seem to be 'any desire for education in Bewdley' and suggested that 'some good **Continuation Classes**' were needed. He pointed out the educational advantages of the Institute, saying, "If eight or ten members wanted a special subject taught and banded themselves together, the committee at Kidderminster would make arrangements for a class and provide a teacher. Or if any member wanted his son or daughter to take up a special subject which was not taught at the Institute, the Kidderminster Committee would grant a 'D' Scholarship, which would enable the young person to attend the classes at Kidderminster. Everything was done to give encouragement to study." It was generally agreed that more publicity was needed for the classes at Bewdley Institute.

On the whole, the **Shorthand Class** during **1906** was very satisfactory, with an average attendance of 8 students who had done 'some really good and progressive work'. The **Art Classes**, however, had been a complete failure because too few students had attended the weekly lessons to make it worthwhile sending a qualified teacher over to Bewdley from Kidderminster. Mr. Birtwistle was disappointed to report that the Kidderminster & District School... had telegraphed[70] him on the very day of the Institute's Annual Meeting to say that the Class was to be closed for the session. Each elementary school in the locality was entitled to send 4 students to the Class, but only 2 or 3 had attended, and sometimes there were only 1 or 2! It seemed that the opportunities for study were not valued - and this despite the facts that the teaching was thorough in character, that no effort was spared to meet the requirements of individual students and that in previous years students had achieved considerable success. Mr. Birtwistle hoped that, after the summer months, "an earnest endeavour would be made to restart the Art Classes". He felt that the loss of the Classes would result in an imbalance between educational and recreational facilities at the Institute, thus thwarting the intentions of Mr. Pease. He could remember when people worked much longer hours than they did currently - "... the great plea for shorter hours [being] that the working classes would be able to devote more time to self-improvement... They incurred no local expenses in holding classes, for the Kidderminster Committee sent the teachers and paid a rent for the room." (Evidently, the rent question of 1898/1899 had been resolved satisfactorily.)

Dr. Pennington said he had tried his best to promote the success of the Art Classes, 'but they had to realize that art and higher education were being centralised more than formerly. The Kidderminster Committee required 8 students before a class could be opened. That condition was enforced at Kidderminster, but he wondered if it was fair that the same standard should be adhered to in a small place like Bewdley. Nowadays young people could gain scholarships by means of which they could continue their studies at Kidderminster, their railway fares to that town being paid and all their books found. Formerly most of the students at the local Art Classes were the **pupil teachers** at the elementary schools. Now they received their instruction at Kidderminster, so that the conditions were changed. Their total subscriptions for the year were only £32-0s-0d. (£32.00) and they could not do much with that. They were forced to encourage those things which would assist the income of the Institute...'

Mr. Hemingway suggested arranging a course of **lectures** and Mr. James thought Mr. Langley Kitching might be willing to speak on his travels in Florida and other places when he returned to England.

The *Wesleyan Church Record and Nonconformist Herald* for December **1906** noted that a **'Women's School'**, a new venture, was 'succeeding splendidly. Held in the Institute, Bewdley, on Thursdays at 7.30p.m. Women and maidens are heartily welcomed. Teachers needed.'

Continuation Classes in connection with the **Kidderminster and District Schoo**l... began in the autumn of **1907** and there was a very fair attendance (*cf* 1898). Subjects taught were **reading, writing, arithmetic, composition, drawing, history, citizenship, shorthand, needlework** and **domestic economy**.

Commercial arithmetic, English, reading, history and geography, drawing, shorthand, domestic economy and **needlework** were taught at **Evening Classes** in **1908**. Fifty-one students had attended during the session. Mr. Birtwistle believed the time would soon come when, on leaving the elementary schools, youths would be compelled to attend Evening Classes.

Forty-two students attended **Evening Classes** during the session **1910-1911**. Subjects taught were similar to those of 1907 and 1908: **arithmetic** and **practical drawing, English, reading, citizenship, drawing, shorthand, domestic economy** and **needlework**. The shorthand classes, however, had finished at Christmas due to lack of support. This was to be deplored, for 6 students had passed First Class in the Midland Counties Examination. Two other students had gained scholarships at Kidderminster School of Science and Art. The Committee earnestly appealed to all employers to advise their young employees of the advantages of these Evening Classes. Any shorthand students who wished to continue their studies were reminded that they could attend classes held at Kidderminster and the [Education] Committee would pay their railway fare... Practical **cookery classes** were held on three days each week for children from the three elementary schools. About 50 girls had attended. Members had not shown enough interest in the first of a planned series of winter **lectures** to justify the Committee in proceeding with the course. An offer by Mr. E. Smith to give an illustrated lecture on *Newfoundland* had been accepted.

Lectures arranged by the Committee during **1911** had not been well attended, but the **Evening Classes** *had* been and the **Shorthand Class** re-started.

A most interesting **Lecture**, *Competition for a living in the plant world*, with lantern views, was given in March **1913** by Mr. T. H. Russell, F.L.S., but the disappointingly small attendance of members lent little encouragement to the Committee to arrange further lectures. There were many causes which militated against education, including apathy among members as well as among the young men of the locality.

The Institute received a fair amount of support from residents, but many people still preferred sport to academic study. An interest in sport was good, but it was also important to remember that knowledge was power. Time devoted to study and to keeping abreast of developments was necessary if England were to retain her position at the forefront of the commercial nations of the world.

At the Institute's 35th A.G.M. in **March 1914** it was recorded with regret that the Bewdley Branch of the **Kidderminster Schools**... *had been transferred to Lax Lane Schools*. The decision to move had been taken by the Kidderminster Management Committee alone and there had been nothing that the Bewdley people could do. Mr. Hemingway thought that on hygienic grounds it would have been better to have held the classes in rooms which had not been used in the daytime for elementary education purposes...

Given this discouraging decision, followed so soon by the outbreak of World War I, it is easy to see why there might never have been any further lectures or courses at the Institute! The Committee, however, remained deeply committed to the Institute's role in education and, in **1922**, a **class for people who were blind** made satisfactory progress under the tuition of an instructress from the Blind Institution, Birmingham. Average attendance was 6, members coming from Bliss Gate, Bewdley, Stourport and Kidderminster. Instruction was given in **netting, cane chair making, basket work** and **Braille reading and writing**. No charge was made for the use of the room: the Class could not have continued without this concession. In making the above report the Institute Committee noted that, although they had not had the educational facilities which they formerly held, the Club was not run for sport alone. It was important to remember that education was vital to a commercial nation such as theirs. The *Chairman* urged members to seek suggestions for more educational schemes for consideration by the Committee.

Three **lectures** on **vegetable growing** were given by Mr. H. Patience, F.R.H.S. in February and March 1927, by arrangement with the Bewdley, Wribbenhall and District Horticultural Society. Admission was free.[71]

Whether or not any other educational proposals were forthcoming is unclear, but, over the years, '[Bewdley] Institute's role as a learning centre had gradually changed and diminished due to education reforms and the availability of modern means of transport to larger education centres. The emphasis had shifted to social and recreational activities.'

At the 49th Annual Meeting in **1928** Mr. Stanley Hemingway recalled the old *Wheatsheaf* buildings and the cobbled streets. "There were no rubber-tyred vehicles then! Bewdley Institute was formed primarily for education purposes." He remembered attending the drawing classes, passing out in the advanced stage and failing in the elementary! He believed that the secondary education system of today had been built on the foundations laid by those pioneers. Ridiculed at the time as mere dreamers, in fact they were altruistic people with the vision to see the right and best way of laying foundations on which others could build. They did not expect to see the fruition of their labours. 'Today the educational side of the Institute had almost ceased to exist, so they had to foster the social side to carry on the Club.' Viscount Cobham told the meeting that his grandfather (Lord Lyttelton, 1823-1889) and the Rev. [Henry] Solly (c1813-1903[72]) had been two of the founders of the movement for Institutes and Working Men's Clubs, "the latter being the driving spirit behind the whole thing. In the 1850s and 1860s Mr. Solly used to pester everyone to support the movement. Lord Cobham senior was Mr. Solly's right-hand man. Mr. Solly set out to raise £1200 (a considerable sum then) and it said much for his energy that he was successful in achieving the result. From a little office in the Strand that movement really originated, with astonishing results. All over the country those Clubs and Institutes could be found, very admirably managed and giving a service of unquestioned value..."

Perhaps no further suggestions for educational classes were made, or there was no time to organize them before World War II overtook the nation. In March 1939 the Government propaganda department arranged a film display at the Institute (identical to one given at Stourport),[73] but it was not until **1940** that the re-introduction of 'normal' lectures and other educational facilities was seriously considered again. Sadly, the idea seems to have come to nothing then, but nowadays occasional talks *are* given.

Some Lectures which took place in the Institute (reproduced by courtesy of the *Kidderminster Shuttle/Times*)

Kidderminster Shuttle, 17th January 1880
'LECTURES AT THE INSTITUTE'
'The course of lectures, which the Committee of the Institute arranged at the commencement of the winter months is being thoroughly appreciated, as is evident by the attendances of the members. Mr. T. Wright, of Birmingham, gave an interesting account of his recent visit to New York, Philadelphia, and other large centres in the United States, and the interest in the lecture was intensified by the fact that Mr. Wright's remarks were illustrated by a large number of lime light views.'

Kidderminster Shuttle, 31st January 1880
' "WELL-KNOWN AUTHORS." - There was a large attendance of members and friends at the Institute, on Tuesday, to listen to an able lecture by

Miss Sturge, on "Well-known Authors." The series of lectures is being thoroughly appreciated.'

The Sun, 6th March 1880 (taken from the reprint in Griffith, G: Reminiscences and records, p.595) 'The Institute in Load-street (sic), Bewdley, was visited on Tuesday by eight gentlemen, who are members of the Birmingham Scientific Midland Society, and who brought with them a large number of microscopical instruments and numerous scientific specimens. The art room in the Institute was on this special occasion thrown open to them at 3 o'clock, and the hour of closing was five. At 7 o'clock a second gathering was held, when the scientific visitors were as follow (sic):- Messrs. C. Pumphrey, T. Bolton, C. J. Watson, James John Morley, W. H. Cox, W. R. Morris, and John Levick. Mr. Cox exhibited Melde's experiment, showing the vibrations of a silk cord, which upon being struck gave the fundamental note, and upon the weight being increased the cord became divided into the neutral segments, the nodes being the portion at rest. Mr. Morris exhibited Professor Hughes' audiometer and induction balance; also the magnetic apparatus and the galvanic apparatus, and the Jablochkoff candles for producing electric light. Mr. Bolton exhibited (under the microscope) a number of live specimens of pond life, showing the circulation of blood in young fish and that of the cell contents in nitella, as also a beautiful collection of mounted sea weeds. Mr. Watson brought crystals of selemite by polarised light, cuttle fish bones, and other curiosities. The principal visitors were - the Rector of Ribbesford, the Rector of Dowles and his wife, Mr. and Mrs. Tangye and daughter, Messrs. Binns, Harradine, Wooldrige (sic), Griffith, and many other inhabitants. The day being very wet, the audience was small at both assemblies.'

Kidderminster Shuttle, 5th March 1881
'BEWDLEY
Lectures at the Institute. The Committee has arranged for a series of lectures to be delivered at the Institute, and on Monday evening the first of the series was delivered by Mr.John Killingbeck - "Heat." '

Kidderminster Shuttle, 12th March 1881
'Fruit culture. The second of the series of lectures to be delivered in connection with the Institute was given on Monday evening in the lecture room by the Rev. W. Lea of Droitwich - "Fruit culture". The attendance was not very large. The lecture was a very interesting and instructive one.'

Kidderminster Shuttle, 2nd April 1881
'On Monday evening Mr. Lloyd Davies delivered the second portion of his lecture descriptive of his tour to the Holy Land. There was a large attendance. -- On Tuesday evening Mr. Harradine, chemist, [see Ref. 230] lectured at the Institute, on "Water," to an attentive audience. - The series of lectures which the committee of the Institute has arranged has been much appreciated.'

Kidderminster Shuttle, 22nd October 1881
'DISSOLVING VIEWS AT THE INSTITUTE -- The committee of the Institute has been fortunate in securing the assistance of Mr. Tomkinson, carpet manufacturer, of Kidderminster, whose interest in workmen's clubs and institutes is well known, and has often been displayed in the most substantial and practical forms. On Monday next, the 24th inst., that gentleman will give his lecture, originally delivered in the Town Hall, Kidderminster, on the "Mutiny on the Bounty," illustrated by exquisite dissolving views, with the powerful lime light. Mr. Tomkinson's apparatus is the best and most effective we have seen, and the lecture which we reported at the time it was delivered to the members and friends of the Workmen's Club here, is a very succinct and graphic narrative of incidents which used to have, and no doubt will have, a fascination for the young, and scarcely less for those advanced in life. For who is there not interested in the story of the Pitcairn Islanders? Our Bewdley friends may expect a rare treat on Monday night. We are glad to learn that Mr. Tomkinson intends to give the children of the Kidderminster Board Schools, and of St. John's, an exhibition of his dissolving views at an early date.'

Kidderminster Shuttle, 18th March 1882

> KS.18-3-1882 **District News.**
>
> **BEWDLEY.**
>
> THE INSTITUTE.—A lecture, the proceeds of which will be devoted to the above, will be given in the Town Hall, on Thursday evening next, at eight o'clock, by Sir Richard Temple, G.C.S.I., on "India." A most interesting and instructive lecture may be anticipated.

Mrs. Parker writes: 'After a lecture at the Institute in 1882 on the wonders of the new ELECTRIC LIGHT, my father [Joseph Tangye] made a dynamo and used to show visitors the light in his workshop. We had to keep on pushing the carbon points together as they burnt out almost at once. As accumulators had not been invented the engine was kept working whilst the light was on, so it was not used in the house.'
(*Source*: Two brothers, p.6).

Kidderminster Shuttle, 17th March 1883
'LECTURE ON THE ATMOSPHERE. - On Tuesday evening Dr. Masterman, medical officer of health for Stourport district, gave an interesting lecture on "The Atmosphere" at the Bewdley Institute. The Rev. J. R. Burton, M.A., presided and there was a large and attentive audience. The lecture was ably illustrated by a variety of experiments which were much appreciated. A hearty vote of thanks was accorded to Dr. Masterman, who kindly promised to give another lecture before long.'

Kidderminster Shuttle, 22nd November 1890
'LECTURE ON INDIA. - Mr. Frederick Sessions, of Gloucester, is announced to give a lecture at the [Bewdley] Institute, on "India" and Alderman George Baker will preside. Mr. Sessions has spent some time in visiting the Mission Stations of the Society of Friends and others in India, and in investigating the social and political conditions of the people. The lecture cannot fail to be full of interest.'

and

'COAL TAR. - A very interesting lecture was given at the Bewdley Institute, on Wednesday evening, by Mr. W. Ray, F.C.S., F.I.C., Master of the Kidderminster School of Science, on "Coal Tar, and what we get from it." There was a numerous and appreciative audience. The lecturer traced the history of coal tar, from the commencement of the discovery of gas, and illustrated by a variety of experiments the methods adopted by English and foreign chemists in their researches for the various products. He gave some practical examples of the application of the products for dyeing cotton and wool. He next exhibited the various extractions which produce scent, those utilised as medicine, and others used as explosives. A vote of thanks to the lecturer was proposed by the Chairman, Dr. Gabb, and seconded by the Mayor, Mr. L. Kitching, and heartily responded to by the audience.'

Kidderminster Shuttle, 21st April 1894

> KS 21 4 **District News.**
>
> **BEWDLEY.**
>
> FRESH EGGS TWELVE MONTHS OLD!—On Tuesday evening Sir John Gabb, J.P. Chairman of the Institute Committee delivered an interesting address to a large audience in the Art room on Poultry. During the address Mr. Gabb exhibited two eggs which were laid twelve months ago, preserved by him. When the eggs were opened it was declared that they were perfectly fresh. Mr. Gabb gave much useful information on the treatment of poultry, and the preservation of eggs. On the motion of Mr. Wallis, seconded by the Rev. J. F. Aust, hearty thanks were tendered to Mr. Gabb for his instructive address.

How we breathe
(reproduced by courtesy of the *Kidderminster Shuttle/Times*)

THE KIDDERMINSTER SHUTTLE—APRIL 28, 1883

LECTURE AT BEWDLEY BY MRS. R. W. DALE.

HOW WE BREATHE.

On Wednesday evening a most interesting and instructive lecture was delivered in the Lecture Hall of the Bewdley Institute by Mrs. R. W. Dale, the wife of the eminent Nonconformist pastor of Carr's Lane Chapel, Birmingham, on "How we breathe." The lecture was delivered under the auspices of the Institute, and Miss E. Sturge, who is now the hon. Sec., occupied the chair. There was a large attendance.

Miss Sturge remarked that when at Birmingham she had the pleasure of listening to one of Mrs. Dale's lectures, and was so charmed that she was exceedingly anxious to bring her to Bewdley, and she was sure all would be profited and interested in the lecture about to be delivered.

Mrs. Dale commenced by remarking that she owed her audience an apology for the kind of lecture she was about to deliver. That was the first time she had visited Bewdley, and she was so charmed with the beauty of the neighbourhood and with the clearness of the atmosphere that she was convinced she ought to have chosen something different to lecture about—poetry, or flowers, or some kindred subject. The fact was she had been bribed into paying Bewdley a visit. She met Miss Sturge at a temperance gathering at Malvern some time ago, and Miss Sturge then asked her to come to Bewdley. Miss Sturge referred to flowers, and said she should have plenty of them if she would come, and as she was passionately fond of flowers she promised to come. She was going to speak about the lungs and the air we breathe. They should understand that she only delivered elementary physiological lectures, dealing with the human body and the laws of health. It was most interesting to know all about the lungs and the various parts and functions of the human body, and if such knowledge was more general and the question more uniformly understood, a great deal of the ill health people suffered would be done away with. The physicians of Birmingham had told her that the hospitals were full because so many persons knew so little about the requirements of the human body. The reason she gave lectures on those subjects was this. In Birmingham there was an association called the Ladies' Association for Useful Work. They took up various subjects, and among them was the holding of classes where health lectures were delivered, and they were attended by the working women and girls of the town. There were about eight women lecturers, and each gave one or two courses per year. Those lectures created a great deal of interest, partly because the subjects were interesting—for a person must indeed be dull that was not interested in physiological subjects—and partly because the leading men of the town rendered valuable assistance. The women were encouraged to write answers to the questions asked on paper, and then prizes were awarded for the most successful students. The last evening of the session, when the prizes were distributed, was made as interesting as possible with singing and short addresses from the Mayor and other leading citizens. Such a system not only obtained in Birmingham, but had been successfully started at Leeds, Nottingham, Wolverhampton, Walsall, and other places. At London the lectures did not succeed so well, and she hoped that something of the kind would be attempted in that neighbourhood. Coming to the subject, Mrs. Dale said they all knew we could not live without air. We could do without eating and drinking for some time, but we could not do without air for a minute; we were feeding on air every moment. When we eat and drank we did not like to take anything dirty or unwholesome; and yet while many persons were most particular about their food they were not at all particular about the air they fed upon. It was quite as necessary for health to breathe good fresh air as to drink pure water. By means of a large diagram, Mrs. Dale described the mechanism of the chest. The chest was not a rigid bony case, but highly elastic, so that it expanded very readily when breathing. If pressed in a crowd a person would be able to sustain great pressure from the front because of the elasticity given to the ribs by the cartilage with which the twelve pairs of rib bones in the chest were tipped; but if the pressure came on the sides there would be greater fear of the ribs being broken. The chest, then, was elastic from the front backwards, and brittle from side to side. At the bottom of the ribs was a great arch-muscle, known as the diaphragm, which assisted us in breathing. The chest had nothing whatever to do with the stomach. The lungs were a pair of spongy elastic bodies, having their sides closely applied to the walls of the chest. When air passed into the lungs, the walls of the chest expanded, and contracted when the air was expelled. They might compare the lungs to a bag of air cells or pockets containing air, with one large pipe, known as the windpipe, with pipes branching out from it. A portion of the air taken into the lungs passed through the air pockets and entered the blood, making it red and healthy. They might ask, What is air? It was a collection of gases, which could not be observed, so that if they were to remove every piece of furniture out of a room it would still be filled with air. It was made principally of two gases, with the smallest quantity of a third gas. One of the principal gases was necessary to life, but if taken alone it would destroy life; therefore it had to be diluted with the other gas. She alluded to oxygen, and the gas which mixed with it was nitrogen, the third gas being carbonic acid. The latter gas was very poisonous. Many had heard of the famous grotto near Naples, where carbonic acid gas flowed out of the earth. Large crowds of visitors went yearly to see the effects of that gas. A poor miserable dog was kept, upon which the operations were made. As soon as the dog was brought into contact with the poisonous gas it became unconscious and showed signs of being poisoned, but as he animal would be wanted for the next batch of visitors it was immediately brought into the open air, and by inhaling oxygen revived. The oxygen gas passed into the blood through the little air cells. The blood was always circulating through the body, and when the blood came from the heart to the lungs it was of a dark colour, but as soon as it came into contact with oxygen the blood was changed into a bright red. The change effected depended entirely upon the quantity of oxygen which entered into the body. If the blood contained much carbonic acid gas it was black or purple; but if, as it should, it contained plenty of oxygen, it was of a bright scarlet colour. They would therefore see the necessity of breathing pure air if the blood was to be kept in a healthy condition. A larger quantity of carbonic acid gas passed from the body than was taken in, and this gas was absorbed by the trees, which gave out in return oxygen. They would see how anxious people were who lived in large towns and cities to get flourishing trees in the streets. Mrs. Dale gave two or three instances of the powerful and injurious effects of carbonic acid gas in a room. Not long ago, on a cold night, she was lecturing in Highbury Chapel. The place was exceedingly warm and comfortable; but by-and-bye some of the women in the audience began to faint away and no less than six persons had to be taken out. She then made enquiries, and found that while the Curator had made the place very warm he had not opened the ventilators, and the result was that the audience were breathing poisonous air. It was because public buildings were not properly ventilated that so many persons fainted away in a large audience. She cautioned her hearers against the usual practice of crowding round a person who had fainted. What was wanted was plenty of fresh air, the upper part of the clothes unfastened, and a little water dashed over the face, and the sufferer would soon recover. It was a good thing that air could find its way through little crevices, or many persons would be nearly suffocated. Many people made the room, especially the bedroom, as nearly air-tight as possible, blocked up the chimney, and kept both door and window closed, shutting out as completely as possible all the pure air from without. They would remember the terrible sufferings of the passengers on board an emigrant ship some time ago. A dreadful storm arose, and the order was given by the Captain that all the emigrants should be put in the room below. The sailors obeyed and fastened down the hatches. The storm raged for several hours, and when the sailors opened the hatches to get the emigrants out, the candle went out. This was repeated three times, and it was not until most of the poisonous gas had escaped that the candle would burn. By closing the door the supply of oxygen gas had been cut off, and nearly all the men, women and children were found lying on the floor, some dead and others unconscious. Then there was another terrible instance driving home the same lesson. They all knew of the Black Hole of Calcutta, a place about 20 feet square, into which 146 persons were packed and left for a considerable time. Their sufferings were horrible to read about. They raved at and entreated the keepers to shoot upon them rather than keep them in that atmosphere. In the morning, when the doors were open, only 23 ghastly men staggered out of the place; all the rest had died, suffocated by the carbonic acid gas. And yet the majority of people would not allow oxygen gas to enter the bedroom during the night. They breathed the same atmosphere over and over again, and then were surprised in the morning that they were not refreshed. They had all noticed what a sickening sensation was frequently experienced on entering a sick chamber, owing to the want of a supply of pure air. There was a great prejudice against opening the bedroom window at night. People had the idea that the night air was bad, but Miss Nightingale had told them that it was the purest air we breathed. Mrs. Dale stated that she always slept with her window slightly open. A strip of wood placed along the bottom of the window would allow the fresh air to enter the room between the two sashes in the middle of the window, and that, in her opinion, was the best way to ventilate the room at night. We could not reconstruct our houses, but we could do our best to ventilate the rooms. She cautioned mothers against allowing children to get into the habit of sleeping with their heads under the bedclothes, which was a very unhealthy habit, and when mothers took their babies out they covered them up with a thick shawl, preventing the pure atmosphere from getting to the children. The climate was severe and changeable it was true, as all had experienced during the last two or three months, but a thin porous wrapper over the face of the child was at the most all that was needed. Because we could not see the bad air, we had great difficulty in understanding how very hurtful it was. They frequently read of men being killed in mines, or sewers, entirely due to the bad atmosphere around them. Mrs. Dale then proceeded to describe the construction of the wind pipe, which extended from the mouth into the lungs. There were two pipes in the throat: the wind-pipe which conveyed the air into the lungs from the nose and mouth, and the gullet which conveyed the food to the stomach. The wind-pipe was very beautifully constructed. There were strong rings of cartilage which went nearly all round the pipe, and being elastic enabled the food to pass easily down the gullet at the back. From the windpipe sprang a pipe going to the right and left lung, and from these large numbers of other tubes, called bronchial tubes, branched out like the branches of a tree. It was when these small tubes were inflamed that people had bronchitis. Looking at the construction of the throat, they would see how important it was not to allow children to put foreign substances, such as pins, pencils, marbles, and other things into their mouths. She was reading in last week's Medical Journal of a case where a boy allowed a pin to pass into the throat. For a few days he suffered a good deal, and then all pain disappeared for over twelve months, when great pain was experienced in the throat. Upon examination, it was found that the pin had been lodged in the throat during the whole of the time, and, by a remarkably skilful operation, the pin was extracted. Among the many complaints from which children sometimes suffered, croup was the most dangerous. It frequently occurred after the child had been in bed a few hours. Sometimes it arose from a membrane growing over the windpipe, and sometimes from excessive inflammation at the top of the pipe. The best plan was to send for a doctor at once. In the meantime the parent should give the child an emetic, and apply hot fomentations to the front. In the absence of anything better, a little mustard and warm water made a good emetic. Consumption was the wasting away of the lung, and was even now almost an incurable disease. It was very common in this country, and hence the great necessity for people to take care of the lungs. The lungs were the great breathing organs, and, along with the skin and kidneys, they got rid of the waste matters from the body. The skin and lungs did very much the same kind of work, for carbonic acid gas was exuded from the skin through the wonderful little glands. Hence it was that when people suffered from lung disease special attention was paid to the skin; and the same was done if the kidneys were out of order. It was important to keep the skin beautifully clean, because there were thousands upon thousands of those little glands sending out the perspiration from the body. We must see that we breathed pure air. We knew how delicate the lungs were, and, in order to assist the lungs in the discharge of their functions, we should make a habit of breathing through the nose instead of through the mouth. People wore respirators so that cold air should not pass directly into the lungs; but the nose was so beautifully constructed that the air was warmed before it passed down into the chest. The Indian mothers always trained their babies to keep their mouths closed, and to breathe through the nose; and that was a custom which English mothers could copy with great profit. A great many people were very careful to keep warm comforters and preservers over the front of the chest, but, if at all, they should do the same to the back of the chest, because the lungs filled the whole of the space. She was never tired of warning mothers against the custom of dressing their infants and young children in low-necked dresses and short sleeves. Of course they might succeed in hardening the children, but the process was a dangerous one. If children were to be healthy and strong, attention should be paid to that matter. We should take care to wear flannel next to the skin in such a changeable climate as ours. We should remember that, just as we took care to keep our bodies in good health, the same care and thoughtfulness should be extended to the dumb animals — dogs, cats, monkeys, horses, cows, etc. They were made very much as human beings were — some of them quite as delicate in their construction; and it was just as necessary that they should have a proper supply of pure air as the human race. Many people lost sight of that very important fact; and it was the duty of parents to inculcate in the minds of their children the importance of being kind and considerate to animals.

Miss STURGE, on behalf of those present, expressed to Mrs. Dale the delight which it had given them to listen to her address, and in their name she tendered hearty thanks to Mrs. Dale for visiting Bewdley on that occasion.

Health Lectures, September and October 1894
(reproduced by courtesy of the *Kidderminster Shuttle/Times*)

KS 15-9-1894

District News.

BEWDLEY.

HEALTH LECTURES AT THE INSTITUTE. — Arrangements are being made for the delivery of a series of six lectures at the Institute under the auspices of the Worcestershire Health Society. The lectures will be free to women, and Mrs. Edith Sykes, associate of the Sanitary Institute, London, will be the lecturer. The series will commence on Friday evening, October 12th, and will be held on each Friday at eight o'clock. Mrs Spencer (Spring Grove), Mrs. Robert Woodward (Arley Castle), and other ladies have promised to preside. The lectures will deal with such important questions as nursing the sick, infectious disease, food, clothing and other points of the greatest importance in the household.

District News.

BEWDLEY.

THE BAPTIST CHURCH. — On Sunday last the annual harvest thanksgiving services were held at this place of worship. The building was tastefully decorated. On Monday evening a social meeting was held, which was well attended.

WORCESTERSHIRE HEALTH SOCIETY. — The course of free lectures to women under the auspices of this society was opened last Friday evening. The Art School at the Bewdley Institute was filled some time before the lecture commenced by a highly appreciative audience numbering 194, representatives from all classes being present, some few being unable to find even standing room. Mrs. Alfred Baldwin presided, and after a few introductory remarks from her as to the importance of the course of lectures and the great benefit to be derived from them, Miss Edith Sykes the lecturer to the Health Society, gave a most interesting and instructive discourse on nursing the sick, the sick room: how to keep it fresh and airy, and the best modes of ensuring a proper ventilation, concluding with a demonstration of how to make the invalids' bed and change the sheets, &c. A hearty vote of thanks to Mrs. Baldwin for presiding was afterwards moved by Mrs. John Gabb, and seconded by Mrs. Langley Kitching, as representing the Chairman and Deputy-Chairman of the Institute Committee. The Ladies' Local Committee are to be congratulated on the interest they have already created in the lectures. This (Friday) evening Mrs. Spencer will preside, the subject being scarlet fever, typhoid, measles, and other infectious diseases.

KS 20-10-1894

District News.

BEWDLEY.

HEALTH LECTURES. — The third of Miss Edith Sykes' interesting and instructive Lectures to Women will be given to-night (Friday), at the Bewdley Institute, at eight o'clock. The subjects will be Poultices, Fomentations, and the Treatment of Bronchitis. The proper mode of making poultices and fomentations will be practically demonstrated in the lecture room. These are matters in which all women having anything to do with the care of a family or the management of a household must feel an interest, and the Worcestershire Health Society is doing a good work in arranging for the delivery of these Free Health Lectures at various centres in the county. We are glad to find that the movement meets with the personal support and encouragement of the ladies of the district. Mrs. Alfred Baldwin presided at the opening lecture, on the 12th, and Mrs. Spencer on the 19th. Mrs. Robert Woodward, Mrs. Reiss, and other ladies have undertaken to take the chair. — A similar course of six lectures, following the same syllabus, is being delivered on Friday afternoons, at three o'clock, at the Kidderminster School of Science. Mrs. Grosvenor presided at the opening lecture.

KS 27-10-1894

Chapter 5:
Library Facilities

The Literary and Scientific Institution

The *Bewdley and Wribbenhall Literary and Scientific Institution*, founded in **1848** at the Old Grammar School,[74] had at least two homes before moving to numbers 21-23 Load Street. Presumably, the organization had built up a collection of books over the years and these may well have formed the nucleus of the library at the Institute.

Interestingly, one of the original *Trustees* of Bewdley Institute was Thomas *Caldwell* Dalley, son of Thomas *Edward* Dalley, who had been a member of the Institute Working Party Committee. Thomas Edward was recorded in 1855[75] as *Secretary, Literary and Scientific Institution, Load Street*. In that year his business premises were in Load Street (probably at numbers 10/11), whence he operated as a 'bookseller, stationer, printer, paper hanger, music seller, Registrar of Births and Deaths, agent to the London Mutual Life Office, and for London and Dublin Stout'. A man of stamina, indeed, to cope with all those activities! Whether or not the *Literary and Scientific Institution* actually *met* at 10/11 Load Street is unclear.

By 1876 the *Bewdley and Wribbenhall Literary Institution* met at 68 Load Street[76] (currently Murray's Chemists and Photo Centre). The move to more permanent accommodation at Bewdley Institute in *c*1878 must have afforded the group a welcome opportunity to expand both their membership and their bookstock.

The Library and Reading Room

Important parts of the facilities at the Institute were the **Library and Reading Room**. Mr. Gething's modified plan shows that they were intended as two separate rooms and confirmation that this was so is provided by local Press Reports of the Official Opening and of the Institute's Annual General Meetings until *c*1927/1928.

Confusingly, there were two **Reading Rooms** at first, as revealed in *Mark's Penny Guide* [published at some time between 1878 and 1887], (p.15): '... Visitors may enjoy the privileges of the **Newspaper** and **Reading Rooms** [at the Institute] on payment of One Penny (approx. 0.42p) per day.' The cost was still one penny per day in 1927!'[77]

At the A.G.M. in January **1885**, the Committee was asked to consider the advisability of **amalgamating the two reading rooms** in an effort to keep running costs as low as possible. Consequently, in October 1885 'it was decided to close the Working Men's Reading Room[78] and to include all its members who had paid a 5s-0d. (25p) subscription for the year in the honorary members' Reading Room.'[79] Intended only as an experiment, the idea evidently met with subscribers' approval.

This Reading Room's opening hours always seem to have been from 8.0a.m. - 9.0p.m., remaining unchanged in 1927, after consideration by members at the Annual Meeting.

In **1892** the Committee increased the number of periodicals and newspapers taken in the Reading Room. New titles were: *The 19th century; English illustrated; Scribner's* and *Century* magazines and *Farm and home* and *Garden work*.

Well supplied with newspapers and periodicals during 1893, additional titles were taken in **1894**.

The Reading Room continued popular in **1903, 1908** and **1909**. Complaints had been made - and the vigilance of members sought - regarding the removal of newspapers and magazines in **1905**. Despite this, the Room was still well-used that year, although Mr. Stonehouse thought, "... the expenses on it might be curtailed, for [it] was not used by a large number of members".

Annual sales of the Reading Room's **newspapers and magazines** appear to have taken place over a number of years: e.g. 'Mr. George Holloway obtained greatly enhanced prices at the sale which he conducted in **1896**'; 'Mr. G. Herbert Banks once again gave his services as auctioneer at a very successful sale in **1903**'; and 'satisfactory prices were obtained from members for the [many] newspapers [and magazines] taken during **1922** and **1933**'.

At the **1934** Annual Meeting it was reported that Bewdley Town Council had approached the County Council regarding the provision of a **Public Reading Room** in the Borough. The suggestion, received favourably, had come before the County Library Committee on 3rd March. It was decided that the Chairman of that Committee (Ald. W. S. Lane) should visit Bewdley, meet the Mayor and discuss thoroughly, although the Mayor thought that Bewdley Council would reject the idea when they realized it would be a charge on the Bewdley rates... It seems that the idea *was* rejected, for the Institute Reading Room was still well patronised in **1942** and **1943**.

The Institute Library

In **1883**, 158 books were circulated. Perhaps because additional books were donated during **1884** and because a *Librarian* had been appointed by then, the year saw an increased use of the Library: 357 volumes were borrowed - 185 being 'books of scientific or educational value' and 172 works of fiction. Mr. Jacob had made a complete catalogue of the books and the effects and fixtures belonging to the Institute.[80]

The first *Librarian* traced so far, **John Humpherson**, was the *only* officer recorded at Bewdley Institute in Kelly's Directory for **1884**. One hopes he never had similar problems to those experienced by the *Parochial Library* in 1887, as reported under 'Local Matters' in the *Church Monthly* for December that year:

'We wish earnestly to impress upon all members [of the Local Lay Helpers' Union] not to take books out of the Library without entering them in the register provided for the purpose. The reason why the Library has been closed [for stock-taking] for so long a period has been almost entirely the difficulty experienced this year in getting all the books returned. In fact in going over the list no less than 33 were found to be out in no one's name. If it is found impossible to remedy this in any other way it will become necessary to close the Library altogether except at certain specified times, and to appoint a librarian. But as this would do away with its usefulness to a great extent, and cause much inconvenience to members, we earnestly hope that it may not be needful to resort to this course.' Presumably, the inconvenience would have been caused by *closing the library* - although, as a librarian myself, I can appreciate that recourse to *appointing* one must have represented the ultimate threat to the customers!

During **1885** the Library proved one of the most satisfactory departments of the Institute. The books had been classified and those no longer required sold. 253 volumes had been in circulation, of which 110 were fiction, 56 magazines and 87 'books of more solid character'. Of the total, 64 were taken from the boxes of the Worcestershire Union of Clubs and Institutes, to which readers were indebted for a variety that the shelves of the Institute Library did not afford.

The *Church Monthly*, October **1887**, had noted an idea to obtain a wider readership for the Institute's books:
'... A suggestion thrown out by the President seemed to be widely approved to the effect that the Union might extend the circulation of its book boxes, upon payment of the usual subscription, to any association of persons who might desire to join together to form a reading society, whether they chose further to organize themselves into a regular club or not. This would seem to offer a still wider sphere of usefulness to the Union than it has at present.'

The Annual report covering **1889** noted: 'The demand on the books in the Library has not been quite as large as in 1888; 463 being the total number of those that have been in circulation during the year. Of these, 109 were taken out by members of Mr. Smith's **Mutual Help Society** [which had started life in the Institute in c1886]. The new books acquired through the [recently formed scheme of paying a] subscription to the Worcestershire Union of Clubs and Institutes were: *The life of W. E. Forster* and Miss Gordon Cumming's *Wanderings in China*. Those which would accrue to the Institute in October, when they had gone the round of the Clubs which united in the **new book** scheme, were: Stead's *Russia*; *The life of Drummond*; *The fairy land of science*; and volume 1 of Mr. C. Booth's *Life and labours of the people*.'

During **1890** 381 books were in circulation from the boxes supplied by the Worcestershire Union of Clubs and Institutes and from the Institute's own shelves. Not as many as in the previous year, this was probably because the members of the Mutual Help Society no longer met at the Institute. Among the new books chosen for the Institute in accordance with the rules of the new book scheme were: *Viceregal life in India*; Arthur Young's *Travels in France*; and *The history of the Jews*.

264 books were issued in **1891**. New ones were needed, especially books on elementary science.

During **1892** 278 books and 9 magazines were in circulation. The Mayor's expressed hope that the Town Council would vote a rate for the establishment of a Free Library was popular with those who attended the Institute's Annual Meeting in 1893.

The Library was well-patronised in **1893**, 500 books were circulated and many new ones were added to stock.

1894 saw a record number of 824 books circulated and the Committee hoped that the satisfactory state of the funds would now enable them to assign an annual sum to buy new titles to meet the demand which evidently existed. The Library had been set apart for **Chess** and **Draughts** on one evening per week.

During **1898** the number of books circulated was 263, compared with 442 in **1897** and 576 in **1896**. Perhaps the decrease in issues was due to two reasons:
(a) although book boxes from the Worcestershire Union of Clubs and Institutes were appreciated, some members felt that the books were 'stiff and antiquated';
(b) by 1898, the Library had been adapted [temporarily] for use as a Social Room.

Although an attractive and successful facility, it had been accomplished by shutting off the books by means of wire doors, thereby perhaps rendering them inaccessible on some occasions when would-be readers were present.

The Library was still used as a Social Room in 1899. The *Kidderminster Shuttle* of 21st October 1899 reported that the eventual intention was to convert 'the **large room now set apart for library purposes** into a social room. The desire is to increase the attractions and usefulness of the library, and with improved accommodation in the new building [the Billiard Room to be built at the rear of the main premises], there ought to be no difficulty in accomplishing this.'

Part of the purpose of a very successful bazaar held in the newly erected Billiard and Recreation Room at the Institute in May **1900** was to raise funds for the Library. In her opening speech, the **Countess of Portsmouth** said that Bewdley 'did not possess a town library and the Library of the Institute - which had been much appreciated in the past - needed replenishing with modern works'.

122 books were circulated in **1900**, 315 in **1902** and 280 in **1903**.

It was reported at the Annual General Meeting of March 1906 that the Library needed yet more new books: 174 had been circulated during **1905** compared with 270 in **1904**.

The reason that only 101 books were circulated during **1906** was thought to be the lack of new titles and the want of funds to buy them.

The Library was not well patronised during **1908**. At the Annual Meeting in March 1909 it was reported that although some of the books were old they contained much good instruction.

A much-needed fillip in the form of new titles acquired during **1909** led to greater use of the Library for a time, but book issues of 162 and 190 in 1911 and 1912, respectively, were still not enough to prove that the Library was as well patronised as it might have been.

A 30 volume set of Encyclopedia Britannica was a welcome gift from Mrs. Sturt in **1913**. That year, to improve facilities for members, the **Library** was overhauled and a selection of in-demand books transferred to the cases in the **Reading Room**.

The combination of new location, new stock[81] and the attention and courtesy of the energetic *Librarian*, **Mr. Johnson**, helped boost book issues to 608 during **1914**, compared with 151 in 1913. It was felt that, generally, a good deal of the literature in libraries was of the popular variety but that there was also a need for more serious books to help prepare for new situations and circumstances which would pertain after the War.

Books circulated during **1915** numbered 633 after further new titles had been purchased. Mr. Johnson having joined the Forces, **Captain Lawson** had undertaken the duties of *Librarian*.

There being no other funds available, a few titles had been purchased with money donated in 1916, but at 273 and 262, respectively, the number circulated during **1916** and **1917** remained fairly static.

Perhaps the end of the War heralded a new interest in reading/studying, for issues climbed to 425 in **1918**. Although this figure fluctuated between 255 and 620 during the next four years,[82] contributory factors may have been:

- the lack of new books. None were purchased in 1922 and it is doubtful if there was any money to spend on them in the aftermath of War - if, indeed, (m)any were published!
- the discontinuance of the book boxes from the Worcestershire Union of Clubs and Institutes in 1922.

By the time of the Annual Meeting in March 1923 the Institute Committee had subscribed to the Village Clubs Association, the understanding being that this Association would recommence the book boxes. The hope that new books would be added in the coming year may not have been realized for volumes circulated during **1923** were 178 fewer than in the previous year! This situation was rectified in **1924**, with new titles being purchased and 622 books circulated.

At the Annual Meeting in 1927 it was agreed that books could be borrowed for a period of 14 days, with power to renew.

In **1927** 1750 books had been used (sic) and in **1928** issues from the **Library and Reading Room** were 1715, so that perhaps each member read over 100 titles per annum during those two years!

During **1929** new books were added and Mrs. Sturt donated a copy of *The Worcestershire Regiment in the Great War*.

By **1933**, however, 'interest in the Club's Library was at a low ebb, doubtless due to the more up-to-date neighbourly opposition of the County Library'.

The Institute Library still lacked support in **1934** and **1935**, but periodicals and daily newspapers maintained their popularity and - as noted elsewhere - the **Club Reading Room** continued to be well patronised almost a decade later, during both **1942** and **1943**.

Over the years, donations to the Library/Reading Room and (in 1889 and 1890, if not in other early years) to the **Reading Room and Coffee Tavern** (*q.v.*) included: *newspapers* from Mr. C. Sturge, the Rev. E. H. W. Ingram, Messrs. J. Tangye, J. R. Thomson and J. M. Sturge: and books from Miss Bromley, Mrs. Enoch Baldwin, Miss E. M. Sturge, the Revs. J. R. Burton, and E. H. W. Ingram, Mrs. Sturt, Mr. F. Porter, Mr. E. Smith, Mrs. Parker and Miss Tangye, J.P. The last two ladies regularly provided *The Spectator*, *The Fishing Gazette* and the *Monthly Review* for use in the Reading Room during the 1930s. Other donors included Mrs. Tangye and Miss Booth.

<u>**Miss Eliza Mary Sturge** (1842-1905), *Librarian*, former *Secretary* of the Institute, and sister-in-law of Mr. Edward Pease</u>

By **1904** the *Librarian* was Miss **Eliza M[ary] Sturge**, daughter of Charles Sturge (one-time corn factor and resident of Wribbenhall). A younger sister of Mrs. Sarah Pease, Eliza was a great support in establishing the Institute.[83] Indeed, both the building and her role there must have held particular poignancy and importance for Eliza[84] since Edward Pease had offered to give the Institute to the town not long before Sarah died.[85] Eliza always played an active part in its life - not least her roles of *Secretary* (from about April 1883 until 1893) and *Fund Raising Committee Member*, with Mrs. I. M. Sturge and others, in 1892.[86] The Committee at the 1894 A.G.M. recorded: 'It was mainly due to Miss Sturge's unselfish devotion to the interests of the Institute that it had been able to accomplish such good work and had now become self-supporting.'

After the death of her mother, Mary Darby Sturge,[87] Eliza was often asked to act as hostess to John Bright, the orator and statesman, for he usually stayed at her father's house in Frederick

Road, Edgbaston, Birmingham when he visited his constituents.[88]

A champion of women's rights and of peace principles, Eliza frequently addressed public meetings in support of these causes. Perhaps she was the Miss Sturge who was the *Secretary* of the Woman's (sic) Suffrage Association, listed at 330 Broad Street, Birmingham, in 1876.[89]

Like her father and her Uncle Joseph Sturge, Eliza was actively involved in philanthropic, temperance and educational movements. She was the first lady member of the Birmingham School Board and, later, was for many years a member of the Worcestershire Education Committee and of the Kidderminster and District Education Committee. She was also *Secretary* of the British Schools at Wribbenhall as well as one of its *Managers*.

For many years Eliza lived with her younger sister, Maria (c1849-1907), on Bark Hill[90] - at number 28 in 1899.[91] Both are buried in the grounds of the Quaker Meeting House, Lower Park, Bewdley.

I. L. Wedley[92] tells of 'the profound respect shown by all classes' at Miss Eliza Sturge's funeral and continues:

'... She was of a kindly and charitable disposition, and on the cards announcing her death these lines were written, which summed up her character admirably:

'Our hearts grew warmer for the presence
Of one, who seeking not her own,
Gave plenty for the love of giving,
Nor reaped for self the harvest sown.
Her greeting smile was pledge and prelude
Of generous deeds and kindly words.'

At their Annual Meeting, held in the Library on Tuesday, 13th March 1906, members of the Institute recorded their great sadness at the death of Miss Sturge. It was a severe loss and they wished to establish a permanent memorial to her, one suggestion being to place an enlarged photograph of her in the Reading Room. This proposal was taken up by her family, and Eliza's portrait still hangs in the Institute today, subscribed:

'This portrait of Miss Sturge
is given to her friends at the Bewdley Institute
knowing they will value it By Mrs. Player's
Daughters in loving memory of their Aunt.
March 22 1906.'[93]

The Wigan Library

The Rev. Thomas Wigan, born in 1743[94] and one-time minister of Wribbenhall Chapel,[95] gave 'to the Rector of Ribbesford and the Master of the Grammar School his library of about 1500 volumes[96] in trust for the clergy and other respectable inhabitants of the town and neighbourhood as a public library' by his Will, proved in 1819.[97]

The books - mainly classics, ancient and modern divinity, history, physical science and philosophy, some being in Latin[98] - were to be deposited with the Master of the Grammar School at the School House, which was in the Park, just off High Street (now a private residence). Apparently, they had actually been deposited, at an unknown date, before Wigan's death.[99]

According to George Griffith, writing in c1870,[100] 'Although the existence of the library was well known in the town, there were few applications for the use of the books.' Certainly, access to the tomes must have been difficult when the school was locked up while its affairs were involved in the Court of Chancery, from 1835-1855,[101] and for about ten years afterwards, there being no schoolmaster between 1840 and 1865/1866 - although Morgan says there is some evidence to suggest that the library was not as neglected as the school![102]

The site for the 'new' Grammar School in High Street was purchased in 1861.[103] At some time between 1876 and 1882 the Wigan Library was removed from the classroom there to the Town Hall - probably during the Rev. John Burton's excellent headship (1871/1872-1885) when the number of pupils at the school increased and the extra space was needed for lessons. Evidently, in 1876 *Mayor* **Whittington Landon**[104] had proposed that the books be removed from the School to the Old Post Office (seemingly, number 12 Load Street[105]) and Morgan writes that the ensuing Council debate, although lacking any legal right to decide the fate of the Library, was not without controversy![106]

The opening of Bewdley Institute in 1878 must have created an ideal opportunity to relieve pressure on space at the Town Hall... Furthermore, the Institute had links with both the Old Grammar School and the 'new' one in High Street which replaced it in c1865/1866:

1. The Bewdley and Wribbenhall Literary and Scientific Institution, which - as noted elsewhere - became part of the Institute, had been founded at the Old Grammar School in 1848;

2. The Rev. John Richard Burton, headmaster of Bewdley Grammar School, High Street was Lecturer on Practical Chemistry at Bewdley Institute in 1879. Joan Hobson thinks he may have used the laboratory at the Institute to teach the Grammar School pupils, too;[107]

3. Edward Pease, Esq., who gave the premises for use as Bewdley Institute, was patron of Dowles in 1876[108] during at least part of the Rev. John Richard Burton's period as Rector there (1876-1885);

4. Thomas Weaver, shoemaker (1609) had left 'five shillings (25p) yearly towards the maintenance of the ... free Grammar School for ever to be paid out of his then House over against the south door of St. Ann's Chapel, Bewdley'.[109]
'His then House' probably refers to a building on the site of today's number 23 - with which premises such a bequest is known to be associated[110] - rather than to
    (a) one of the buildings which surrounded the old wooden chapel in 1609 or
    (b) a building near the chapel on the contemporary bridge.

Having lived and/or worked nearby, Thomas must have known the pupils by sight, if not by name. Clearly, he was greatly interested in local education and very impressed when the first known Bewdley Grammar School (founded in c1591[111]) was built in c1599-c1606 - only a few years before his Will was proved!

By 1904 the Rev. **Wigan's** volumes had found a new home at Bewdley Institute[112] which, as noted elsewhere, already had its own library as well as housing the former Literary Society. The cleric's **Library**, however, continued to be under-used - perhaps because of the unsettled periods between the Boer War and the onset of World War I, then the Depression and the Second World War.

By 1940, the Institute having been commandeered by the Army, the books had been 'moved to the attic of an ancient cottage, where their weight threatened imminent collapse.'[113]
Was the attic that of number 23 - the 'Forestreet Chamber' - where, according to his Inventory, baker Thomas Weaver [senior's] 60 books were kept in c1717?

That same year (1940) *Worcestershire County Librarian* Miss S. Fergusson's proposal that Wigan's Library be removed to Birmingham University was welcomed enthusiastically by the *University Librarian*, Dr. Bonser. The actual transfer to the University, however, did not take place until 1946 - perhaps due to the constraints of the Second World War.

A new scheme was drawn up by the Charity Commissioners in 1950 which, among other measures, substituted as a Trustee the *University Librarian* for the *Master of the Grammar School*, which no longer existed as a separate entity. By 1958 all the books had been catalogued and were in a good state of repair, the latter task evidently having been an enormous undertaking![114]

The latest Charity Commission Deed regarding Trustees was drawn up in c1980 and the Wigan Library is currently (mid-1990s) enjoying a new lease of life.[115]

The County Library

Meanwhile, Bewdley's first County Branch Library was officially opened on 28th April 1931 on Bewdley Institute premises, the occasion being accompanied by music and a grand parade followed by refreshments.[116]

This Branch replaced the original County Library service to the town which had begun in 1925 as deposit collections of two boxes containing about 150 books in total which were exchanged three times per annum at the local schools - Lax Lane originally and, later, at Wribbenhall too.[117]

The new Branch library was housed in a room 'formerly used as a Library and Committee Room' (the dress shop, *Dorian's*, number 22b). Some renovation was needed to adapt this room for use as a public library. Among other conditions imposed on him, the contractor who undertook this work had to 'cover up and protect from injury the Bagatelle table'![118] Small wonder, for much money had been expended on buying and keeping equipment for this popular activity in good repair over the years.

At first the library was open to the public at restricted hours: 'two evenings each week for adults, from 7 to 9p.m., when the librarian would be in attendance, and one afternoon each week from 4 to 6p.m. for children of 'ten years of age and upwards',[119] with voluntary librarians - Councillor J. Bates and Mr. Harry Mountford, who had acted as honorary librarians at the Lax Lane and Wribbenhall Schools, and Mr. G. Tarratt.[120]

The first *Branch librarian* was **Mr. B. Plevey**[121] who, in 1931, added this work to his duties as *Steward* of the Institute. His wife helped him in both aspects of his job and Miss Fergusson, County Librarian, could not speak too highly of their efficiency.

Miss Nora(h) F. Plevey joined her father as an assistant in 1934 and was herself *Branch librarian* from 1939 until 1967, when she was succeeded by Mrs. Frances Virr.

In 1957 the Branch Library moved to a building in the Institute yard[122] known today as the **Wheatsheaf Room**. The letterbox in the left-hand door of the entry which leads to the yard still bears the legend 'Library' in white lettering!

Opened to the public on 12th September 1957, the hours were increased from 13.5 to 30 per week. The stock was doubled to 7,000 books and - for the first time - separate provision was made for children.[123]

Provision of a different kind was made for a local dog which, from behind some fencing, enjoyed barking at library customers: they brandished umbrellas and sometimes hurled imprecations in his general direction - but to no avail, apparently!

The library remained in the Assembly Hall until 1970, when a purpose-built Branch Library was opened[124] on the present-day site in Load Street Car Park - the building being on ground which was formerly part of the garden belonging to a doctor's surgery/house, numbers 70-72 Load Street.

Bewdley Library:
Book Issues & Opening Hours, March 1944 & Opening Hours, September 1957
(reproduced by courtesy of the *Kidderminster Shuttle/Times*)

County Library — The issues the month up to last Satlu were — Fiction 1653, literature and juvenile 274, making a to of 2,143 books issued. The librarian is still concerned about the lack of interest shown in the non-fiction section and now that new arrangements for display of this branch are in hand he that there will be an incre interest shown. The Libra wishes to point out that in junction with the County rarian and the Chairman of Library Committee she has ranged for the Library to be opened from Monday for adults on Mondays and Wednesdays from 6 to 9 p.m. and Fridays 3 to 4 p.m. and 7 to 9 p.m. The new hour for juveniles are: girls Monday 4 to 4.30 p.m. and boys Wednesdays 4 to 4.30 p.m. It is hoped that these new hours will enable the Library to be used by a wider range of readers.

Worcestershire County Library
BEWDLEY BRANCH

The enlarged and reorganised Bewdley Branch Library, in the former Assembly Hall, off Load Street, will be OPEN TO THE PUBLIC as from THURSDAY, SEPTEMBER 12, 1957. The hours of opening will be:

MONDAY: 2.30-5.30; 6.30-8.
TUESDAY: 10-1.
WEDNESDAY: 10-1; 2.30-5.30.
THURSDAY: 10-1; 2.30-5.30.
FRIDAY: 10-1; 2.30-5.30; 6.30-8.
SATURDAY: 10-1.

The Library in the present Load Street premises will close down at 9 p.m. on Wednesday, September 11, 1957.

R. R. LAWSON
County Librarian.

Chapter 6:
Some Other Occupants of Bewdley Institute Premises

The Coffee Tavern

The term 'coffee tavern' calls to mind the seventeenth century when *coffee houses* became popular in England. The earliest of these were rather like taverns which sold coffee, tea and other drinks such as ale, beer, etc. Gossip was exchanged, politics were discussed and newspapers spread out on the trestle tables in the premises. The coffee houses became gentlemen's clubs and the buildings developed their own distinctive bay windows[125] - these seemingly being very similar to the bay window at today's **George Hotel**, Load Street, which had boasted a *coffee room* in at least 1807,[126] and to a former bay window at number 23 itself (*see* photograph on p.13). What a delightful coincidence that the first *London Coffee Shop* is said to have opened in 1632,[127] the date on the collar beam above the attic window of number 23!

A **Coffee Tavern** 'adjoining and forming part of the Institute' occupied number 23 from October **1886**[128] and perhaps until *c*1928.[129] Maybe it eventually became the 'refreshment' room noted in Kelly's Directory for 1932, when the Institute was described as 'comprising reading, refreshment, social and billiard rooms...'

The Coffee Tavern probably developed from the original service of 'refreshments supplied by the steward at moderate charge' mentioned in *Littlebury's Directory* of 1879 after the Institute first opened. Perhaps this, in turn, was inspired by - or evolved from - the small *coffee room* which was established *circa* May 1878[130] in Bewdley by the Church of England Temperance Society (C.E.T.S.) which had formed in the town by March that year.[131] By October 1878 (the month in which the Institute was officially opened) the *coffee room* had proved so popular that it needed larger premises and, in November 1878, was referred to as the *Coffee Tavern!*[132] The [C.E.T.S.] Coffee Tavern proper was inaugurated towards the end of **1879**, and seems to have been located in the Parish Rooms which the Church of England opened at about the same time.[133] The writers of the *Bewdley Parish Magazine* of November 1880 were able to report that: '... the prospects of the Coffee Tavern seem to be much more hopeful than they were at one time'.[134]

While it is certainly true that there may have been more than one Coffee Tavern[135] in Bewdley at about this time, it seems worth noting here several interesting points:

(a) On 4th October **1879**, the County and City of Worcester Coffee Tavern Co. Ltd. opened a small branch at 53 Load Street,[136] a former mission room which had been especially refurbished to accommodate the Bewdley Coffee Tavern[137] (on premises occupied most recently by *Sweet & Juicy*, greengrocers who retired in September 2001).

In opening the Tavern to the public, Lord Lyttelton, *Chairman* of the Directors of the Company said:
"The objects of those persons who founded that company were, he hoped and believed, almost entirely of a beneficent character. They wished to do what they possibly could to promote the great and sacred cause of temperance, but they intended to do that not by means of any charitable organization, but by means of a purely commercial organization. The Directors hoped and expected to pay shareholders an annual dividend: and they took good care not to open any tavern where there was not a fair prospect of the concern paying its way."

The financial results at the Bewdley Coffee Tavern, however, were never as good as hoped, culminating in a loss of £92.00 over the 15 months between January 1883 and March 1884. 1883 was evidently a difficult year for the Worcester Company, due to a general slump in trade and to competition from private ventures. In March 1884 the Worcester Company Directors reluctantly decided to close the Bewdley Tavern, reporting that: 'They never thought the Bewdley Tavern would be a success.

It was taken up at the request of a most excellent gentleman at Bewdley, rather against their own judgment. They had a local guarantee; and ... a benevolent fund which they had power to apply to make good *small* losses... but that the time had come when that guarantee could go on no longer.'[138]

(b) Lord Lyttelton, *Chairman* of the Directors of the Worcester Company when the Bewdley Coffee Tavern opened, was also *President* of Bewdley Institute. The large attendance at the opening ceremony included many ladies and several officers and members of Bewdley Institute: e.g. the Revs. E. H. W. Ingram and J. R. Burton, Messrs. C. Sturge, Giles Shaw, J. Gabb, Hemingway and Miss Sturge.[139]

(c) The Rev. E. H. W. Ingram (the *Rector of Ribbesford* and a *Trustee of Bewdley Institute*) was present at the 1st and 3rd ordinary meetings of the County and City of Worcester Coffee Tavern Co. in February 1880 and in March 1882.[140] *Was he 'the most excellent gentleman at Bewdley' at whose request the Worcester Coffee Tavern Co. had opened a small branch in the town - at about the same time in 1879 as the C.E.T.S. Coffee Tavern proper was inaugurated? Was it not strange that two such ventures should start at about the same time in the town with many of the same people involved? Were the two Taverns one and the same?*

(d) A Coffee Tavern evidently continued in Bewdley after the withdrawal of the Worcester Company, for at the Annual Meeting of the Institute in February 1886 a move by Mr. Birtwistle was carried, namely that the *Committee be asked to consider the desirability of uniting the Coffee Tavern and the Institute.* As noted elsewhere, this was achieved within eight months. 'In consequence of the transference of the Coffee Tavern' to the Institute 'at the end of the present month' [September 1886], the Rector of Ribbesford appealed in the *Bewdley Parish Magazine* for 'two or three rooms in a respectable house, which he might hire as Parish Rooms'...[141] *Did the Coffee Tavern continue to be run at 53 Load Street after the departure of the Worcester Company? Was number 53 Load Street ever used as Parish Rooms, or were the Parish Rooms [always] entirely separate premises? Did the Worcester Company 'take over' or partner the existing Bewdley C.E.T.S. Tavern in 1879 and (if number 53 were the Parish Rooms at about that time) did they use Church of England premises in which to house it, the organization of the Tavern reverting to the Church of England after 1884?*

Interestingly, issues of the *Kidderminster Shuttle* for 18th October 1890, 17th November 1894 and 13th April 1895 refer to **53 Load Street** as being **the people's hall**. Was the erstwhile *mission room* renamed the *people's hall* after the County and City of Worcester Coffee Tavern Co. Ltd. had vacated the premises?

Certainly, the Coffee Tavern facilities at the Institute would have been favoured by Mr. Pease. Temperance was one of the objectives of the Quaker founder of the Institute; at least two people connected with the C.E.T.S. were original *Trustees* of Bewdley Institute;[142] and the C.E.T.S. regularly organized Boxing Day teas at the Institute in the 1890s. Furthermore, Mr. Pease would have approved of the 1878 C.E.T.S. *coffee room* committee's efforts to supply poor and destitute children with a free hot breakfast or tea in winter...[143]

One of the earliest teas at the **Institute Coffee Tavern** must have been that prepared for the Diocesan Lay Helpers' Association on Wednesday, 24th November 1886, which was enjoyed by 'about 80 of the country members... Some of our own Lay Helpers presided at the tables, to which they and others had kindly sent presents of cakes, buns, fruit, &c. to supplement the plainer fare which had been contracted for.' [144]

The newly-transferred Bewdley Coffee Tavern evidently did not confine its hospitality to the Institute building, for a charming outdoor picture is painted by the September 1886 issue of *Bewdley Parish Magazine* (p.89):

'The women attending the Ribbesford and Bewdley Mothers' Meeting, to the number of 50, assembled for Tea at Ribbesford, on Tuesday August 24th, at 4p.m., the Gardens at Ribbesford House having been kindly thrown open for the occasion by Mrs. W. Brinckman. The husbands also were invited, but owing to the early hour only 14 were able to be present. Tea was provided by the Bewdley Coffee Tavern, in the Ribbesford Meadow, under a rick sheet kindly lent by Mr. Willis. After tea the women walked or sat about the gardens, while most of the men joined in a game of bowls on the lawn. At 7p.m. a short service was held in the Church, and the party dispersed home about a quarter to eight.'

The **Institute Coffee Tavern** yielded a net profit of £6-14s-3d. (£6.71) during 1888, having taken receipts totalling £201-9s-10d. (£201.49).

The following year, however, the **Coffee Tavern** had increased its debit balance by £4-7s-2d. (£4.36), largely due to erecting a substantial - but rather expensive - sign board near the bridge.

As a result of this publicity, many excursion parties came to the coffee tavern during the summer 'and Mr. Shaw had kindly allowed the manager to provide for them at Winterdyne. This entailed some extra expense in sending and fetching, but the Committee was most grateful to Mr. Shaw for giving them the advantage and attraction of his beautiful grounds.'

At their 12th Annual Meeting the Institute Committee was delighted to be able to report that, at last, the Coffee Tavern had not only paid its way during **1890** but had reduced its debt to the Institute Account from £6-1s-11d. (£6.10) to £5-2s-10d. (£5.14).

The **1891** Census revealed that **William H[enry] Tomes** was *Coffee Tavern Manager*, aged 39, born in Aston, Warwickshire and that he was living at number 23 Load Street with his wife (Ellen, aged 36, born in Rudge, Shropshire). His father-in-law (William Hotchkiss, aged 66, a *Market Gardener*, born at Church Stretton, Shropshire) was present at least on Census night, if not actually living on the premises, as also was Emily Fowler, aged 16, who was born in Bewdley and whose occupation was *Inn Barmaid*.

The *Church Monthly* for March **1892** noted: '... in future the Institute Committee will be free from all responsibility in connection with the **Coffee Tavern**, which is of course affected from time to time by fluctuations in trade. The last year has been particularly unfortunate, and has left a deficit of nearly £30 [to add to the total liabilities of the Institute]. **The Tavern has now been let to a tenant** [Mr.Tomes][145] at a nominal rent, and although the Institute will not make anything by this arrangement, it will at least be free in future from any call upon its resources on this account.'

If - as seems likely - **Henry Tomes**, *Manager*, mentioned in Kelly's Directory for 1896 was the same person as **William Henry Tomes**, Manager of Bewdley Coffee Tavern at number 23 in 1904, then he was evidently a busy man! By 1904 William Henry Tomes was a member of Bewdley Corporation, due to retire in November of that year and he was foreman of the *Fire Brigade Station* which was located in the Town Hall (but he lived at 39 Load Street).[146]

Kelly's Directories for **1912** and **1916** describe **Edward Southan** as *Proprietor, Bewdley Coffee Tavern*. Although no location is given, since he was probably the Edward Southan who was the *Steward* of Bewdley Institute, it seems reasonable to suppose that the Coffee Tavern was still on these premises.

A **dresser**, owned by the proprietor of Victor's Hairdressers, number 23, is inscribed 'COCOA, TEA, COFFEE' and may be part of the original furniture at the Coffee Tavern on these premises. (Photograph: David W. Brown, *c*1980s, reproduced by courtesy of the proprietor of Victor's Hairdressers)

The opening of the Bewdley Coffee Tavern, October 1879
(reproduced by courtesy of the *Kidderminster Shuttle/Times*)

OPENING OF THE BEWDLEY COFFEE TAVERN
KS 11-10-1879

On Saturday afternoon the Bewdley Coffee Tavern, established in connection with the County and City of Worcester Coffee Tavern Company, was opened to the public by Lord Lyttelton, chairman of the directors of the company. The Tavern is situate in Load-street, near St. Ann's Church, the premises formerly used as the mission room having been admirably fitted up by the company's contractors for that purpose. The ceremony was looked forward to with much interest by many of the residents, who have long desired that some counter attraction to the numerous public-houses should be established in the borough, and it is to be hoped that the well-wishers of the borough will do all they can to make the tavern one of the permanent institutions of the place. There was a large attendance at the opening ceremony, including Lord Lyttelton, the Revs. E. H. W. Ingram, G. D. Boyle, C. B. Bathe, J. R. Burton, Joseph Lea, J. L. Chesshire, — Flintoff (Woodbury Reformatory), F. Burd (Noon Savage); Messrs. Giles Shaw, C. Sturge, J. Gabb, Hemingway, Capt. Spenser, Capt. Manby, R. Woodward, junr., F. Everill (secretary to the company), Rothera, G. Wright, Miss Sturge, and many ladies.

Lord LYTTELTON said he had already had the pleasure of opening three or four similar places to that, and it required an abler orator than himself to infuse any special interest or freshness into the subject. One *[great reason]* had induced him to be present, and that was he was chairman of the company under whose auspices — with the energetic & valuable assistance of the Rector of that parish — *[chairman of the company, under whose auspices, and with the valuable assistance of the Rector of that parish]* — that tavern had been established, and he felt it his duty to come over and wish God-speed to that newly-born institution, and, as far as his personal presence could do it, to give that institution a fair start on what he hoped would turn out to be a prosperous career. The objects of those persons who founded that company were, he hoped and believed, almost entirely of a beneficent character. They wished to do what they possibly could to promote the great and sacred cause of temperance—(applause)—but they intended to do that, not by means of any charitable organisation, but by means of a purely commercial organisation. The directors hoped and expected to pay the shareholders an annual dividend; and they took good care not to open any tavern where there was not a fair prospect of the concern paying its way. In Bewdley they expected the tavern would pay, and he called upon the residents to assist in carrying out the anticipations of the directors. They had to struggle against such a combination of powerful and varied interests that were arrayed against them, that it was necessary not to rely upon the fitful assistance that charity could give, but to have the permanence which commercial stability alone could give to that kind of undertaking. At the present time there was all the more reason why they should rely upon what they could honestly earn, rather than trusting to charity. They hoped to be able to attract people from public-houses, where they had been in the habit of spending a good deal of their money, to those taverns, where they would have drinks cheaper and more wholesome at the same time. Charitable contributions, he was sorry to say, owing to the bad times, were falling off in a remarkable and lamentable degree; therefore they were justified in starting such places on a commercial basis. The objects of the company were obvious. They neither intended nor hoped to improve public-houses off the face of the earth. He believed that a well-conducted public-house was a necessity, and might do some good; for in times past they had bourne their share in the political and social education of the people in this country. They were not going to *[interfere with public-houses]* where they were wanted, but they did propose to interfere very much with public-houses that existed where they were not wanted. There were no more mischievous things in this country than public-houses that were not wanted—that was, a public-house which depended for its existence upon custom which otherwise would not be given; and great stimulus was necessary in order to secure that custom. He could not help thinking that in Bewdley there was a large proportion of public-houses to the population—(hear). It would be a benefit not only to the population, but to the holders of those superfluous licenses, if they would adopt some livelihood which would be more conducive to the interests of the public and he did not think those taverns would have been established in vain if such a result could be accomplished. They did not expect to attract the regular frequenters of public-houses from those places; but there were large numbers of people who habitually drank strong drinks, who would like to have the chance at certain times of the day to drink something not so potent; especially early in the morning, workpeople going to their work would prefer the chance of having a cup of warm coffee or cocoa, and that would be far more palatable, strengthening, and useful than beer or spirits. They wanted to give such people that opportunity. Then there was the case of people who had not acquired, as yet, a preference for strong drinks; and there were large numbers of women who never cared for alcohol, but preferred coffee, tea, lemonade, or other light beverages. It was extremely important—nothing more important than for them to consider what shall become of the young people, and that was a way in which they might be more useful than in any other direction—to prevent the youth of the land acquiring a love for strong drink. There was also the case of hungry people. In a vast majority of public-houses no solid refreshments could be obtained, and doctors told them that alcoholic drinks never did a person so much harm as when taken on an empty stomach. His experience as a magistrate taught him that persons, when hungry, with only threepence or fourpence in their pocket went into a public-house to assuage the pangs of hunger by drinking away their few coppers, and then appeared before the Bench with the plea—and it was often a truthful one—that being hungry the beer overcame them, which had brought them within the clutches of the law. He hoped that now such an excuse would not exist at Bewdley, as they would be able to get wholesome refreshments, which could do them no harm. He hoped all present heartily approved of the objects of the company, as he had set them forth. He would leave the general question of intemperance to succeeding speakers, but would say a few words with regard to the depression in the trade and agriculture of the country. He feared there were not many gleams of light in the picture; but this much he could say, that whereas during the reckless times of prosperity, when wages increased with such suddenness, which they would remember, there was a vast increase in the quantity of strong drink consumed, and he feared a corresponding increase in drunkenness. The ray of light in the present blackness was this, that the consumption of strong drinks was rapidly decreasing and so far as he could judge from observation, assisted by statistics, drunkenness was also on the decrease. Now they would agree with him that, if, as a result of bad times, there could be a permanent self-denial on the part of the people in the matter of strong drink, it would be worth while having even three or four more years of depression, such as they had been going through of late years. He was not going to quote them the millions of money spent on drink in this country every year, or dwell on the melancholy extent to which our prisons, lunatic asylums, and workhouse were filled with the victims of that terrible disease – for it was nothing less than a disease—but he would only ask them to remember one thing—and he could point to the case of France as an illustration of what he was saying—that the distress was aggravated by the want of self-denial among the people. France was a country which only nine years ago passed through the most terrible war from which any country had survived. It was a country more thinly populated, considering its area, than England, and certainly, as ████████████████████████, their enterprise ████████████████████████ was far ████████████ notwithstanding that fact, they found, although the French had had a bad harvest; although the vine, one of the most important industries in the country, would be very unproductive this year, that the wealth and prosperity of the country was extending in a most marvellous degree, and her sources of revenue were rising, whereas in England they had this deplorable fact presented to them, that almost without a single exception the sources of revenue were becoming less and less productive every day. He did not wish to be a prophet of evil, yet he could not help pointing to this fact, which was significant, that although the depression might be due to temporary causes, still, the economical superiority of France over England must in a great measure be due to the habits of frugality, thrift, and what always accompanied those great qualities, habits of sobriety, which distinguished the people of that country in comparison with the people of England—(hear, hear). The state of things which he had ventured ████████████████ shame and a curse upon us as a ████████████████ incumbent upon every person, whatever his rank in life, to do what he possibly could to stem that great evil, and he called upon the people of Bewdley to do what they could in that direction, by supporting that humble institution; to encourage a place where those among them who had not the safeguards and the luxury of well-provided homes, might go and be received without being exposed to the temptations of excess and sin; and where the women and children of the place might safely enter without risk of being exposed to contaminating influences, bad example, and demoralising sights—(cheers). He now declared the tavern open for the use of the people of Bewdley, and, as a practical way of declaring it open, he would drink a cup of coffee, which his lordship declared to be remarkably good.

The Rev. G. D. BOYLE, in moving "Prosperity to the Bewdley Coffee Tavern," regretted that such a tavern as that one had not been opened at Kidderminster; but he hoped that soon the obstacles which had been in the way of that movement would be surmounted. The clergy did not wish to improve all public-houses off the face of the earth, but they did desire to see them exist in such numbers and proportion as the population demanded, and made worthy of a great, civilised, and Christian nation. There were some who said that the tendency to the highest elevation of the classes in England was not so perceptible as a few years ago; but, while all could not agree with that, everyone would say, in the words of the great social reformer, Matthew Davenport Hill, brother of the late Sir Rowland Hill, that "wherever we move in the direction of improvement, we find our steps clogged by the evils which intemperance brings in its train, besetting us before and behind;" and he, for one, rejoiced to see any movement set on foot which was calculated to remedy the present state of things.

The Rev. JOSIAH LEA seconded the motion, and spoke of the degrading effects which the multiplication of public-houses had upon the rural districts, and of the importance of some places being established to counteract such pernicious influences.

The motion having been carried,

The Rev. E. H. W. INGRAM moved a hearty vote of thanks to Lord Lyttelton for his presence that day, and said he hoped it would be distinctly understood that that was purely a commercial undertaking, and that charity was in no way connected with it. What they wanted to see was a reform in public-houses and if publicans could see that the sale of tea and coffee could be made to pay, those taverns would do much in that direction.

The Rev. F. BURD said there was an impression abroad that that tavern was established in opposition to the Institute in that town.

Capt SPENSER seconded the vote of thanks, which, having been carried, Lord LYTTELTON, in reply, said the best answer he could give to the impression referred to by Mr. Burd, was that while he was chairman of the directors of that company, he was also president of the Bewdley Institute.

The company freely patronised the tavern at the close of the proceedings.

Museum

At the Annual General Meeting of Bewdley Institute in **January 1885** it was reported that a room had been set aside for a **Museum**.[147] Mr. Langley Kitching had arranged a display of various interesting objects which he had collected during his travels in South Africa, Madagascar and elsewhere. One side of the room had been fitted with a handsome mahogany case[148] in which fossils were on display. More cases were needed, but twelve months later there was still not enough money to purchase these despite kind donations amounting to £2-17s-0d. (£2.85) from Mr. E. Baldwin, the Rev. J. Burton, Miss Doncaster and Mr. J. M. Downing. The last-named also gave many artefacts over the years.

The *Church Monthly* for April 1887 reported:
'Many of our readers may have seen the curious old drain pipe discovered during the excavations for the new wall at Ribbesford Churchyard, and now exhibited in Mr. Dalley's window. The following letter from one of the authorities at the British Museum, to whom the question was referred by the Churchwarden, will be read with interest. It is proposed to place the pipe eventually in the Museum at the Bewdley Institute.

British Museum, 5th March 1887

Dear Sir,

The pipe of which you have sent a sketch is of a type which we have considered Roman and placed among our Roman antiquities. There is however a great want of neatness in the execution, and I have recently found a pipe of somewhat similar character and stated to have been found at Friskney Abbey, and which therefore must I presume be considered medieval. At any rate the pipe you have found seems well worth preserving in a local collection such as you mention.

Yours faithfully,
AUGUSTUS W. FRANKS.'

The Museum also housed some local geological specimens, gathered by keen Bewdley naturalist Edward Baugh,[149] a son of the Rev. Edward Baugh.[150] Much of his collection was deposited at the British Museum, but the remainder - complete with cases - was presented to the Institute by Mrs. T. Baugh as the intended nucleus of 'a good local museum'.[151]

Could the inspiration to found the former Tickenhill Museum in Bewdley have arisen from the earlier Museum at Bewdley Institute - and the even earlier Museum owned by Alderman Edward Best who, Mr. Hayley (*c*1760-1821) remembered, *had lived in part of Tickenhill?*[152]

Mrs. J. F. Parker (nee Alice Tangye, daughter of Joseph Tangye[153]) and her husband started and ran Tickenhill Museum in their home from *c*1930s until *c*1960s.[154] Afterwards, the major part of the collection was relocated to Hartlebury Castle,[155] where it formed the nucleus of today's County Museum; while part went to the Museum of Science and Industry in Newhall Street, Birmingham;[156] and their collection of children's books to Birmingham Reference Library.

Registrar[157]

In **1940 John Crossley** attended the Institute on Wednesdays - from 3.00 to 4.00p.m. - in his capacity of **Registrar of Births and Deaths for Bewdley sub-district**.

One hundred years earlier, the Registrar's Office had been in Lower Park, with W. N[ichols] Marcy as *Registrar of Births and Deaths*. A busy man, he was also an attorney, town clerk and clerk to the magistrates.

By 1850 Samuel Danks of Load Street had included this role among his duties and, as has been seen, in 1855 Thomas Dalley, *Registrar of Births and Deaths*, had provided this service from his Load Street premises (probably number 10/11).

By 1916 the *Registrar of Births and Deaths for Bewdley sub-district* was Thomas Wall, at 13 Load Street; in 1924 and in 1928 at 20 Load Street; and in 1932 at 2 Load Street (although this may be a misprint).

Chapter 7:
[If only he could speak...] then what a proud history he could tell!

The Assembly Room

Nowadays called the **Wheatsheaf Room**, the building in the yard behind Bewdley Institute is probably the one described as 'the new Assembly Hall' in 1931,[158] suggesting that there had been an earlier Assembly Hall. If so, then was the new Assembly Hall on roughly the same site as the old one, and did the old one develop from the Working Men's Club Room of 1878?

The Plan attached to the Trust Deed dated 31st December 1877 shows a building in the yard with internal measurements of **14 feet 6 inches by 53 feet** (4.5 metres by approx. 16.3) standing on or near the site of the 'new' Assembly Hall. This was evidently the Working Men's Club, described in both the 1878 Press report and the 1879 Directory as being '**14 feet by 48** (4.3 metres by 14.8), divided in two by a movable partition'.

Or perhaps an even earlier Assembly Room had first been designated *inside* the former *Wheatsheaf* building when it evolved as an inn during the eighteenth century. At that time it was fashionable to create such Rooms as places to hold general meetings.

- Maybe the Assembly Room was where newspapers were read to the *Wheatsheaf's* customers in the days of coaching. If so, then what delightful coincidences that - about 100 years later - the first Branch of the town's County Library was opened nearby (in number 22b, 1931), and that another 26 years later it was removed to the 'new' Assembly Room - which itself possibly occupied the site of the original Assembly Room, as already noted!

- Whist Drives and Dances were held in the New Assembly Hall at the Institute. Evidently popular events, the great success of one held on Easter Monday 1931 was reported in the *Kidderminster Shuttle* for 11th April. Not only was it supported by local people but also by many from Kidderminster and Birmingham. 'The Riverside Dance Band provided the music for dancing. Mr. E. P. Shepherd was M.C. for whist and Mr. A. G. Humpherson M.C. for the dance.'

Many other enjoyable dances took place in the New Assembly Hall, among the most appreciated of which were those organized during the Second World War by the late Harry Gillam of High Street, baker.

- The 1st Bewdley Scout Troop entertained a large gathering in the Assembly Rooms at the Annual Parents' Night in 1935.[159] The anniversary of the founding of this Group was commemorated there with a supper on the last Saturday in February 1946, followed by an Anniversary service at the Baptist Church the next day. Dr. U. W. N. Miles was *President* and Mr. S. K. Quayle, *Scoutmaster*.[160]

- A furniture store which was accommodated in the 'new' Assembly Hall in the yard behind the Institute during *c*1970s/1980s may not have been the first on the site! Over 250 years earlier, the Inventory of Thomas Weaver [senior] - a baker at number 23 from *c*1693 to *c*1717 - had included mention of 'Bowen's House'. Bowen was a *joyner* (sic). Did his 'House' once occupy that very location and did it constitute a store for '15 chairs and stools and 1 oval table' which, perhaps, he had made himself?

- Over the years the *Wheatsheaf's* Assembly Hall has been used for a variety of social gatherings, private and public; sales; and auctions. Some of these events continue to be held there and, currently - as well as being available to hire for Wedding Receptions, functions, etc. - the *Wheatsheaf Room* is home to a Judo Club and a Weightwatchers' Club...

The Institute

In addition to its own Annual Meetings, held at different times in different rooms,[161] the Institute was host to various other local organizations.

- It seems ironic to note that the **Bewdley Life Boat Lodge, I.O.G.T.** met at the Institute in **February 1881** - just two days before the Severn flooded the town to an even greater degree than it had in 1852, when the greatest local flood on record is said to have occurred! (cutting reproduced by courtesy of the *Kidderminster Shuttle/Times*)

THE KIDDERMINSTER SHUTTLE—FEBRUARY 19, 1881

District News.

BEWDLEY.

THE RECENT FLOOD.— The Severn rose at Bewdley last week higher than it has done since 1852, when the greatest local flood on record is said to have occurred. Several dwellings on Saturday night were inundated to the depth of five or six feet, and even on the road to Wribbenhall houses had nearly two feet of water. The flood invaded the gas works, and for some time the supply of gas was cut off. Head Constable Fisher had a narrow escape. Having disembarked a number of children whom he had conveyed in a boat along Coals Quay, the boat capsized, and Mr. Fisher fell into the stream. Fortunately, he was able to grasp a pole which was near, and sustained his head above water till assistance arrived.

BEWDLEY LIFE BOAT LODGE, I. O. G. T.— On Thursday last a tea and entertainment took place in the Bewdley Institute. The tables were presided over by Mrs Cooper, and the Misses Lees and Johnson. Mr. H Jacobs occupied the chair, giving an able address on the evils of intemperance. The following was the programme of the entertainment:

Trio..The Palace of the King....Misses Lees, Johnson and Cooper
Song....Over the Severn side ......Mr. G. M. Davies
Recitation...Edward and Angelina......Mr. W. Page
Song..Man the Life Boat................Mr. B. Mole
Duet..Mother, I've come home to die.....Misses Lees and Johnson
Reading..Speculation.............Mr. G. M. Davies
Song..Kitty Gray...................Miss E. Crump
Recitation..The Christmas Tree..........Miss Lees
Trio..Far away ....Misses Cooper, Lees, and Mr. R. Hughes
Song..The Noble 24th.............Mr. G. M. Davies
Reading..Children's influence ....Mr. G. Styles
Recitation..The Drunkard's Wife ......Miss Lawley
Sacred Song......................The Company
Address .Good Templarism ....Mr. Bird
Song..The Vacant Chair ....Miss Crump
Reading..William Bruce............Mr. C. Ricketts
Sacred Song ....The Company
Song..The Old Sexton............Mr. G. M. Davies

- In March 1881 it was asserted that a new recreational **Boat Club** would shortly be formed 'in connection with the Bewdley Institute' - apparently, as a rival to one which met at the *George*.[162]

- **Bewdley Rowing Club** (established in 1877[163]) held its Annual Meetings at the Institute in at least 1896, 1906, 1909, 1915, 1916, 1917, 1919, 1920, 1921, 1924, 1925, 1927, 1929, 1930 and 1937.[164]

- The *Kidderminster Shuttle* of 14th April 1888 reported on a meeting of **Bewdley and Wribbenhall Mutual Help Society** held at the British Schools. Started in 1886 by Mr. Edward Smith after he came to live at the Heath, Wribbenhall, the Mutual Help Society had '**commenced in a small room at the Bewdley Institute**, but the society grew so rapidly that soon the largest room was needed for holding the ordinary meetings... The Rector of Ribbesford presided at one of the meetings... [The present meeting] was the last meeting of the society for the season, but members would have access to the **Institute library**, and it was intended to start a Band of Hope for the children. The qualification for membership of the society was simply attendance at either the early morning Sunday School or at the pleasant Sunday afternoon meetings...'

- Founded in 1854,[165] **Bewdley, Wribbenhall & District Horticultural Society** met at the Institute from c1900 until c1905 when, as noted in Table 1, they gave up their room to make way for the establishment of a bagatelle room there. Perhaps they managed to meet elsewhere on Institute premises afterwards: they certainly held their Annual Meetings there in 1910, 1920 and 1924,[166] although in 1921, 1922 and 1939[167] their A.G.M.s were at Bewdley Town Hall.

- There were meetings of the **[Riverside] Allotment Holders of Bewdley** in at least 1919 and 1922. The Allotment Holders formed in 1918 'when the Severn Meadow was broken up'. At the 1919 meeting a resolution was passed to affiliate with Kidderminster which, in the allotment movement, 'stood top in all the Worcestershire towns'. Institute member Mr. T. Hobbs belonged to the group. Mr. J. R. Homfray was *Chairman* in both 1919 and 1922.[168] Was he the Institute's bagatelle-playing Mr. J. Homfray?

Besides hosting these activities, Bewdley Institute regularly provided (as it still does today) hospitality for various entertainments and group meetings. Not least in popularity were

- the **Boxing Day Teas**, organized for several years by the Church of England Temperance Society [C.E.T.S.], as can be seen from the following articles in the *Church Monthly* (dates as indicated):

January 1891: 'The tea and entertainment promoted by the C.E.T.S. on Boxing Day at the Institute was as successful as usual, though there were 15 fewer tickets sold than last year. The number present at tea was 175, and for the entertainment the room was packed to its utmost capacity. Everyone was very kind in helping, and the entertainment was the means of revealing talent in unsuspected quarters which will we trust be placed at our disposal at some future time.'

January 1892: 'On Boxing Day (Saturday, December 26th), for the 4th year in succession the same society [the C.E.T.S.] organized a Tea and Entertainment, which was held at the Bewdley Institute... The large room was crowded, and accommodation had to be provided for a considerable number in the square room. Altogether at least 220 sat down to tea at 5.30p.m. After tea the room was cleared, and the entertainment commenced at 7p.m., and lasted till 9.30. As to how many were present then we prefer not to hazard a conjecture. We know that 34 more paid to come in, besides performers, and that there was not even standing room, several remaining outside on the stairs and passage all the evening, and many going away disappointed. The Committee are to be congratulated upon the success of both tea and entertainment, which ought, between them, to add a substantial sum to the resources of the Society. The best thanks are due to all who so kindly contributed to the tea, or gave help so readily in the entertainment.'

December 1892: 'On December 26th (Boxing Day), the C.E.T.S. are organizing their usual tea and entertainment, to be held at the Institute. Tickets taken beforehand will be 6d. (2.5p) each. It is possible that prices at the door may be raised this year. Admission to the Entertainment only will be 3d. (1.25p). Any contributions towards the tea will be gratefully received by the Secretary, Miss Mary Nott. As a counter-attractive movement on a day of particular danger to sobriety, this effort deserves the support of all temperate people.'

Disappointingly, the *Church Monthly* of January 1893 noted:
'The C.E.T.S. Tea and Entertainment was held this year in the Town Hall, as it was not possible to have the use of the Institute. Whether on this account, or because of the intense cold, or the superior attractions of skating by moonlight,[169] cannot be said, but the numbers at the tea were considerably less than in most previous years...'

During 1887 the Church of England Temperance Society had met every Wednesday at 8.00p.m. in the large room at the Institute, although by 1891 they were meeting on Tuesdays at 8.15p.m. in the Park Lane School (which stood almost opposite Burlton's Almshouses until the early 1960s). New members were always welcome.

- Other social events were held for charitable purposes and as rewards for good attendance, e.g: from the *Church Monthly* (dates as indicated):

December 1887: 'We would draw attention to a series of Tableaux Vivants which are being arranged by some kind friends on behalf of the Ribbesford Poor Fund. It is always a matter of difficulty to keep this Fund adequately supplied during the winter months, as it is well known that our offertories are just at their lowest ebb when the need is greatest. We are therefore very grateful for any efforts of this kind to help the fund. The Tableaux will be presented in the large room of the Bewdley Institute on the evenings of December 20th and 21st, and will be interspersed with other varieties of entertainment. Mr. G. E. W. Holmes has kindly consented to act as show man.'

February 1893: 'Band of Hope[170] On Tuesday, January 24th, the Members of the above had their tea in the upper room of the Institute. About 150 children, out of a membership of 200, who had made the requisite number of attendances at the meetings during the four months previous, sat down at 5 o'clock to a capital tea at tables laden with good things which disappeared in a very short space of time. After tea they went across to the Park Lane School-room for the Entertainment which consisted of "Punch and Judy" and a Magic Lantern...'

Today's **Bewdley Institute** has a proud history. Through its bar licence, the *Institute* retains a connection with the former *Wheatsheaf Inn*, which in turn links back to *c*1693 - only approximately 60 years after the building was constructed or altered!

Doubtless, the carved watcher at the roof's ridge witnesses just as much conviviality, camaraderie and gossip there today as ever he observed at the Inn and at the baker's shop which preceded it. Long may he continue to do so!

Find by Steward James Geddie leads to 'surprise' centenary for Institute, February 1976
(reproduced by courtesy of the *Kidderminster Shuttle/Times*)

Find leads to 'surprise' centenary for Institute

BEWDLEY Institute is 100 years old . . .

But the "birthday" would have gone by un-noticed if club steward Jim Geddie had not stumbled across the record in the loft.

The damp and almost illegible parchment is the only record of a public meeting held in the Town Hall on December 22, 1875 when a subscription list was opened.

Seventy two men signed it — and they can be regarded as the club's very first members.

Now, there are 200. And some of the officers feel there could be a "boom" time ahead.

"We are certainly on the up," secretary Dave Acton told me. "I think we could double that number. But strange though it may seem a lot of people in Bewdley don't even know we exist."

So far the change for the better has been somewhat slow — starting about 15 years ago when women were first allowed to enter the men's stronghold. Until then, the club, in the words of president Bill Millichip, was "at a very low ebb."

'SIGN OF TIMES'

"I think it was a sign of the times when the only attraction was snooker," said Millichip, a member for 40 years.

But it was a year or two before when I, as a very junior reporter, first visited the club to cover an annual meeting.

One man provided the headline when he said the club was "like a morgue."

Today he is the steward who found that piece of paper in the loft.

"It got me into deep trouble — but it was true," said Mr Geddie pulling me another half.

"Just look at the difference now."

Well, the 346 years old building — once a meeting place for a temperance organisation and a Masonic Lodge before that — is now the headquarters for two darts teams who play in a newly-formed club league in Kidderminster, and three snooker teams who play in the Stourport League . . . And for the women, Friday night is bingo night.

Social evenings with "big names" to boost the funds — and membership — are being planned for the future.

But one link with the past will still remain.

That is the downstairs reading room which a 100 years on is still used daily by members of the public . . .

For, as those 72 men decided all those years ago, "the advancement of science, art and literature."

[If only he could speak...] then what a proud history he could tell!

President Mr Bill Millichip . . . He has been a member for well over 40 years. Other long-serving members include Vic Humpherson, Albert Warrilow and Ted Bath — now all life members.

Alan Acton (left) and his brother Dave make up the chairman and secretary team.

Full-time steward Jim Geddie . . . He uncovered the true age of the club.

Billhead: James Geddie, 22 Load Street (1970)

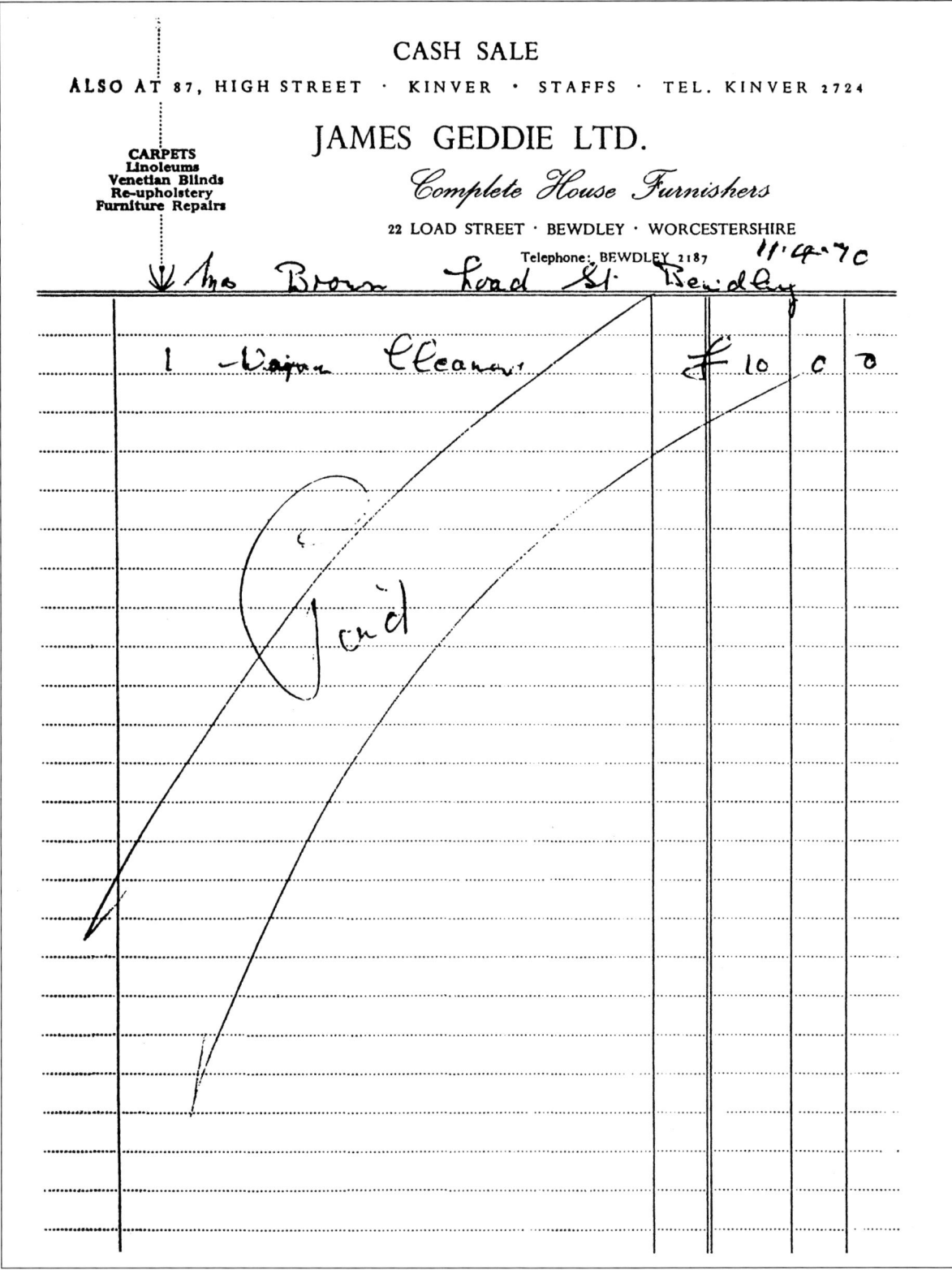

Appendix I

Officers, Committee Members and Members

Officers, Committee Members and Members (where known, year of birth and/or death is given in round brackets immediately after their names & status/qualifications).

Key to symbols: ^ One-time member of Bewdley Council
  # One-time Mayor of Bewdley
  ## One-time Deputy Mayor of Bewdley
  ~ One-time J.P.

- Unless otherwise indicated, the following information is taken from *Kidderminster Shuttle* or *Kidderminster Times* reports of the Institute Annual Meetings. There were some reports which I could not find in either newspaper (*see* Ref. 26) and some which did not name the officers appointed.
- The names and dates listed are those actually found in the newspaper reports or deduced from them. It follows, therefore, that neither is a complete list.
- The Institute's year ran from 1st January to 31st December, but the Elections (or Nominations for later ballot) took place at the Annual Meetings, which were normally held in the following February or March. Committee members were often elected for more than one year, with some members retiring in rotation. They were usually eligible for re-election. Dates such as e.g. 1880-1883 indicate that that member served for 3 years (from the date of the Annual Meeting in 1880 to the date of the Annual Meeting in 1883).
- Using the symbols shown, the following list is an attempt (not necessarily complete) to indicate some of the Offices held by some of the members in the town:

Members of the Working Party Committee[171]
The Revs. **J. Fortescue** and **J. R. Burton**, Messrs. **J. Gabb, T. E. Dalley, R. Hemingway, Whitcombe, Newman, Nicholls, Birtwistle, Parrott, Binns, Nellist** and **Tangye**.

Original Committee of Management [172]
21 members: **Edward Pease**, the **Rev. Edward Henry Winnington Ingram**, the **Rev. John Fortescue**, the **Rev. John Richard Burton**, **John Gabb**, **Joseph Tangye**, **Robert Henry Whitcombe**, **John Nicholls**, **Richard Hemingway**, **Joseph Tonks**, **James Parrott**, **Thomas Caldwell Dalley**, **Jonathan Birtwistle**, **Watson Binns** and **Thomas Nellist** and **Charles Harrison** of Areley Kings in the County of Worcester, Esq., M.P., **Giles Shaw** of Winterdyne near Bewdley, Esq., the **Rev. Augustus William Gurney**, Vicar of Wribbenhall, **John Marshall Downing** of Dowles, Farmer, **Thomas Owens** of Bewdley, Grocer and **James James** of Bewdley, Tanner.

Trustees

The 15 original *Trustees* of 'Bewdley Institution' 31st December 1877:

Binns, Watson (d. by the time of the 1906 A.G.M.)
Birtwistle, Jonathan (*c*1836-1911[173])
Burton, the Rev. John Richard, M.A. (*c*1847[174]-*c*1939/1940)
Dalley, Thomas Caldwell (b. *c*1855[175]) (d. by the time of the 1911 A.G.M., although the 1929 A.G.M. says 'died at some time between March 1928 and April 1929.' Was the latter a relative of the same name?)
Fortescue, the Rev. John
Gabb, Dr. John # ~ (1821-1908[176])
Hemingway, Richard
Ingram, the Rev. Edward Henry Winnington (d.1930[177])
Nellist, Thomas (d. by the time of the 1911 A.G.M.)
Nicholls, John # ~ (*c*1802-1895[178])
Parrott, James (b. *c*1826[179]) (d. by the time of the 1911 A.G.M.)
Pease, Edward (1834 1880)
Tangye, Joseph ^ (1826-1902)
Tonks, Joseph (*Chemist* on Conveyance of October 1877, but Rector [of Dowles] by 1892 A.G.M. and this seems to have been confirmed when the death of the Rev. was reported at the 1938 A.G.M. '... it was said that he was one of the original *Trustees*)'.[180]
Whitcombe, Robert Henry (snr.) (*c*1822[181]-*c*1909/1910)

Only 4 of the original *Trustees* still survived by the time of the Annual Meeting in **1911**, namely Archdeacon Ingram, the Rev. J. R. Burton, the Rev. J. Tonks and Mr.

R. Hemingway.[182] It would cost £3 or £4 to make appointments to fill the vacancies but, after discussion and a vote, a resolution to do so was taken.

Trustees appointed in 1912 or 1913[183]

Bawdon, E. A. ^ [184] (d. *c*1931/1932)
Green, J. # ~ (d. by time of 1940 A.G.M.)
Harcombe, R. A.[185] 1912-1940+
Harcombe, W. S. ## [186]1912 until his d. at some time between March 1940 and March 1941
Hemingway, S. 1912-1940+
Longbottom, A[lfred] (*n.b.* the *Kidderminster Shuttle* report of the 1925 Annual Meeting of the Institute said that Mr. Longbottom had been a *Trustee* for 20 years) (*see also* Ref. 23)
Shepherd, E. P. (joined H. M. Forces in October 1916[187]) 1912-1940+
Smedley, R. N., C.C. # 1912-d. *c*1914/1915
Stonehouse, H. (d. by time of 1940 A.G.M.)
Whitcombe, Major R. H. (jnr.) (D.S.O. by 1919) # ~ (*c*1860-1935[188])

By **1938** the number of *Trustees* had fallen below the 6 specified in the Deed, but a planned special general meeting to consider the appointment of new *Trustees* had to be postponed while the Committee was negotiating for the purchase of the reversionary interest. At the **1940** Annual Meeting a move towards rectifying this situation was made when, on the suggestion of the *Chairman*, it was agreed to recommend that 8 new names[189] be added to the list of 4 *Trustees* currently serving in this capacity (*viz*: Messrs. R. A. Harcombe, W. S. Harcombe, S. Hemingway and E. P. Shepherd).

In the event, only 5 new **Trustees** were **appointed in 1941** (also noted at the A.G.M. in 1942!):

Barth, E. S. 1941+
Hemingway, E. C. 1941+
Hemingway, L. 1941+
James, W. E. # 1941+
Taylor, Joseph 1941+

E. C. Hemingway was not on the list of 8 names in 1940! He was probably elected in recognition of his major part in accomplishing a successful conclusion, in August 1939, to negotiations to purchase the reversionary interest in the Institute from the Countess of Portsmouth's estate.

Noted at 1942 A.G.M. that Cllr. C. R. Pritchard declined to become a *Trustee*.

Managers/Stewards/Custodians

Sherwin, H. *Steward* 1879
Tomes, William Henry 1892   ) perhaps the
Tomes, Henry 1896; 1899; 1900   ) same
Tomes, Henry *Steward* (fruiterer) 1904) person
Southan, Edward ('Uncle Ted') *Steward* 1912; 1916
  • was elected a Life Member at the Annual Meeting in 1937
  • one of the few remaining original Committee members when he d. at some time between April 1939 and March 1940
Johnson, Charles *Steward* (d. *c*1931/1932) 1924
Simmonds, Capt. William Albert *Custodian* (d. *c*1938/1939) [1925-]1928 (left part-way through the year to take up a similar appointment at Stourbridge Conservative Club)
Johnson, Charles   part of 1928 (succeeded Capt. Simmonds but relinquished the post for health reasons)
Plevey, B[ert] *Steward* remainder of 1928 until his retirement, described as 'recent' at the A.G.M. in April 1946
Simkiss, W. A. (a retired policeman and before that a gamekeeper) *Steward* before April 1946 until he retired (again!) on 31st August 1949

Presidents

The Rev. John **Fortescue** (d. *c*1879 - *see* Ref. 8) was *President of the original 'working party', from c1875 until c1878.*

The first *President* of the newly-formed Institute was the **Right Hon. Lord Lyttelton** (Richard Plantagenet Campbell, 1823-1889[190]), Lord High Steward of the Borough of Bewdley and representative of the Borough on the County Council: *President from c1878/1879-1889.* Lord Lyttelton was an active campaigner and worker in support of Clubs and Institutes such as that eventually established at Bewdley. In December 1875 and in February 1877 he was present at public meetings to discuss the proposed Bewdley Institute. Indeed, it was said that without him there probably would not have been such a meeting as the first-mentioned... He chaired the A.G.M. in 1886.

The second *President* was **Lord Cobham** (Charles George, 5th Baron Lyttelton, 8th Viscount Cobham, 1842-1922 - a descendant of Sir Thomas, 4th Baronet, and Lady Christian Lyttelton (nee Temple) d.1740)[191]), Lord High Steward of the Borough of Bewdley; and M.P.

for Worcestershire from 1868-1874.[192] *President* from 1890-1922. He presided at the Annual Meetings in at least 1890, 1892 and 1898 and had agreed to preside at the A.G.M. in 1901, but this had to be postponed due to the death of Queen Victoria. By the time of the newly-fixed date he had gone abroad until after Easter... By 1920 Lord Cobham was unable to visit Bewdley very often but he continued his long-standing deep interest in everything affecting the welfare of the Borough. In his absence from the Annual Meeting in 1922 he was 'unanimously and cordially re-elected *President*, members voting to send a letter to Lady Cobham expressing sympathy with her in the illness of her husband and assuring her of the deep affection in which he was held... He had done great work for Institutes in the County for more years than the *Chairman* [Mr. Davies] could remember, and always maintained an interest in the advancement of youths...' Members at the 1923 A.G.M. recorded the sad blow to the Institute which had occurred with the death of Lord Cobham. 'Although he was unable to attend many of the Annual Meetings, no appeal for help ever failed to secure his hearty co-operation and support. An annual subscriber, he was a generous donor to Institute funds and always took a kindly interest in its affairs.'

The third *President* was **Viscount Cobham** (John Cavendish, K.C.B., T.D., 9th Viscount Cobham, 1881-1949 - son of the 2nd *President*[193]),. High Steward of the Borough of Bewdley; M.P. for Worcestershire from 1910-1916 (Mid-Worcestershire or Droitwich Division); and Lord Lieutenant for the City and County of Worcester. C.B.E. by 1944. *President* from 1923-1949. Viscount Cobham chaired the Annual Meeting in the Institute's Jubilee year (1928) but was not well enough to attend in 1934. Due to his commitments as Under-Secretary of State for War in 1939-1940 he was unable to be present and by 1941 he was serving in H. M. Forces. In accepting his re-election as President in 1928, Viscount Cobham referred to his family's long association with Bewdley, saying that if anyone cared to look into the history they would find it most interesting and in some instances humorous. It was Sir Thomas Lyttelton who was put in charge of the town to defend it for Charles I against Cromwell's army... Another title Viscount Cobham held - that of Lord High Steward of the Borough - was one of the oldest and most important titles he had. "It was a splendid link with the glorious past. Bewdley was once one of the first seven towns in England. Today it might be thought that Bewdley was in a backwater but after all, it was not so when they came to think that one of her sons was Prime Minister. They should be proud of Bewdley's past, proud of its present and not afraid of its future."

The 4th *President* was Mr. W[illiam] E[dgar] **James**, elected in 1950 in succession to the late Viscount Cobham. Mr. James was a well-known grocer in the town for many years and was elected Mayor of Bewdley in 1954.[194]

Vice-Presidents

Adam, Peter ~ (d.1925[195]) 1918-1925

Adam, Lt. Col. W., D.S.O. 1926-1927

Baker, G. # (1826-1910[196]) c1884-1886; 1888-1889; 1892-1893; 1909

Baldwin, A[lfred], M.P., (d.1908[197]) 1892-[1894]; 1907-1908

Baldwin, Enoch, M.P. 1884-1886; 1888-1889; 1892-1893

Baldwin, Stanley, M.P. (later P.C.) (1867-1947[198]) (elected in the place of the late Alfred Baldwin) 1908-1918; 1921-c1946

Barth, E. S. 1936-1946

Beacall, [? of Severn Tannery[199] 1917-1918

Binnian, J. (of the Summer House) 1933-c1946 (one wonders if he ever knew that his house once belonged to the daughter of the founder of the Institute!)

Binyon, T. W. (of Spring Grove) 1904; 1909-1913

Brockhouse, J. T. 1928-1934

Brown, W. J. 1937-d. c1941/1942

Butcher, J. H.^ 1930-c1946

Chapman, Frank[200] 1936

Chappell, H. C. 1928-d. c1934/1935

Chase, R. W. 1917-1918; 1921-c1927

Chumbley, P. 1947

Coldrick, J. 1940-c1946

Coldrick, T. 1943-c1946

Conant, Capt. R. J. E., M.P. 1940 c1946

Dixon, J. A. (d. c1997/1998) (Head Teacher at Lax Lane School, he became the first Head Teacher at St. Anne's School, Wyre Hill when the former transferred there in c1960s) 1946-1947

Downing, J. M. (d.1897[201]) 1891-1893; [1894-1895]

Dudley, the Rev. S. G., M.C., 1935-c1938

Elkington, E. G. 1933-[1934]

Fisher, T. Norman (d.1932[202]) 1928-1932

Foster, George (Wassell House) 1932

Frost, H. N., (C.C. by 1937) # ~ (d.1943[203]) 1927-1943

Gabb, Dr. J[ohn] # ~ c1884-1886; 1888-1889; 1892-1893; [1894-1895]

Gardner, W. 1943-*c*1946

Goodman, G. F. 1936-*c*1946

Goodwin, Laughton 1936

Green, J[ohn] # ~ (in the place of the Rev. A. Hodgson) 1907; 1909-1918; 1921-1927

Griffith, J. P. 1929-*c*1931

Hales, L. Gordon 1936-*c*1946

Harcombe, R. A. 1935-[*c*1946]

Harrison, Charles, M.P., (d.1888[204]) 1878-1879; *c*1884-1886

Hector, R. A. ^ ~ 1928-*c*1946

Hemingway, E. C. 1930-*c*1946

Hemingway, Lance 1931-1932 (same person as Mr R.L. L. Hemingway, below?)

Hemingway, R. 1899-1900; 1909-1913

Hemingway, R. L. L. 1933-*c*1946 (same person as Mr. Lance Hemingway, above?)

Hemingway, Stanley 1899-1900; 1909-*c*1946

He was also a *Vice-President* of the Bewdley and Wribbenhall Workmen's Club in 1892[205]

Hodgson, the Rev. A. (in the place of the late Sir Edmund A. H. Lechmere, Bart.) 1895; 1906 (had left the district by the time of the 1907 A.G.M.)

Hollis, the Rev. C. Raymund, M.C. 1930-*c*1946 (left Bewdley in 1949[206])

Ingram, the Rev. E. H. W., M.A. 1878-[1887]; 1888-[1890]; 1891-1893; [1894-1908]; 1909-d.1930 (left the area in *c*1894; Archdeacon by 1914)

Jackson, R. B. # 1920-*c*1946

James, W. E. # 1944-*c*1946

Jenks, T. 1936; 1939-*c*1946

Johnston, Dr. 1900

Kitching, Langley (of Rosenhurst, Park Lane) # (d.1910[207]) ('an authority on botanical matters') 1891[-1895]; 1909

Lawrence, Dr. G. S. 1941-*c*1946

Lechmere, Sir Edmund A. H. of the Rhydd, Bart., M.P. (High Sheriff of Worcestershire in 1852 and 1862[208]) (*c*1826-1895[209]) 1886; 1888-1889; 1892-1894

Lederer, F. 1910-1913

Lees-Milne, (of Ribbesford House) 1912-1913

Marlow, A. T. 1937-1938

Marlow, J. ~ 1910-*c*1913

Miles, Dr. H. N. ('Dr. Bob') 1936-*c*1946

Miles, Dr. U. W. N. ~ (*c*1872-1954[210]) 1921-*c*1946

Money-Kyrle, the Rev. R. T. A. 1899-1900

Mountford, F[ergus] E[dward] (proprietor of Sabrina Co. of Bewdley) ^ ~ (*c*1879-1948[211]) 1931-*c*1946

Nicholls, A. G. 1937-*c*1946

Nicholls, J[ohn] # ~ *c*1884-1886; 1888-1889; 1892-d.1895

Owens, T[homas] # ~ (in the place of Mr. John Nicholls) 1895; 1909 (he resigned in *c*1910 on leaving the district)

Palmer, P. W. ^ 1939-*c*1946

Parker, J. F. 1919-*c*1946

Parman, H. W. 1943-*c*1946

Plevey, B. 1950

Poignand, M. E. 1921

Potter, T[homas] D[ownes] ~ (d.1932[212]) 1923; 1926-1932

Price, Samuel # ~ (*c*1826-1886[213]) 1878-1879

Pritchard, C. R. # (d.1950[214]) 1935-*c*1946

Ransom(e), R. M. (d.1912[215]) 1911-1912

Robinson, J. (of the Park) (d. *c*1926/1927) 1915-*c*1926/1927

Rowe, S[amuel] J[ames] (*c*1902-1959[216]) 1937-*c*1946

Rowe, T. 1936

Shaw, Giles (d. *c*1902/1903) *c*1884-1886; 1888-1889; 1892-1893; [1894-1895]

Shepherd, E. P. (a genial man) 1931-*c*1946

Simpson, F. F. (of Beau Castle (sic)) 1912-*c*1918

Smedley, R[obert] N., C.C., # 1904; 1909-d. 1914/1915

Smith, Edward (of the Heath) ~ (1849-1916[217]) 1889; 1892[-1895]; 1909-1916

Starbuck, S. T. 1945-*c*1946

Stonehouse, H. 1909-1913

Sturge, Charles (1802-1888) *c*1884-1886; [1887-1888]

Sturge, J[oseph] M[arshall] (1838-1916[218]) (brother of Sarah Pease and of Eliza Mary & Maria Sturge[219]) 1892-[*c*1895]

Sturge, Marshall 1889 (same person as Joseph Marshall Sturge?)

Sturt, G. C. N. (Capt. by 1919) 1910-*c*1946

Tangye, J[oseph] ^ 1889; 1892-[1895]

Taylor, J. 1942-*c*1946

Tonks, the Rev. J. (Rector of Dowles) 1892; 1893[-1895]

Weatherhead, L. H. 1947

Webb, Major W. Harcourt (Spring Grove) 1932

Westley, C. H. 1910-d. *c*1924/1925

Whitcombe, P. W.~ 1914-1918; 1921-*c*1946

Whitcombe, Major R. H. (jnr.) D.S.O. by 1919 # ~ 1910-1935

Winnington(-)Ingram, the Rev. E. H. see Ingram, the Rev. E. H. W.

Chairmen of Committee

Gabb, Dr. John # ~ 1878-1879

[**Harrison**, Charles, M. P.] 1880

Price, Samuel # ~ 1884

Gabb, John # ~ 1885

Ingram, the Rev. E. H. Winnington [1886-1887]; 1888-1893 (*Chairman*, whose letter of apology for absence from the Annual Meeting in 1894 announced his retirement. Although it was noted at that Meeting that he had presided on the Committee for the last 10 years, this does not quite tally with reports of the Annual Meetings in 1884 and 1885).

Gabb, John # ~ 1894-1895

Dudfield, E[dwin] A. # (d.1902[220]) 1899

[**Money-Kyrle**, the Rev. R. T.] 1900 (he presided at the 1900 A.G.M. and Stanley Hemingway was present)

Hemingway, Stanley 1901-1904

[**Pennington**, Dr. [Thomas]] (of Ivy Cottage, Wribbenhall) (c1859-1915[221]) 1905-1907 (he presided at these 3 A.G.M.s and Stanley Hemingway was present in 1905 and 1907)

Hemingway, Stanley 1908-1915; [1916]

Hemingway, R. [1917]

Green, J[ohn] # ~ [1918]; 1919; 1920

Davies, F. W. (d. c1929/1930) 1921-1928

Shepherd, E. P. 1929-1937

Palmer, P. W. ^ 1938-1939

Webster, B. T. (d. c1942/1943) 1940-1941

James, W. E. # 1942 until part-way through 1944; 1945-1947; [1948; 1949]

Vice-Chairmen

Kitching, Langley 1894

Robinson, J. (of the Park) [1924]-d. c1926/1927

Harcombe, R. A. [1931]-1934

Tarratt, George ^ (d. c1937/1938) 1936-1937

Humpherson, V. J. 1938

James, W. E. # 1939-1941

Taylor, J. 1942-1944

Ryder, A. W. 1945-1947; [1948-1949]; 1950

Hon. Secretaries

Birtwistle, Jonathan 1877; [1878]; 1879

Peach, T. 1880-[1883]

Sturge, Miss E. M. c April 1883-1893
(described as 'indefatigable' at the 1890 A.G.M.)

Whitcombe, R. H. (jnr.) (D.S.O.by 1919) # ~ 1894-1896

Hemingway, Stanley 1897-1898

Mackay, Sgt. W. S. (c1876[222]-c1899) (killed in action in South Africa) part of 1899
• It was largely due to his energetic action that the new Billiard Room was erected and opened in 1900

Mackintosh, E. A. remainder of 1899-1900

Dudfield, [Edwin A.] # c1900-1901
• Through his efforts there was a considerable increase in the number of members during 1900

Shepherd, Ernest P. 1902-1925

+ Mr. **Clark**, appointed *Assistant Secretary* in 1921 (perhaps for that year only)
• When elected *Secretary* in 1902, Mr. Shepherd was the youngest member of the Committee and at that time often worked from 7.0a.m. until 11.0p.m. He realized the responsibility of following in the footsteps of his worthy predecessors in that office and remembered Dr. Gabb and the Rev. Money-Kyrle pressing him to undertake the work
• Mr. Shepherd was described by Mr. S. Hemingway in 1913 as, '... one of the best officials the Institute has ever had'

Barth, Edward S. 1926-1927

Thomas, J. P. 1928-[cOct. 1929]

Johnson, C[harles] (d. c1931/1932) (took over as *Hon. Sec.* in about Oct. 1929) until at least May 1931

Humpherson, A[lec] G. 1931-1942
+ assistance from Mr. F. E. **Russell** in 1932
(At the A.G.M. in 1933 Mr. Russell was elected *Assistant Secretary*)

Small, W. H. [part of 1942]; 1943; 1944
(It seems from the 1943 Minutes that Mr. Small may have taken over as *Secretary* at some time after the Annual Meeting in March 1942)
• At the Annual Meeting in March 1944 Mr. Small accepted the office of *Secretary* for a further 2 months while several sub-committees were set up to help him run various aspects of the Institute's activities, since he felt unable to accept the entire organization single-handed. Should the experiment prove successful, he was willing to continue in office for a further period. Members were appreciative of Mr. Small's energetic and enthusiastic work for the Club.

Bates, J. ^ 1945-1947

Thompson, C. H. 1950

Institute Billheads list **Hon. Secretaries** as follows:

J. Balis, (sic), 29th August 1946 (*cf* A.G.M. 1946 says 'J. Bates');

M. Crawley, 12th May 1956

Hon. Treasurers

Tangye, Joseph ^ 1878-1879: 1884-1885 [and presumably in the intervening years]

Hopkins, [T.] (d. *c*1893/1894) *c*1893/1894
Birtwistle, J. *c*1910
Harcombe, W. S. ## (d. *c*1940/1941) 1911-1937
Shepherd, E. P. 1938-1943
Starbuck, S. T. 1944-1946
Perrin, H. M. 1947-1950

Auditors/Hon. Auditors

Potter, T[homas] D[ownes][223] ~ [*c*1878-1883]
(In accepting the office in February 1901, Mr. T. D. Potter said he had been Auditor for 20 successive years and in 1904 he said that he had served in that capacity for 25 years! It is probably safe, therefore, to assume that he was *Auditor* from the year that the Institute was opened. It is not known whether he served alone at that time)
Potter, T[homas] D[ownes] ~ and **Whitcombe**, Major R. H. (jnr.) (D.S.O.by 1919) # ~ 1884-1885; 1888-1893
Potter, T[homas] D[ownes] ~ and **Hemingway**, S. 1894-1895
Potter, T[homas] D[ownes] ~ and **Mackay**, D. [*c*1897 and] were re-appointed in 1898
Potter, T[homas] D[ownes] ~ and **Duncan**, J. B. 1899-1904
Duncan, J. B. and **Stonehouse**, H. 1906-1912
Duncan, J. B. and **Wall**, T. 1913-1920
Wall, T. and **Brown**, C[yril] C. (d. *c*1925/1926) 1921-1925
Wall, T. and **Humpherson**, A. 1926-1931
Wall, T. and **Harcombe**, R. A. 1932-1935
Wall, T. and **Barth**, E. S. were elected/re-elected in 1936-1937
Wall, T[homas] and **Wilson**, W. S. 1938-1942
Plevey, Bert (jnr.) and **Starbuck**, S. T. 1943
Plevey, Bert (jnr.) and **Stowe**, H. S. 1944
Plevey, A. B. and **Stowe**, T. H. 1945
Plevey, A. B. and **Humpherson**, A. G. (appointed at 1946 A.G.M.)
Plevey, A. B. and Stowe, T. H. (re-appointed at 1947 A.G.M!)
Plevey, A. B. and **Clements**, F. 1950

Librarians

a) The Institute Library
Humpherson, John 1884
Parrott, Joseph 1892

Hayden, Joseph[224] 1896
Sturge, Miss Eliza M[ary] (1842-1905) 1904 until her death in 1905
Wooldridge, N. 1912
Johnson, Charles 1914-*c*1915/1916 (joined H. M. Forces at some time between March 1915 and March 1916)
Lawson, Captain from the time Mr. Johnson joined H. M. Forces [until d. *c*1925/1926]
Fryar, C. 1928-1929; [1930-]1933

b) The County Library
Plevey, B. 1931-1934
+ help with the Children in 1931 given by *Voluntary Librarians* Messrs. Harry **Mountford**, J. **Bates** ^ and G. **Tarratt** ^
Plevey, Miss Nora(h) 1939-1967
Virr, Mrs. Frances 1967-*c*197(6?)

Members, Friends and/or Subscribers (many of whom held Office and/or were *Vice-Presidents* at various times - *cf* separate lists)

One of the rules of the Institute required one year's membership before election onto the the Committee. This still applied in 1906 and, presumably, had been an original rule.

Committee members, where known, are indicated with a C.

Those marked ** joined H. M. Forces during the latter part of 1914

Adams, G. 1943-1944
• Sports Committee member for *Salute the Soldier Week* 1944
Ainsworth, F. 1921
• runner-up in Bagatelle Team competition for member winning highest number of games 1921
Albert, A. 1921
• *Captain* of the Institute Billiard Team in the Kidderminster and District League 2nd Division 1921
Alexander, H. R. 1910-d. *c*1932/1933
Allcock, C.** 1910
Allen, W. 1922-1923
Allen, the Rev. W. 1875
Anderson, P.**
Andrews, R. A. 1910
Ansell, A. R. (d. *c*1930/1931)
Ashcroft, E. 1906-1907

Aust, the Rev. F. J. (Baptist Minister, d.1911[225]) 1892-1893; 1895C; 1897-1898; 1900-1905; 1908-1911

Awdry, W. C. (d. c1891/1892) ('a good friend of the Institute')

Bailey, S. (d. c1935/1936)

Baker, A. Had joined H. M. Forces by March 1916

Baker, R. C. [1884]; 1885C

Baldwin, Alfred, M.P. [1895-1898]; 1899; [1900]; 1901C; 1902-1904; [1905]-1906
(Mr. Baldwin's Parliamentary duties in London meant he was unable to preside in Lord Cobham's place at the newly-arranged date for the 1901 A.G.M: the original date had been postponed due to the death of Queen Victoria)

Baldwin, Mrs. Enoch c1880/1890s

Banbury, W. J. 1932-1933; 1935-1936

Barnfield, F. 1905-1906; 1907C; 1908-1909; 1911C; [1912-1915]; 1916-1917 Had joined H. M. Forces by March 1916
- winner of silver medal and silver challenge cup for Airgun Shooting 1907

Barnfield, H. 1906

Barth, E. C. [1923]; 1924C; 1936   ) possibly

Barth, E. S. [1925]; 1926-1927C; 1928;   ) the
1929-1930C; 1931; 1932-1933C;   ) same
1934-1935; 1936-1937C; 1940-1942C   ) person

Bates, J. ^ 1914[-1931]; 1932-1934; 1936-1937; 1942-1944; 1945-1947C
Had joined H. M. Forces by March 1916

Baugh, Mrs. T. in at least 1884

Bawden/Bawdon, A. E./ E. A. ^ 1899-1901: 1903C; 1906C; 1907; 1909C; 1910; 1911; 1912C; 1913; [1914-]d. c1931/1932
- one of two *scrutineers* appointed to conduct the ballot for the election of members of the Committee in 1901 - there being 15 nominations for 9 places

Bell, T. 1929; 1930C; 1932C

Bennett, J. 1907

Bentley, Private Thomas
- 46066, killed in action, F[rance] and F[landers], 14th October 1918 (*see* Ref. 28)

Betts, Thomas 1902; 1903C

Binns, Watson [1884]; 1885C

Binyon, T. W. (of Spring Grove) 1903

Birch, C. [1930]; 1931-1936C

Birch, Calvin (d. c1938/1939) 1936; 1937-1938C

Birtwistle, Jonathan ~ 1877C; [1878C]; 1879C; 1880 [-1884]; 1885C; [1886-1887]; 1888-1889; [1890]; 1891-1892; [1893-]1894; 1895C; [1896]-1899; 1900C; 1901-1902; 1903C; 1904-1906; 1907C; 1908-1909; 1910C
(in 1907 he claimed to be the oldest member)

Bishop, W. 1941-d. c1942/1943

Bishop, W. O. 1922-1923

Booth, Miss 1892

Botfield, H.** 1914[-1920]; 1921

Bowdler, F. 1905

Bowdler, R. 1907

Bradley, 1915-1916
- one of two *scrutineers* appointed to conduct the ballot for the election of members of the Committee in 1916 - there being 11 nominations for 7 places

Brettell, F. P. (of Midland Bank) ~ 1922-1924; 1925C; 1927C; 1928; 1930; 1931-1936C

Brierley, the Rev. H. (Rector of Ribbesford & Incumbent of Bewdley, 1893-c1898[226]) 1894; 1895C; 1897-1898

Briggs, the Rev. James (d. c1933/34) c1933/1934

Brinton, John ~ 1877

Bristow, P.** 1910

Bromley, Miss [1879]-d. c1885/1886

Brown, 1901-1903; 1919C

Brown, C[yril] C. 1906; 1907C; 1909; 1910C; 1913C; 1916-1917C; 1921-d. c1925/1926C
- one of two *scrutineers* appointed to conduct the ballot for the election of members of the Committee in 1909 - there being 13 nominations for 7 places

Brown, J. (d. c1939/1940) c1939/1940

Brown, W. J. 1910-1911; [1912]-1932; [1933]-1936
- won a sports prize in 1940

Bullock, J. H. H. Had joined H. M. Forces by March 1916

Burton, the Rev. John Richard, M.A. (*cf* B.A., F.G.S. in 1879) 1877-1884; 1885C; 1886-c1939/1940
- Rector of Bitterley - Shropshire - when aged 90, he was thought to be the oldest Rector in the country still in charge of a parish![227]

Bury, J. 1875

Campbell, 1899-1900
- one of two *scrutineers* appointed to conduct the ballot for the election of members of the Committee in 1900 - there being 13 nominations for 8 places

Campbell, A. J. 1897-1898; 1900C (resigned at the 1901 A.G.M.)

Chapman, Frank 1934

Childe, Maj.
- killed in action during Boer War

Clamp, F. (d. c1933/34) c1933/1934

Clark, 1921C
- one of two *scrutineers* appointed to conduct the ballot for the election of members of the Committee in 1921 - there being 12 nominations for 7 places (Could this have been Mr. H. H. Clarke?)

Clarke, H. H. 1918; 1919C; 1920; 1921C; 1922

Clements, F. 1950C

Coates, John 1936
- winner of most Snooker games 1936

Coldrick, Private B. [Herbert] 1914-d.1917 Had joined H. M. Forces by March 1916
- 15/1600, killed in action, F[rance] & F[landers] (including Italy), 6th October 1917 (*see* Ref. 30)

Coldrick, J. 1909; 1910C; 1911C; 1914-1917C; 1922C

Coldrick, J[ohn] (snr.) (d. *c*1927/1928) [1922]; 1923C; 1925C; 1926C; *c*1927/1928

Coldrick, J[ohn] (jnr.) [1929]; 1930C; 1931; 1932C; 1933-1934; 1937-1938; 1939C; 1942-1948C
- Sports Committee *Chairman* 1931-1932; 1934
- Emergency Committee 1937-1938

Coldrick, Lieutenant T[homas] 1910; [1911]; 1912-d.1918 Had joined H. M. Forces by March 1916
- winner of a Cue and Case in the Kidderminster and District Billiard League 'A' Team 1912
- killed in action in France, March 1918. He had been appointed Bewdley Rate Collector when Mr. Ja[me]s Humpherson retired 'and was highly respected in the Bewdley district' (*see* Ref. 29)

Coldrick, W. 1910-1911
- winner of silver Challenge Cup and prize in Bagatelle Tournament 1910

Coles, C. 1929

Coles, E. E. 1919; 1921
- winner of Bagatelle Challenge Cup and prize for player winning most matches 1919

Coles, E[dward] 1932-1933
- one of two *scrutineers* appointed to conduct the ballots for the election of members of the Committee:
  (1) in 1932 - there being 10 nominations for 7 places and
  (2) in 1933 - there being 11 nominations for 8 places

Coles, S. 1925-1926

Conchie, J. R. Had joined H. M. Forces by March 1916

Cope, G. 1905-1906

Corbet, Mrs. Miller (*see* Ref. 38) 1885

Cornish, H. W. (d. *c*1933/1934) [1890]; 1891-[?1893]C; 1894; *c*1933/1934
(The 1934 A.G.M. noted: '... his chief interest was in the literary department of the Institute and he would be greatly missed in the Reading Room')

Cox, H. [1946]; 1947-1950C

Craddock, A. 1916

Crawley, W. H. [1949]; 1950C

Crew, A. 1921
- *Captain* of the Institute Bagatelle Team in the Kidderminster and District League 1921

Cross, G. [1944]; 1945-1947C

Dalley, 1880

Dalley, T[homas] C[aldwell] 1877; 1880; 1885C; 1888-1889; 1891C

Dalley, T[homas] E[dward] 1875; 1888-1889

Darke(s), G. 1897-1898; 1900C

Dauglish, the Rev. A. F. 1928

Davey, B. A. 1932
- Sports Committee member 1932

Davies, F. W. *c*1896-1917; 1918C; 1919; 1920-1928C

Davies, T. 1891

De Vit, 1875

Denison, 1890-1892

Doncaster, Miss 1885

Downing, J. M. 1880; 1885C

Dudfield, E[dwin] A. # 1891-1894; 1897-1898; 1899-d.1902C
- the first *Secretary* of the Billiard Room

Dudley, the Rev. S. G. (M.C. by 1937) 1934; 1935-1937C

Duncan, [J. B.] [1898]; 1899-1904C; 1906-1920C

Dunn, F. 1910

Elliott, H.[228] 1884-1885

Emslie, R. [1944]; 1945-1947C

Evans, W. L.**

Ewins, Private Arthur J[ohn]
- 63527, killed in action, F[rance] & F[landers], 24th October 1918 (*see* Ref. 31)

Exley, E. 1935-1936) brothers they
- member Sports Committee 1936) organized

Exley, R. A. 1935-1936) dances
- member Sports Committee 1936) in 1936

Exley, S. 1934
- with others, organized dances in 1934

Ford, the Rev. O. Parker 1880

Fortescue, Mrs. 1879-1880

Frost, H. N., C.C. # ~ 1927; 1928C; 1929-1931; 1935-1938C

Frost, Mrs. H. N. 1929; 1931

Fryar, C. [1927]; 1928C

Gabb, H. O. 1899; 1900C

Gabb, Dr. J[ohn] # ~ [1876]; 1877; 1878-1879C; 1880; [1881-1883]; 1885C; [1887]; 1889C; [1890-1891]; 1894-1895C; [1896]; 1897-1898; 1899C; 1900-1901; [1902]; 1903C; 1904-1905; 1906C; [1907]-d.1908

Gabb, O. 1897-1898

Gardner, Norman J. 1934; 1935-1938C; 1940; 1941-1946C;
- *Captain* of the Snooker Team 1934
- *Captain* of the Institute's Number 1 Snooker Team 1936; and *Captain* again 1938 (was this team Number 1, too?)
- Sports Committee member for *Salute the Soldier Week* 1944
- won Snooker Cup in 1940 with 10 wins and was said to be the only member to play the complete number of games in that and the Billiards Cup Championship competitions

Gardner, T[homas] ^ 1878-1905; 1906C; 1907-1910; 1911-1917C; 1918-1921; 1922C; 1923C; 1924; 1925-1926C; 1927-d. *c*1928/1929
- one of two *scrutineers* appointed to conduct the ballot for the election of members of the Committee in 1915 - there being 10 nominations for 7 places (one of the Club's oldest members when he died at some time between March 1928 and April 1929)

Gardner, W. 1905-1906; 1908; 1909C; 1910; 1912C; 1915C; 1916; 1919C; 1920; 1921C; 1922-1923; 1925C; 1927C; 1931-1936C; 1937; 1940-1945C; 1947
- one of two *scrutineers* appointed to conduct the ballot for the election of members of the Committee in 1916 - there being 11 nominations for 7 places
- was elected a Life Member in 1947

Gazeley/Grazeley, H. G. ^ [1940]; 1941-1946C
- with Miss Plevey organized a special competition which raised £13.00 towards Building Fund 1943
- ran weekly football sweep during at least 1944, allocating 25% of profits to Building Fund

Godwin, W. H. ^ 1942-1943

Godwin, W. J. [1941]; 1942C; 1944-1947C

Goodman, G. F. 1934

Goodwin, H. J. 1934-d. *c*1935/1936

Goodwin, Laughton 1934; 1935

Gorfankl, H. 1938
- *Captain* of one of the Institute's two Snooker Teams 1938

Gray, G.**

Grazeley, H. G. (see Gazeley)

Green, J[ohn] # ~ 1906; 1907C; 1908; 1910C; 1913C; 1916-1921C

Griffiths, W. [1911]; 1912-1913C; 1920; 1921C) poss.
Griffiths, W. M. [1915]; 1916-1917C: 1919C) the
Griffiths, William [1915]; 1916-1917C)same person

Gurney, the Rev. A[ugustus] W[illiam] (Incumbent, All Saints', Wribbenhall, 1864-1878[229]) 1875; 1877

Hales, L. Gordon 1934-1935

Hall, H. E. 1939; 1941-1946C
- Sports Committee member for *Salute the Soldier Week* 1944

Hancox, C.**

Hancox, W. H.**

Hanglin, P.**

Harcombe, R. A. (of Load Street) [1894]; 1895-1937C; 1938+
- won the St. Dunstan's Certificate for billiards in competition 1921

Harcombe, W. S. ## 1910; 1911-1937C; 1938-d. *c*1940/1941
the above **Harcombes** - brothers, they retired and left the area in 1938 but continued in membership although living hundreds of miles away

Harradine, [H. G. chemist[230]] 1880; 1881
Harris, F. 1907)
Harris, F. W. [1909]; 1910C) the same person?
Harris, T. F. W. [1912]; 1913C;)
1916-1917C; 1921; 1939; 1940)

Harrison, Charles, M.P. 1875; [1876]; 1877; 1880C; [1881-1883]; [1887-d.1888]

Hawkins, A. B. 1932-1933
- Sports Committee member 1932

Hayden, W. J. 1910-1911

Heath, Private Reginald E. ** 1914-d.1916
- killed in action during the First World War (*see* Ref. 32)

Hector, R. A. ^ ~ 1900-1901; 1904-1905

Hemingway, C. 1909
- one of two *scrutineers* appointed) were
to conduct the ballot for the election) these
of members of the Committee) 3
in 1909 - there being 13 nominations) the
for 7 places)

Hemingway, Cecil 1920-1921) same
Hemingway, E. C.** 1910; 1911-1917C;) person ?
[1918-1919]; 1928
- was elected a Life Member in 1940

Hemingway, L[ance] 1934-1935; 1944-1945 (same person as R. L. L. Hemingway?)

Hemingway, R. 1877; 1885C; 1897-1898; [1917C]

Hemingway, R. L. L. 1940-1945C (same person as L[ance] Hemingway?)

Hemingway, Stanley 1892-1893; 1894-1895C; 1897-1898C; [1901]; 1902-1904C; 1905-1906;1907-1917C

Heydon, 1888; 1889

Heydon, F.[231] 1916

Heydon, J. [1890]; 1891-[1893?]C; 1894; 1895
- *Hon. Secretary* of Billiard Room Sub-Committee 1892; 1894; 1895
(Could he have been Joseph Hayden (sic), *Librarian* in 1896 - and/or the same person as the Mr. Heydon, member in 1888 and 1889?)

Hinton, W. R. [1927]; 1928C

Hobbs, Tom 1878-1939+
- was elected a Life Member in 1939, when he was 'one of only two inaugural members still surviving'

Hodgson, the Rev. A. 1894; 1895C

Hodgson, the Rev. E. T., M.A. 1891

Hollis, the Rev. C. R. (Rector of the United Benefice of Ribbesford with Bewdley, 1923-*c*1949[232]) 1925; 1928

Holloway, E. G. 1936-1938
- member of Sports Committee 1936 (during which year he, Mr. J. Taylor, Mr. Alan Lawson and Mr. W. E. James arranged whist drives); 1937-1938

Homfray, J. 1914-1916; 1918C; 1919; 1920C; 1921-1924
- *Captain* of the Institute Bagatelle Team 1914

- 'an old member' when he was elected *President* of the Kidderminster and District Bagatelle League before the Institute's Annual Meeting of April 1922
- shared bagatelle prize, total value 10s-6d. (52.5p), with J. Taylor 1923

Hopewell, E. W. 1888-1889

Hopkins, T. 1884; 1885C; 1888-1889; 1891-d. c1893/1894C

Humpherson, Alec. G. 1926-1946C; 1949-1950   )
- *Collector* for the Outing Fund 1930   )
- *Captain* of the Institute Snooker Team 1932   )
- winner of most games and runner-up for   )
  the highest break prize, after a tie,   )
  in the Kidderminster & District Snooker   )
  League 1932   )
- *Captain* of one of 2 Institute Snooker   )
  Teams 1934   )
- represented the Institute in the Burroughs   )
  & Watts Snooker Championship   (brothers)
  in 1934, but after several interesting   )
  matches was defeated in the 7th round   )
- Emergency Committee 1937-1938   )
- won Billiards Cup in 10 games 1940   )

Humpherson, V[ic] J. 1921; [1924]; 1925C;   )
1927C; 1930; 1931-1936C; 1937; 1938C;   )
1946-1948C   )
- winner of most games in the Billiard   )
  League 1921   )
- Sports Committee *Secretary* 1930-[1932] ;   )
- one of two winners of the annual Snooker   )
  Handicap 1934   )
- Emergency Committee 1938   )

Hunt, E. 1905-1906; 1910; 1911C; 1912-1913; 1914-1917C; 1922-1923C; 1925-1926C; 1928C
- winner of a Cue and Case in the Kidderminster and District Billiard League 'B' Team 1912

Hunt, F. 1910

Hunt, W[illiam] 1877; 1891-[d. c1934/1935] ('an old and respected member')

Hyrons, H. J. 1888-1889

Ife, T. 1899-1900

Ingram, the Rev. E. H. W. (Rector of Ribbesford, 1876-c1893 & Incumbent of Bewdley, 1892[233]) 1877; 1885C; [1886-1887C]; 1888-1893C

Jackson, [R. B. # ?] 1916-1917

Jacob, H. [1884]; 1885C
(was it he who catalogued the effects of the Institute and the books in the Institute Library c1884?)

James, J. [1941]; 1942-1944C
- *Chairman*, Sports Committee for *Salute the Soldier Week* 1944

James, J. O. [1946]; 1947-1949C

James, W. 1906-1907; 1913-1914

James, W. E. # 1932-1933; 1935-1938; 1939-early 1944C; 1945-1947C; [1948-1949C]; 1950C
- member of Sports Committee 1936 (during which year he, Mr. Alan Lawson, Mr. E. G. Holloway and Mr. J. Taylor arranged whist drives); 1937-1938
- Emergency Committee 1937-1938

Ja(c)quis(s),[234] 1923

Jenks, T. 1930; 1934; 1937-1938

Johnson, Charles c1912-1914; 1915C; [1916-1927]; 1928C; 1929-1930C; still a member when he d. c1931/1932
Had joined H. M. Forces by March 1916
(according to the 1932 A.G.M. Mr. Johnson had been a member for 20 years)

Johnston, M.[235] 1899; 1900C (was he the same person as Dr. Johnston, a *Vice-President* in 1900?)

Jones, C. F.**

Kitching, Langley # [1884]; 1885C; 1888-1889
- one of two *scrutineers* appointed to conduct the ballot for the election of members of the Committee in 1889 - there being 12 nominations for 9 places

Lakin, J. H. 1899-1900

Lancashire, 1899

Lawley, L. 1910   ) were they
Lawley, Leonard 1932-1935   ) the same
Lawley, T. L. 1935; 1937-1938   ) person?

Lawrence, Dr. G. S. 1940

Lawson, Capt. [1911]; 1912C; 1915C; 1916; 1918C; 1920-d. c1925/1926C
- one of two *scrutineers* appointed to conduct the ballot for the election of members of the Committee in 1922 - there being 10 nominations for 7 places

Lawson, A. W. 1940; 1941-1943C   ) were they
Lawson, Alan 1923; 1924C; 1934-1937;   ) the
1938C; 1939; 1946-1948C   ) same
- Sports Committee *Secretary*   ) person?
  1934-1936 (in 1936 he, Mr. J. Taylor, Mr. W. E. James and Mr. E. G. Holloway arranged whist drives); member [possibly still Secretary] 1937
- joint *Secretary*, Reconstituted Sports Committee 1938; and (joint *Secretary*?) 1939
- almost single-handed collected donations to Restoration Appeal 1937

Lawson, B. [1940]; 1941-1943C

Lawson, R. [1934]; 1935-1937C; 1943; 1944-1946C

Lea, Josiah 1877

Lea, Thomas 1877
(unable to be present at the Public Meeting in December 1877, he sent £10-10s-0d. (£10.50) subscription towards the establishment of the Institute at Bewdley)

Leacock, E. P. (one-time of the Manor House, High Street[236]) 1901; 1902; 1906
Lee, Albert 1937; 1938C
Lewis, J. 1905-1906
Lloyd, Simon 1938; 1940-1941
- won 2nd prize in a Snooker Competition 1940

Lloyd-Davies, Mrs.   ) (of Wyre Court?) 1897-1898
Lloyd-Davies, the Misses[237]
Lockwood, R. S. [1942]; 1943-1945C
Long, H. P.**
Longbottom, A. 1899; 1903C; 1906-1907; 1910; 1911-1917C; 1921; 1922-1923C; 1924-1925
- one of two *scrutineers* appointed to conduct the ballots for the election of members of the Committee: (1) in 1921 - there being 12 nominations for 7 places and
(2) in 1922 - there being 10 nominations for 7 places (*n.b.* the KS report of the 1925 Annual Meeting of the Institute said that Mr. Longbottom had been a Committee member for 24 years) (*see also* Ref. 23)

Longmore, 1923
Mackay, D[aniel] [of Lower Park House] 1894; 1897-1898C   ) father &
Mackay, D. R. 1899-1900   ) 2 of his
Mackay, Sgt. W. S. 1897; 1898-d. c1899C) sons (*see* Ref. 222)
Mackintosh, E. A. 1899-1900C
Mapp, J. (d. c1939/1940) c1939/1940
Marlow, A. T. 1936
Mason, 1893
Miles, Dr. H. N. ('Dr. Bob') 1934; [1935]
Miles, Dr. U. W. N. ~ 1919-1920
Millichip, W. 1936-1939; 1940C; 1946-1947C
- *Captain* of the Institute's Number 2 Snooker Team 1936
- *Chairman* Reconstituted Sports Committee 1938; and member 1939 (*Chairman?*)

Millington,   1899; 1910-1913   ) were they the
Millington, A. J. (c1866-1933[238])   ) same person?
(one of the oldest members when he d. in February 1933) c1890-1917; 1918C; 1919; 1920C; 1921-1933
- one of 3 people nominated for election as an *Hon. Auditor* in 1913, there being 2 places
- runner-up in Bagatelle Challenge Cup 1919
- a former student at Bewdley Institute, in 1890 he became Assistant Master to Jonathan Birtwistle at Beauchamp Schools, Wribbenhall (the former Bewdley and Wribbenhall British Schools). On the latter's retirement in 1899 he became Head Teacher there and remained in post until his own retirement in 1925.[239]

Minton, Lance-Corporal Cha[rle]s E. ** 1914-d.1916
- 66, d[ied] of w[ounds], F[rance] & F[landers] (including Italy), 3rd September 1916 (*see* Ref. 33 & photo. p.19)

Minton, W. **
Moles, J. F. (d. c1941/1942) c1941/1942
Money-Kyrle, the Rev. R. T. A. (Rector of Ribbesford & Incumbent of Bewdley, 1898-c1902[240]) 1900C; 1901
Moore, G. A. 1907
Moore, the Rev. H[erbert] A[ugustine] (Rector of Ribbesford & Incumbent of Bewdley, 1905-c1922[241]) 1906-1907
Moore, Lieutenant J[ohn] A[ubrey] (son of the Rev. H. A. Moore[242]) ** 1914-d.1915
- killed in action on 7th August 1915, during the Gallipoli campaign (*see* Ref. 34)

Morris, 1875
Morris, P[eter] W. [1921]; 1922C; 1925-1926C; c1927/1928; still a member when he d. c1927/1928
Mountford, G. [1890]; 1891-[1893?]C
Mountford, P. F. ^ 1910; [1911]; 1912C; 1915; 1920-1921; 1923C; 1925-1926C; 1929C; still a member when he d. c1939/1940 (probably the master plasterer whose copperplate signature, 1889, is on an inside wall of the author's house in Bewdley)
Muir, Dr. (d. c1930/1931) 1927; 1928-1929C
Nellist, Mrs.
Nellist, Miss
Nicholl, the Rev. Lewis Harold (Rector of Ribbesford & Incumbent of Bewdley, 1902-c1904/1905[243]) 1902-[c1904/1905]
Nicholls, A. G. 1936
Nicholls, D. Had joined H. M. Forces by March 1916
Nicholls, J[ohn] # ~ 1885C
Nipe, S. 1921-1923; 1926; 1927C
- achieved the highest break - 39 - in the Billiard League 1921

Oakes, H. N. Had joined H. M. Forces by March 1916
Oakes, J. (d. c1920/1921) 1888-1889; 1895C; 1903C; 1912C; 1915C; 1920C   ) the same
Oakes, James [1908]; 1909C; 1918C   ) person?
(probably the James Oakes who built the new Billiards Room c1900)
Osborne, F. [1914]; 1915C
Owens, T[homas] # ~ 1884; 1885C; 1888-1889; 1891-[1893?]C; 1894; 1895C; 1897-1898; 1900-1902; 1903C; 1904-1905; 1906C; 1907
Page, 1906
Page, C. (d. c1935/1936) c1935/1936
Page, E. 1905-1907
Pain, T. G. 1908; 1909C

Palmer, E. J. [1935]; 1936-1938C
Palmer, J. [1931]; 1932-1935C
Palmer, P. W. ^ 1920-1921; 1928-1930C; 1932C; 1933-1936; 1938-1939C
- Emergency Committee 1938

Parker, Mrs. Alice (c1873-1960) during the 1930s, at least
Parker, J. F. 1907-1908; 1944
Parman, W. (or H. W.) 1944-1946C
Parmenter, J. [1933-1939]; 1940-1941
- one of two winners of the annual Snooker Handicap 1934
- won 1st prize in Snooker Competition 1940

Parrott, J[ames] 1884; 1885C
Parrott, Joseph 1892
Pass, E. 1906-1907; 1922-1924
- one of three *scrutineers* appointed to conduct the ballot for the election of members of the Committee in 1923 - there being 14 nominations for 7 places

Peach, T. 1880-[1883]C
Pennington, Dr. [Thomas] 1894; 1895C; 1900-1901; 1903; 1905-1907C; 1908; 1909C) probably the
(had resigned from the Committee) same
by March 1911)) person
Pennington, T. 1899-1900; 1903C   (*see* Ref. 221)
Perks,   1910-1911
Perks, W. 1922-1923; 1925C; 1927C; 1931-1936C
Perrin, H. M. 1946; 1947-1950C
Pitt, R. 1928; 1929-1930C; 1931; 1932C
- *Treasurer* of the Outing Fund 1930

Plevey, A. B. [1944]; 1945-1948C; 1949; 1950C
Plevey, B.** [1908]; 1909C; 1910; 1912C; [1913-1920]; 1921-1927C; [1928]-1947+
- won the St. Dunstan's Certificate for snooker in competition 1921
- was elected a Life Member in 1947

Plevey, Bert (jnr.) 1943-1944C
(was he the same person as A.B. Plevey?)
Plevey, Miss N. with Mr. Gazeley organized a special competition which raised £13.00 towards Building Fund 1943
Porter, F. 1914-1915
Potter, F. [1944]; 1945C
Potter, Thomas Downes ~ 1878-1885C; 1886-1887; 1888-1895C; 1896; 1897-1904C; 1905-1922; 1924-1925
Powell, H. L. 1898; 1899C; 1900C (resigned at the A.G.M. 1901)
Poyner, Sgt.**
Price, A. 1906-1907; 1916
Price, Alfred 1921
- won Bagatelle Cup 1921

Price, S[amuel] # ~ [1883]; 1884-1885C
Pritchard,   1922-1923
- one of three *scrutineers* appointed to conduct the ballot for the election of members of the Committee in 1923 - there being 14 nominations for 7 places

Pritchard, S. 1907; 1910; 1911-1917C
Ransom(e), R. M.
(his death was noted with regret at the Annual Meeting in March 1913, where he was described as 'having been long associated with the Institute')
Read,   1888-1889
Reeve, E.**
Reynolds, C. 1924; 1925C
Reynolds, T. E. 1888-1889
Rhodes, C. R. 1899-1900
Robinson, J. [1914]; 1915C; 1918C; 1920-d. c1926/1927C
Rowe, S[amuel] J[ames] 1936
Rowe, T. 1934
Russell, F. E. 1931-1932; 1933C
- Sports Committee 1932
- the Institute's *Assistant Secretary* in at least 1933 (left the district c1933/1934)

Ryder, A. W. [1938]; 1939C; 1942-1947C; [1948-1949C]; 1950C
Sambrook, A. 1949-1950
Schulhof, the Rev. J. (Headmaster of Bewdley Grammar School, September 1907-April 1912[244]) 1911-[April]1912
Shaw, Giles 1875; 1890; [1891]; 1896-d. c1902/1903
Shepherd, E. P. 1896; 1897C; 1898-1901; 1902-1925C; 1926; 1927-1943C
- one of two *scrutineers* appointed to conduct the ballot for the election of members of the Committee in 1915 - there being 10 nominations for 7 places
- *Secretary* Institute War Savings Committee 1917
- Emergency Committee 1937-1938
- was elected a Life Member in 1944

(at the 1940 Meeting it was reported that he had resigned from the Committee after 46 years!)
Silk, T. [1905]; 1906C
Simmonds, C. H. 1906-1907
Simmonds, Capt. William Albert [1920]; 1921-1927C
Slater,   1945
Small, W. H. [1941]; 1942-1947C
Smedley, R[obert] N., C.C. # 1903; 1905; 1908
Smith, Edward (of the Heath) ~ 1888; 1899; 1903-1904; 1906; 1907C
Smith, J. 1890; 1891C; 1892
Southan,   1922-1923
- one of three *scrutineers* appointed to conduct the

ballot for the election of members of the Committee in 1923 - there being 14 nominations for 7 places

Southan, A. R. (d.1932[245]) 1920-[1932]
- formerly *Secretary* of the old Workmen's Club, Wribbenhall (probably the Mr. A. R. Southan who played the Wribbenhall Church organ at the funeral of Mr. A. Longbottom in 1925)

Southan, Edward ('Uncle Ted') [1878-1924]; 1925-1929; [1930-]1934; [1935-]1936; 1937[-d. *c*1939/1940]
- was elected a Life Member in 1937

Southan, R. [1902]; 1903C: 1906C; 1910

Southan, R. E. 1925

Southan, Reg.**

Southerton, T.~ 1897-1898
(was he Thomas Southerton, Mayor 1893-1896?)

Stairmand, 1900-1901; 1903

Stairmand, Mrs.[246] 1900-1901

Starbuck, S. [T.] [1940]; 1941-1946C

Stephenson, A. J. 1910; 1911C

Stephenson/Stevenson, S. C. 1899-1900; 1906C; 1907

Stephenson, W. H. 1898; 1899C

Stone, A. 1941; 1942-1944C

Stone, Thomas (d. *c*1932/1933) 1925-1926; 1929-1930C; 1932C
- one of two *scrutineers* appointed to conduct the ballots for the election of members of the Committee:
(1) in 1926 - there being 11 nominations for 8 places and
(2) in 1932 - there being 10 nominations for 7 places
- Sports Committee member (*Chairman?*) at least during 1929-1930

Stonehouse, H./H. E. [1898]; 1899C; 1900; 1903C; 1906-1912C

Stonehouse, W. H. 1899-1901

Storve/Stowe, H. 1942; 1943-1945C

Stowe, H. S. [1943]; 1944C

Stowe, T. H. 1935; 1945-1947C; 1949-1950

Stowe, W. H. 1925-1926
- one of two *scrutineers* appointed to conduct the ballot for the election of members of the Committee in 1926 - there being 11 nominations for 8 places

Sturge, Charles 1877-1883

Sturge, Miss Eliza Mary 1877-1883; *c*1884-1893C; 1894; 1895C; 1896-1899; 1900C; 1901-1902; 1903C; 1904-d.1905

Sturge, J[oseph] M[arshall] 1890; 1891-[1893?]C
(same person as Marshall Sturge?)

Sturge, Miss M[aria] (*c*1849-1907[247]) 1897-1898

Sturge, Marshall 1888; 1893C (retired 1894)
(same person as *Joseph* Marshall Sturge?)

Sturt, (Captain by 1919) G. C. N.**

Sturt, Mrs. B. M. (of Winterdyne) 1928-1930; 1939 (she became a member - rather than a friend - of the Institute before the 1929 Annual Meeting)

Tangye, Miss 1880

Tangye, Miss ~ *c*1930s

Tangye, Mrs. 1889; 1890; 1892; 1904-1905

Tangye, Joseph ^ 1878-1879C; 1880; [1881-1883]; 1884-1885C; [1886-1888]; 1890; 1891-[1893?]C; [1896-1898]; 1899C; [1900-1902]

Tarratt, George ^ 1931-1933; 1935-1937C
- one of two *scrutineers* appointed to conduct the ballots for the election of members of the Committee:
(1) in 1933 - there being 11 nominations for 8 places and
(2) in 1937 - there being 7 nominations for 6 places
- Emergency Committee 1937

Taylor, J. 1913-1915; 1922-1923C; 1924; 1925-1926C; 1927-1928; 1932-1933; 1936-1938; 1939C; 1942-1944C
- shared bagatelle prize, total value 10s-6d. (52.5p), with J. Homfray 1923
- won the Godsall Cup as the best bagatelle player in the League 1927
- one of two *scrutineers* appointed to conduct the ballot for the election of members of the Committee in 1937 - there being 7 nominations for 6 places
- Sports Committee (*Treasurer*) 1936 (in which year he, Mr. Alan Lawson, Mr. W. E. James and Mr. E. G. Holloway arranged whist drives); 1937-1938
- Emergency Committee member 1937-1938
(was this Mr. Joseph Taylor, *Trustee*, *Vice-President* and *Vice-Chairman* in the 1940s? - and the same person as J. H. Taylor?)

Taylor, J. H. 1907

Taylor, L. W. [1949]; 1950C

Teague, J. ^ 1891-1892; 1897-1899; 1902-1907; 1910-1915

Teague, R. 1920-1921

Thomas, J. P. [1925]; 1926C; 1928-1929C; 1935-1936C; 1937-1939; 1940-1946C

Thompson, Bert 1936-1938
- Snooker Team *Captain* 1936
- Sports Committee 1937-1938

Thompson, C. H. 1938-1939; 1946; 1947-1949C; 1950C
- joint *Secretary* of the Reconstituted Sports Committee 1938; 1939 (joint *Secretary?*); 1946 (*Secretary*)
- Billiards Team *Captain* 1938

Thompson, E. (snr.) 1937; 1938C

Thompson, E. H. [1939]; 1940-1942C

Thompson, Harry 1940-1941
- won 2nd prize in Billiards Handicap Competition 1940

Thomson, H. 1925

Thomson, J. R. 1891

Tolley, Lance-Corporal Frank ** 1914-d.1915
- 17261, killed in action during the First World War, F[rance] & F[landers], 12th March 1915 (*see* Ref. 35)

Tolley, W. E. 1899

Tomes, W. H. 1899-1903: 1906
- it was probably this Mr. Tomes who was one of two *scrutineers* appointed to conduct the ballots for the election of members of the Committee:
  (1) in 1900 - there being 13 nominations for 8 places and
  (2) in 1901 - there being 15 nominations for 9 places

Tonks, the Rev. Joseph (Rector of Dowles) [1877-]1891; 1896-d. c1937/1938

Trout, 1923

Varcol, G. Had joined H. M. Forces by March 1916

Vickrage, W. H. [1884]; 1885C (*see* Ref. 24)

Waghorn, H. C.**

Wall, C. 1905-1906

Wall, T. 1905-1908; 1909C; 1910-1911; 1912-1944C; 1946-1947+
- *Captain* Billiard Team 1910; 1911
- Emergency Committee 1937-1938
- was elected a Life Member in 1947

Wallis, S. [1890]; 1891-[1893?]C; 1895C

Warrilow/ Warrillow, A. 1922-1923; 1945C

Watkins, A. 1947+
- was elected a Life Member in 1947

Webb, T. 1902; 1903C

Webster, G. L. 1888

Webster, Baron T. 1938-1939; 1940-1941C; still a member when he d. c1942/1943

Webster, Dr. Trevor[248] 1894; 1895C; still a member when he d. c1902/1903

Wells, 1891

Whitcombe, J. 1875

Whitcombe, R. H. (snr.) [1877-1878]; 1879; 1885C; 1888-1889; [1894] -d. c1909/1910 (*see also* Refs. 36 & 181)

Whitcombe, Major R. H. (jnr.) D.S.O. by 1919: (mentioned in a Despatch of the Commander in Chief of H. M. Forces in France c1916) ** # ~ 1878-1883; 1884-1885C; 1886-1887; 1888-1893C; 1894-1896C; 1897-1899; 1900C; 1901-1902; 1903C; 1904-1909
- it was probably this Mr. Whitcombe who was the 1st Life Member, elected at an unknown date (one of the oldest members when he d. in 1935, 'a pioneer of the Institute and a member of the Committee for 20 years') (*see also* Refs. 36 & 181)

Whitmore, H. T. [1920]; 1921-1927C

Wilcox, A. C. 1932; 1933C
(left the district c1933/1934)

Williams, T. [1944]; 1945C

Willis, Reginald (of Ribbesford House, he had only recently moved into the area when he died at some time between March 1936 and March 1937)

Wilson, the Rev. H. 1888-1889; 1891
- one of two *scrutineers* appointed to conduct the ballot for the election of members of the Committee in 1889 - there being 12 nominations for 9 places

Wilson, S.**

Wilson, W. S. [1937]; 1938-1942C
(were any of the Wilsons relatives of the Sturge family through the Albright & Wilson connection? *see* Title no. 4 in this series)

Winnington(-)Ingram, the Rev. E. H. see Ingram, the Rev. E. H. W.

Winter, E. A.

Woodward, D. 1943-1944
- Sports Committee member for *Salute the Soldier Week* 1944

Woodward, L. A. 1922-1923; 1925-1926; 1933-1935C; 1939C; 1942-1944C

Wooldri(d)ge, Mr. 1880

Wright, W. A. or W. E. 1943-[1946]; 1947-1950C
- Sports Committee member for *Salute the Soldier Week* 1944

Class Secretaries

Owens, T[homas] # ~ c1884-1885

Hon. Secretaries of the Bewdley Branch of the Kidderminster & District School(s) of Science and Art

Whitcombe, R. H. (jnr.) D.S.O. by 1919 # ~ 1891 and for many years

Birtwistle, Jonathan 1904-1905

Leacock, E. P. 1905-1906

Birtwistle, Jonathan c1910-d.1911

Representatives of the Institute on the Board of Management/ Executive Committee of the Kidderminster & District School(s) of Science and Art

Sturge, Joseph Marshall 1891
Birtwistle, Jonathan 1899-1904

Representatives of the Institute on the Council of the Worcestershire Union of Clubs and Institutes

Lancashire, Mr.   appointed 1899
Birtwistle, J.   1900-1904

Appendix II

Some of the Examination Results and Free Studentships, Prizes and Certificates gained by Students at Bewdley Institute[249]

Distribution of prizes at the Bewdley Institute, October 1879
(reproduced by courtesy of the *Kidderminster Shuttle/Times*)

)ERMINSTER SHUTTLE—OCTOBER 11, 1879

DISTRIBUTION OF PRIZES AT THE BEWDLEY INSTITUTE.

LORD LYTTELTON ON SCIENTIFIC EDUCATION.

The prizes won by the successful students of the classes held in connection with the Bewdley Literary Institute were distributed on Monday evening at the Institute, by Lord Lyttelton. Prior to the distribution, a public tea was held in the Club room, which was attended by many of the leading families in the district. The trays had been given by the ladies, and the following presided at the urns: Mrs Ingram, Mrs Price, Mrs Lutwyche, Miss Clinch, Miss Fleming, Mrs Gabb, Mrs Birtwistle, Miss Whitcombe, Miss Price Miss Davies, Mrs Hemingway, and Miss Rhoades.

The Lecture room was crowded at the public meeting, many being unable to secure seats. Lord Lyttelton presided; and amongst those present were the Revds. E. H. W. Ingram, J. L. Chesshire, J. R. Burton, Beresford-Potter, (Malvern), O. Parker Ford, Messrs. J. Gabb, J. Birtwistle, C. Sturge, J. Tangye, Crane, and others.

Lord LYTTELTON said he regretted the absence of Mr Charles Harrison, M.P., who was expected to have been present, but his excuse was contained in the following letter, which had been received from him: "I am very sorry indeed to disappoint you to-night, but I am obliged to start immediately to Frankfort to see my daughter, who is ill. Pray apologise for my absence to Lord Lyttelton. I hope you will have a good meeting. You have my best wishes for your success." The Rev. G. D. Boyle, M.A., (of Kidderminster) also apologised for his absence. Having expressed the pleasure it gave him to be present as President of the Institute, the noble Chairman said he was glad to find as far as the educational objects of the Institute were concerned that it seemed to be in a very prosperous way. The classes had been extremely well-attended, and a satisfactory number of prizes had been obtained for work done. That was the more satisfactory as in this county, and indeed in this part of England, it had been extremely difficult to keep up institutes of that kind in a satisfactory manner. There had been but little difficulty in maintaining clubs of every description for recreation, and in many cases those Institutes had gradually dropped into clubs for social and convivial amusement, and had lost sight of their educational objects. He was glad to find that was not so in Bewdley. Seeing that such satisfactory results had been obtained, it was all the more a pity that financially the Institute was not flourishing. He was one of those who thought that Institutes ought to be self-supporting. Of course in the first instance the expense of the building must be defrayed by special contributions, and if any special work had to be done afterwards that could not be defrayed out of the current income; but in a town of that size the Institute ought to pay its way so far as the current expenses were concerned, and if that could not be done they would be piling debt upon debt until they got into a very serious financial position. As for the heavy debt still upon the building he did not think the members of the Institute should be expected to defray that, but it should be discharged by the well-wishers of the Institute, by the richer residents of the district, and he hoped he might be able to induce some who had not hitherto contributed towards the Institute to do their best to get it out of the difficulties in which he feared it was at present involved. It was only a few days ago that he was present at the opening of the magnificent School of Art building, at Kidderminster. That was one of the finest buildings they could wish to see in a provincial town, and had been provided by the town, almost entirely by the contributions of the richer citizens, and chiefly by the manufacturers. It was a great credit to their liberality and foresight, that they had provided such a noble building for the town. He knew that Bewdley was not a manufacturing town, and was not anything like so rich as Kidderminster, and they could not be expected to keep up such a School of Art, but they could in their measure emulate Kidderminster, and by doing so they would help themselves. It was possible that, although Bewdley was not a manufacturing place, if that building could be kept up some day they would find a Watt or a Stephenson,—whose inventive faculties would have lain dormant but for the instruction given there—rise up, who would be not only a credit to the town, but of immense use in the world. Such a thing was within the bounds of possibility, so that it was essential that that building should be efficiently maintained; and he called upon the richer inhabitants to do what they could if not in a spirit of benevolence, perhaps in a spirit of what he might call enlightened self-interest. The attendances at the classes had been remarkably good. The total average attendance at the classes was no less than 75, which was exceedingly satisfactory. The number of students was very high and the number of passes bore a favourable proportion to the total number of students. In Chemistry there were 27 who had passed, out of a total number of 34. There were 61 students in Freehand and Model Drawing, of whom 36 were presented for examination. Nine sets of satisfactory drawings were sent up to the Departments, and nine Prizes were secured — a most unusual thing. There were upwards of 700 volumes in the library. He was glad to see that the artistic subjects were not the only ones taken up. As long as there was a solid proportion of students, who took up the more repulsive studies such as chemistry, mathematics, and the like, they would always find plenty who would go in for the more attractive studies such as Freehand and Model Drawing. It was satisfactory to see in such an Institute that out of a total average attendance of 75, nearly half represented attendances at purely scientific classes. He would have been glad to have seen more attending the mathematical classes. To a scientific student there was nothing so useful as for him to prepare the way by a good sound mathematical training. He did not mean in the higher mathematics, but let him get a firm grasp of mathematical principles, and when once he did that, he would find the way comparatively easy before him. They had been told that mathematics were the basis of all science. It was only the study of mathematics which could give them those habits of accurate thought and logical reasoning which were so essential in anything like scientific investigation. He could speak with greater authority upon chemistry, having worked rather hard in that study. He was glad that such a large number had taken up the science of chemistry. The number who attended the Inorganic Chemistry was 25, Practical Chemistry 9, and a large number had passed satisfactorily. Whether they regarded that science as a means or an end, there could not be a more important educational agent than the study of Chemistry. He had as some people would say the good, and others the bad, fortune to have been educated at one of our large public schools in the days when little else but Latin and Greek were taught. He was not going to run down the study of Latin and Greek, for the knowledge of those languages was the key to a wide and grand literature, and no scientific study could hold out such inducements as Latin and Greek could ; but in other respects he did not believe there was any branch of science or instruction which was better worth taking up by a boy or an intelligent girl than Chemistry It encouraged habits of logical reasoning and accurate thought, it also encouraged the power of analysis and keen observation and it was absolutely necessary for anyone to make anything of Chemistry that he should learn to possess delicate touch and manipulation. It was a science which entered into nearly every science and manufacture, but speaking of it as an educational agent alone, he had said enough to prove that it was an extremely valuable one. Then there was Freehand Drawing—a very useful acquirement, whether regarded as a recreation or a source of profit, and, speaking at Bewdley, there were special reasons why the Bewdley Institute should patronise the Drawing Classes. Everybody who had the slightest faculty for drawing ought to draw at Bewdley situated as it was in the midst of scenery such as very few other towns in the Kingdom could boast. He could not exaggerate from an artist's point of view the beauty of the district in which the residents were fortunate enough to live There was every kind of scenery—rock scenery, hill scenery, wooded valleys, and the beautiful River, and he could not conclude without expressing the fervent wish that some day the might be able to turn out a portrait or landscape painter of the first class. His Lordship concluded by congratulating those students who had earned prizes, and encouraged those who had not passed, to make their want of success the stepping stone for many future successes.

The prize list was as follows :—

Building Construction.
Class II.—W. Hunt and W. F. Morris, local prizes.

Mathematics.
Stage 2, Class II.—P. W. Whitcombe.
Stage 1, Class I.—H. Humpherson, Queen's prize.

Chemistry.
Advanced stage—Class I.—R. C. Finney, local prize.
Elementary stage — Class I.—E. E. Morrall, P. W. Whitcombe, W H. Vickrage, Miss F. B. Whitcombe, Miss A. E. Fleming, and Miss A. J. Tangye, Queen's prizes.—Class II.—R. Brinton, G. Baker, C. Grist, A. W. Tangye, A. Rollason, T. Webster, Miss M. M. Fleming, Miss E. A. Whitcombe, local prizes.

Practical Chemistry.
Class II.—R. C. Finney.
Elementary—Class I.—E. E. Morrall, local prize.—Class II.—T. Webster, J. Birtwistle, A. Longbotham, A. Rollason, W. H. Vickrage, local prizes.

SPECIAL PRIZES.
Mathematics (given by Mr J. Tangye)—H. Humpherson, 1 ; F. Pritchard, 2 ; A. Darkes (arithmetic), 3.
Penmanship (given by Mr J. Nicholls).—T. Reynolds, 1 ; T. Davies, 2.
Satisfactory Sets of Drawings, sent to Science and Art Department.—Mary Mountford, Blanche Ford, Mary Gilmour, Esther Hunt, Laura Smith, Fred. Pritchard, T. Reynolds, and W. A. Humpherson, local prizes.
'For *best Set of Drawings* (examiner, Mr Tucker).—Fred Pritchard.

PASSES IN DRAWING.
Freehand.—Miss E. Gabb, Miss A. Fleming, F. Pritchard, H. J. Bishop, H. R. Fisher.
Model.—Miss E. Gabb, Miss A. Fleming, F. Pritchard, and H. R. Fisher.

FOR ATTENDANCE.
Miss E. Clark Miss M. Barnett, W. A. Humpherson T Reynolds, J Carter, J. Harris, and T. Morris.

The Rev. E. H. INGRAM in moving a hearty vote of thanks to Lord Lyttelton for distributing the prizes, spoke of the financial position of the Institute. When that building was being erected they anticipated a grant of £500 from the Government towards the fund, but owing to some little technicality that grant had as yet been withheld. It was hoped, however, that the sum would yet be received from the Government. In addition to that sum, however, there was a debt of over £200 still to be raised, so that in reality there was a debt of over £700 upon the building He had little doubt if they received the Government grant, but that the remaining sum would be raised. The working expenses of the Institute were about £90 per year, and at present the income about £70, but he thought if certain gentlemen in the town, who ought to take an interest in the Institute, could be induced to do so, there need be no fear about the Institute meeting its current liabilities.

Mr CLARK (chairman of the Institute Committee) seconded the motion, which was carried.

Lord LYTTELTON, in reply, said he hoped the next time he was present on an occasion similar to the present he should find that the financial difficulties of the Institute had been surmounted, and that the debt owing to them by the Government had been honourably and faithfully discharged.

A musical entertainment followed, which was much enjoyed by the company.

During 1892:

Science and Art Department, South Kensington Art Division

Freehand Drawing (First Class): Miss Eleanor M. Mackay [aged about 14 - *see* Ref. 222]; Miss Daisy E. Pochin; George H. Wooldridge; F. Arthur Dalley; J. Sydney Reeve.
(Second Class): Mrs. M. Field; Miss Louisa Insull; Miss A. Dalgity; Miss H. A. Howarth; Miss V. Hope Lloyd-Davies; Miss Catherine M. Tangye; Arthur Southan; L. W. Page; William Phillips; Fergus E. Mountford [aged about 13 - see Appendix I, *Vice-Presidents*]; Walter Gardner; Thomas Ife; Edmond J. Westrope.

Model Drawing (First Class): George H. Wooldridge.
(Second Class): Miss V. Hope Lloyd-Davies; F. Arthur Dalley; J. Sydney Reeve; Walter Gardner; J. H. Brunn.

Science Division

Theoretical Chemistry, Elementary Stage (Second Class): Ralph A. Daniell; William Denison.
Practical Chemistry, Elementary Stage (Second Class): Thomas E. Wrather.[250]
Principles of Agriculture, Elementary Stage (First Class): John Gardner.
(Second Class): Simpson Williamson; Samuel Wallis; Frederick Baynham; Ernest W. Stone; Walter Green; Horace Bale.

Worcestershire Chamber of Agriculture

Fruit Growing and Insect Pests: 1st Prize, £1 - William Tolley; 2nd Prize, 12s-6d. (62.5p) - Samuel Wallis; 3rd Prize, 2s-6d. (12.5p) - J. Marshall Sturge; Miss E. M. Sturge [aged about 50]; Joseph Hollington (equal).
Prizes for regular attendance, 4s-0d. (20p) each: T. Lewis; T. Wood; S. Wallis; W. Bourne; J. Albert.
General Agriculture: 1st and 2nd Prizes not awarded; 3rd, 10s-0d. (50p) - Joseph Hollington.
Prizes for regular attendance, 4s-0d. (20p) each: J. Hollington; H. Nellist; J. Williamson; Ernest W. Stone; W. Pattison.

Worcestershire County Council - County Dairy School

Butter-making competition at Shire Hall, Worcester: 1st Prize - Miss Mansell; 2nd Prize - Mrs. George Baker; 3rd Prize - Miss E. Hartland; Reserved and Very Highly Commended - Miss L. Hartland; Highly Commended - Miss Lawley; Mrs. Cornish; Miss Booth; Commended - Mrs. Hollington; Miss Davies.

Kidderminster School of Science and Art, Bewdley Institute/Branch Exam. Results, September 1893
(reproduced by courtesy of the *Kidderminster Shuttle/Times*)

KIDDERMINSTER SCHOOL OF SCIENCE AND ART.

The following successes have been gained by the students of the School of Science during the past session.

SCIENCE AND ART DEPARTMENT EXAMINATIONS.

BEWDLEY INSTITUTE.
Freehand.—First Class.—Miss Lizzie T. Mackay, Second class, Miss Fanny J. Brunn, Miss Annie Dalgetty, Miss K. L. Elgood, Miss Constance M. Gabb. Wm. Heydon, Miss Louisa Insull, Miss Violet K. Lloyd Davis, Fergus F. Mountford, Wm. Phillips
Model Drawing.—First Class.—Miss K. L. Elgood, Miss Eleanor Mackay, John S. Reeve. Second Class— Thos. Ife, Fergus E. Mountford.
Drawing in Light and Shade.—First Class.—Miss Lizzie T. Mackay. Second Class.—Miss Edna Annie Sturge.
Outline from the Cast.—Second Class.—John S. Reeve.

BEWDLEY BRANCH CLASSES.
MATHEMATICS: 1st *Stage*: Walter Green.
AGRICULTURE—*Advanced*, 2nd Class: Minnie S. W. Topley. *Elementary*: Celia H. Hingley, Arthur J. Millington, Walter Green, Joseph Hollington.
HUMAN PHYSIOLOGY—*Elementary*: Arthur J. Millington, Katherine L. Elgood, George H. Wooldridge.
HYGIENE—*Elementary*: Arthur J. Millington, Katherine L. Elgood.

An extract from Kidderminster School of Science and Art Report, October 1893

(reproduced by courtesy of the *Kidderminster Shuttle/Times*)

KS 21-10-1893 AN EXTRACT FROM
KIDDERMINSTER SCHOOL OF SCIENCE AND ART. REPORT

A quarterly meeting of the General Committee was held on Thursday afternoon, the Mayor (Mr. G. W. Grosvenor) in the chair. The attendance included the Revds. F. A. Reiss and J. R. Burton, Messrs. J. Stooke, J. Killingbeck, B. Hepworth, W. Chadwick, J. Morton, R. H. Whitcombe, Junr. (Bewdley), W. Tucker (Art Master), H. E. Hadley (Science Master), and F. Perkins (General Secretary).

Apologies for absence were announced from Mr. A. F. Godson, M.P., Mr. L. Kitching (Mayor of Bewdley), and the Rev. T. Simcox Lea.

THE REPORTS.

The Finance Committee reported that the following amounts had been received and paid into the Bank:— Grant from the County Council, £1,000; Kidderminster Corporation, £75; dividend on Consols, £9 12s. 8d.; subscriptions, £61 8s. 6d.; fees, Art Department, £78 16s. 2d., Science Department, £35 1s 2d.; analytical fees, £1 13s.; total, £1,261 11s. 6d. Payments amounting to £471 18s. had been made, leaving a balance in the bank at date of £811 5s. 3d.

The report of the Executive Committee showed that the whole of the classes carried on in Kidderminster and district under the auspices of the school were doing satisfactory work, with the exception of the class for Wool-Dyeing, the attendance at which was not what it ought to be, considering the importance of the subject and its bearing upon the staple trade of the town. The committee regretted the small attendance at the Shorthand classes at Stourport, and hoped the residents there would take greater interest in the subject and attend in larger numbers. In the Art department the grants on personal examinations had increased from £104 16s. 6d. to £147; on works sent up, £192 16s. had been received; and three prizes were awarded for works in the national competition. The grants earned in the Art department at Kidderminster were £271 16s.; Stourport, £12 10s.; Bewdley, £7 10s.; Wolverley, £2 10s.; Cookley, £2; Hartlebury, 10s.; total, £296 16s.; against £208 16s. last year.

In the Science Division the amount earned was £50 at Kidderminster, and £17 10s. at Bewdley.

The report of the Lecture scheme showed that the balance on the season was £4 19s. 2d., which, with £12 17s. 11d. brought forward from last year, made the present balance £17 7s. 1d.

The Mayor moved the adoption of the various reports, and said it was a great disappointment to the committee of the school that more young men, who must be interested in the dyeing department of the staple trade of the town, did not see that it would be to their advantage, and to that of the trade of the town, if they would qualify themselves for a more perfect knowledge of this most important subject. There were many apprentices in the town who surely ought to be brought into the class. The Head Master and Mr. J. Stooke had done all that could be done to induce an interest being taken in the class, the teacher of which was most capable in every way. The appliances in the laboratory were as complete as could be desired, and the great wish of the committee was that they should be utilised as much as possible. His Worship mentioned that as the grant of £1,000 from the county could not be relied upon as being of that amount in the future, owing to the increased number of applications which the County Council were receiving from different parts of the county, the committee of the school desired to be as economical as possible in their management of all the departments. Although the school might do much more good to the town than at present, the committee must congratulate themselves on the satisfactory increase— notwithstanding the increased difficulty of obtaining grants from the South Kensington Department. The last session was the first under the mastership of Mr. Hadley, and the committee had such confidence in his ability and energy in promoting the work of the school that they felt quite sure that another session would prove a great advance on the last. The Kidderminster school received such a large grant from the County Council because it served the districts round. Excellent work was being done at Bewdley and in the various villages, and it would be the constant endeavour of the committee to supplement the facilities which now existed.

Mr. Killingbeck seconded, and the reports were passed.

The Rev. J. R. Burton brought up a report dealing with the extension of the work of the school in certain departments, and advocating advanced teaching in those sciences which are associated with the staple trade of the town.

The report was referred to the committee for consideration, and the name of Mr. Burton was added to the Executive Committee.

Bewdley Institute Annual Meeting and distribution of prizes, February 1894

(reproduced by courtesy of the *Kidderminster Shuttle/Times*)

KS. 24-2-1894

THE BEWDLEY INSTITUTE.

ANNUAL MEETING AND DISTRIBUTION OF PRIZES.

On Tuesday evening the annual meeting of the Bewdley Institute was held in the large Art-room, when the prizes and certificates gained by the students of the Art and Science Classes were distributed by Mr. G. W. Grosvenor, D.L., Chairman of the County Council Technical Education Committee. There was a moderate attendance of members, and Mr. Grosvenor presided. Among those present were the Rev. W. W. Stromberg; Messrs. Langley Kitching, R. H. Whitcombe, Stanley Hemingway, D. Mackay, H. E. Hadley (Head Master of the Kidderminster School of Science), J. Birtwistle, L. A. Dudfield, T. Owens, Cornish, and others.

Mr. Grosvenor announced letters of apology from Viscount Cobham, Mr A. Baldwin, M.P., Mr. M. Tomkinson, the Rev. B. H. W. Ingram, who expressed great regret at severing his connection with the Institute, and the Rev. J. Brierley, Rector of Bewdley. Mr. Grosvenor said he felt sure the regret expressed by Mr. Ingram was felt by the whole of the inhabitants.

Mr. R. H. Whitcombe read the 15th annual report of the committee. This congratulated the members upon a prosperous and successful year. It was believed to be the first time in the history of the institution that the annual expenditure had been met by the income, and a balance carried forward—(hear). The committee deeply regretted the retirement of their able colleague and chairman, the Rev. E. H. W Ingram. He had taken a large share in the work and responsibility of carrying on the institution since it was founded in 1877, and had always shown the deepest interests in its welfare. He presided on the committee for the last ten years, and always displayed the greatest tact, discrimination, and courtesy. The committee regretted also the death of the treasurer, Mr. Hopkins, as well as the retirement of Mr. Marshall Sturge and Miss E. M. Sturge, who was for many years the hon. sec. In the retirement of these, the Institute had sustained a very great loss. It was mainly owing to Miss Sturge's unselfish devotion to the interests of the Institute that it had been able to accomplish such good work, and had now become self-supporting. With their retirement, the last link with the founder of the Institute, the late Mr. Edward Pease, had been severed. They would ever remember with affectionate regard the liberality and munificence of their founder—(hear, hear). The balance in hand was £25 3s. 6d. The satisfactory state of the funds had enabled the committee to paint and clean the exterior and interior of the building, as well as insert a new window in the art school. An addition of £5 per year had also been made to the salary of the steward. The educational work of the Institute continued to show progress. Classes were held each evening except Saturday, and most of them were well attended. The successes at the last examination were as numerous as could be expected. The object which the founder had in view of promoting secondary and higher education was now being realised, and was much appreciated. The library was well patronised, many new books having been added, and the reading room was well supplied with newspapers and periodicals. The billiard room was an attractive feature, and had handed over a substantial balance to the fund. There had been an increase of nineteen members for the Institute during the year—(applause).

Mr. Stanley Hemingway, as one of the auditors, presented the annual statement of receipts and expenditure of the Institute and the Science and Art Classes.

Mr. Whitcombe then read the second annual report of the Bewdley Branch of the Kidderminster and District Schools of Science and Art. The local school continued to improve, and show signs of further development. Good work of a practical and useful character had been done. In the examinations held last May twenty-eight certificates were secured, and the grant earned was £24. The committee endeavoured to arrange for a class in dairy work and butter making, but the number of students was not sufficient. The new session had commenced favourably, classes being held in drawing, theoretical and practical chemistry, principles of agriculture, cookery, mathematics and physiology, elementary and advanced, the total number of students, exclusive of those attending the cookery classes, being 132—(applause). The attendance at most of the classes was good and regular. The committee regretted that the class in agriculture failed to draw the number of students which it ought, and unless the attendance at the chemistry classes was increased, the classes would either have to be discontinued or reconstructed on new lines. Of the fourteen free studentships granted last year ten were renewed, and six other free studentships had been presented. The committee expressed satisfaction that a considerable number of pupil teachers and monitors of the elementary schools took advantage of the free admissions to the science classes. The teachers of the classes had fulfilled their duties in a zealous and able way. The work of the school could not be carried on without the aid of a grant made by the County Council, and that grant would only be continued on condition that it was supplemented by local subscriptions. They ought to raise from £15 to £20 per year to pay the rent of the lecture room, and establish a prize fund. The school was appreciated and was doing good work, and therefore the committee appealed to private generosity to support the institution.

Mr. Langley Kitching moved the adoption of the report, with the direction that the same be printed. He remarked that last year, when Mr. Grosvenor presided at the annual meeting, he (Mr. Grosvenor) was Mayor of Kidderminster while he (the speaker) was Mayor of Bewdley, thus showing that the heads of the two corporations were united in promoting technical education. They welcomed Mr. Grosvenor that night, because they recognised the interest which he took in the Kidderminster and District Schools of Science and Art and other kindred institutions. The report was unique in the history of the Institution for never before had they received such a satisfactory statement both with regard to the management and the position of the finances. He was sure they would not have been able to produce such a satisfactory statement but for the fact that they possessed such an efficient and excellent honorary secretary—(applause) The committee had given their best attention to the management of the Institute, and rejoiced to know that their labours have not been in vain. The economical management of the Institute had engaged a large share of the attention of the committee. Something had been done to diminish the cost of the gas without diminishing the brilliancy of the light given—(a laugh). He should like to see a Naturalist Field Club or a Natural History Society formed in connection with that Institute—(hear, hear). Such an organisation would take the members into the country and teach them to enjoy the works of nature—(hear, hear). It was surprising how many people went through the world with their eyes virtually closed. One of the works which took hold of his juvenile attention was by Lindley Murray's, entitled, "The Teacher and his pupils:—Eyes and no Eyes, or the Art of seeing "—(hear, hear). He received considerable instruction from that book. There was no better hobby for anyone to take up than to exercise the eyes upon the works of nature whether Botanical, Conchological or Geological—gathering any kinds of specimens and taking them home to examine them at leisure—(applause). It was, even in a rough kind of way, an intellectual enjoyment. There were so many young men who did not seem to enjoy themselves when out in the country, and he had heard of visitors who came to lovely Bewdley, regarding the best form of enjoyment to enter a public house or spend their time in smoking—(laughter). He should be glad to assist in the formation of a Natural History Society—(applause) The work which the Institute was now doing must give satisfaction to those who assisted in its formation 17 years ago—(hear, hear).

Mr. J. Birtwistle seconded the motion and congratulated the committee on presenting such an encouraging and stimulating report. Without any self laudation he might claim to be the pioneer of art and science classes in Bewdley, for he was the first to ~~introduce teaching~~ of these subjects in the borough. He regretted that more of the youths of the Institute did not take greater advantage of the Institute. At present the ladies seemed to have everything their own way. He strongly advocated the establishment of continuation schools, where the boys and girls leaving the elementary schools could learn the elementary sciences, and then they would be ready to take advantage of these classes. The continuation schools would be attended with gratifying results.

Mr. Grosvenor supported the motion. He congratulated the members of the Institute and the town on the good work which was being done there. It was a source of satisfaction to find that there was a balance on the right side. Since he was last with them they had greatly embellished the building and made it more attractive to the members. That ought to increase the popularity of the Institute. He regretted that the report spoke of slightly diminished numbers in some of the classes. He trusted that was only a temporary defection, and that the numbers would greatly increase during the year. There was much point in the observations made by Mr. Birtwistle with regard to continuation schools. It would seem that those who left the elementary schools had not acquired a sufficient knowledge of elementary science to enable them to appreciate the higher education which was given in those classes. What was needed was continuation schools or classes, which would lead up to those classes. Then it was a question whether they would be able to ensure attendance. He feared that in the elementary schools the chief ambition of the boys and girls was looking forward to the time when they would be free from the trammels of school altogether and would have nothing more to learn. There seemed to be some flaw in the present system of the elementary teaching, for it left the boys and girls in a condition of eagerness to throw off all desire for further learning. The drawing classes were attractive but that was probably because drawing was taught in the elementary schools, but science was not taught in the elementary schools, and it was the lack of application to study which seemed to be the besetting sin of the rising generation—(hear, hear). The technical education which seemed to be most in favour with the youths of the country was football—(laughter). Football was very well in its way, it was an excellent recreation and developed the physical frame, but to many it meant watching the game, not always with the best motives and results. He trusted that the football mania would end in favour of a mania more intellectual, and if the continuation classes could be established he was convinced that great good would result. He hoped such men as Mr. Birtwistle would do all they could to promote continuation classes. The Education Dept now gave encouragement to the work and made grants.

doubt whatever that technical education was sadly needed by the British people, not only from a commercial point of view, but as Mr. Kitching had said to enable them to take a keener and more intelligent interest in life. From a commercial point of view Great Britain must take care lest for want of technical education—not the want of opportunity, but the want of a desire to take advantage of the opportunities offered—she was not outpaced in the commercial race with other countries—(hear, hear). No doubt British manufacturers were very much handicapped by foreign competition. That to a large extent meant that foreign countries took more pains to cultivate technical education among the artizan population than was done here. It was really deplorable to see so many things in daily use and consumption brought into England and manufactured abroad. He heard of a curious incident only a few days ago. A German gentleman, living in England, went into one of the large shops of Birmingham. He was anxious to send to a young relative in Germany an English made toy. He asked the lady attendant for an English made toy. She looked rather surprised, and said she did not know that she could find one. After great search she found one article of English manufacture. All the rest of the goods in the shop had been made either in Germany, Switzerland, or other foreign countries. He trusted that the impetus which had of late been given to the spread of technical education would lead to England taking her right place once more as the manufacturer of those articles which were needed by the people, for there was no reason why all those things should not be made equally as well and as cheaply, by the intelligent population of these islands—(applause).

Mr. Hadley (Master of the Kidderminster School of Science) also addressed the meeting, after which the reports were adopted; the prizes and certificates gained by the students were distributed by Mr. Grosvenor; and thanks were tendered to the committee, the teaching staff, and Mr. Grosvenor for their services.

The following is a list of the Prizes and Certificates gained by Students:—

Prizes.

Miss Lizzie T. Mackay, Freehand Drawing 1st Class, Model Drawing 1st Class, Shading from the Cast 1st Class.

Miss K. L. Elgood, Physiology (elementary stage), Hygiene (ditto), Model Drawing 1st Class, Freehand Drawing 2nd Class.

Arthur J. Millington, Physiology (elementary stage), Hygiene (ditto), Agriculture (ditto), Shading from the Cast (2nd Class).

Walter Green, Mathematics (1st stage), Agriculture (elementary stage).

Certificates.

Science and Art Department, South Kensington Art Division.

Freehand Drawing—1st Class: Miss L. T. Mackay. 2nd Class: Mrs A. Dalgity, Miss K. L. Elgood, Miss F. Brunn, Miss C. Mary Gabb, Miss L. Insell, Miss Hope Lloyd-Davies, F. E. Mountford, W. J. Heyden, W. Phillips.

Model Drawing—1st Class: Miss L. T. Mackay, Miss K. L. Elgood, J. Sidney Reeve. 2nd Class: Thomas Ife, Fergus E. Mountford.

Shading from the Cast—1st Class: Miss L. T. Mackay. 2nd Class: Miss Edna A. Sturge, Arthur J. Millington.

Science Division.

Practical Chemistry—Advanced, 2nd Class, W. A. Vickrage.

Agriculture—Elementary stage, Arthur J. Millington, Walter Green, Joseph Hollington.

Mathematics—1st stage, Walter Green.

Physiology—Elementary stage, Miss K. L. Elgood, Arthur J. Millington, George H. Wooldridge.

Hygiene—Elementary stage, Miss K. L. Elgood, A. J. Millington.

Successes gained in connection with the Kidderminster and District School of Science and Art during 1894:
(reproduced by courtesy of the *Kidderminster Shuttle/Times*)

> **KIDDERMINSTER SCHOOL OF SCIENCE AND ART.**
> **ART DIVISION.** KS 25-8-1894
>
> The reports from the Science and Art Department as to the recent examinations have now come to hand, and the results have been as follows:—
>
> **BEWDLEY BRANCH.**
> FREEHAND.—*First Class.*—Miss Jane Heydon, James Lewis, Fergus Mountford, Arthur Payne.
> *Second Class.*—Miss Kath. L. Elgood, Walter Gardner, Miss Blanche Hunt, Miss Louisa Insull.
> MODEL DRAWING.—*Second Class.*—Henry L. Vickrage.
> ELEMENTARY SHADING.—*First Class.*—George H. Wooldridge.
> *Second Class.*—Miss Annie Belling, Miss Kath. L. Elgood.
> OUTLINE FROM THE CAST.—*First Class.*—W. S. Mackay.
> *Second Class.*—Miss Ethel Elgood, James Lewis.
> SHADING FROM MODELS.—*Second Class.*—Miss Lizzie Mackay, Geo. H. Wooldridge.
> SHADING FROM THE CAST.—*Second Class.*—Miss Lizzie Mackay.
>
> **STOURPORT BRANCH.**
> FREEHAND.—*First Class.*—Frank H. Hardwick.
> *Second Class.*—Harry R. Poole, Claude Shaddock, Joseph H. Davis.
> MODEL DRAWING.—*Second Class.*—Miss Lilian Edith Grose.
> EXTERNAL CANDIDATE: FREEHAND.—*Second Class:*—Miss Janet Smith.

Art Division
Advanced Shading (2nd Class): Miss L. T. Mackay.
Shading Models (2nd Class): Miss L. T. Mackay; George H. Wooldridge.
Advanced Freehand (1st Class): William S. Mackay [aged about 18 - *see* Ref. 222].
Advanced Freehand (2nd Class): Miss Ethel Elgood [*see* 'successful students', p.32]; James Lewis.
Elementary Shading (1st Class): George H. Wooldridge.
Elementary Shading (2nd Class): Miss A. Belling; Miss R. L. Elgood.
Model Drawing (2nd Class): H[enry] L. Vickrage [aged about 16 - *see* Ref. 24]
Elementary Freehand (1st Class): Miss Jane E. Heydon; James Lewis; Fergus E. Mountford; Arthur J. Payne.
Elementary Freehand (2nd Class): Miss R. L. Elgood; Walter Gardner; Miss Hunt; Miss L. Insull.

Science Division
Practical Inorganic Chemistry (Advanced) (2nd Class): W[illiam] A. Vickrage [aged about 21- *see* Ref. 24].
Physiology (Advanced) (1st Class): Miss Blanche Hunt.
Physiology (Elementary) - Pass: Miss A. Belling; Miss Jane E. Heydon; Alexander Campbell.
Physiology (Elementary) - Fair: Miss Caroline Campbell; Miss Mabel Payne.
Principles of Agriculture (Elementary) - Pass: Frederick Baynham.

Free students, 1894-1895
Bewdley National Schools: Arthur J. Payne; Alfred Percy Vickrage [aged about 15 - *see* Ref. 24]; and Kate E. Newell all renewed. William H. Channin, September 1894; Ethel Mountford, special, September 1894.
British Schools, Wribbenhall: William J. Heydon; Florence E. Stone; Alice Phillips;
and Nellie S. Coldrick all renewed. Amy Payne; Marjorie Heydon; and Maud Stone all special, September 1894.
Wribbenhall National Schools: Ellen Glover; and Rosamond Lawley both special, September 1894.

During 1896 examinations held at Bewdley Branch of the Kidderminster and District School of Science and Art obtained 19 1st Classes and 14 2nd Classes in the Elementary and First Class Advanced Stage [no subjects named]. 56 students joined the various classes.

Kidderminster Schools of Science & Art, Exam. Results, August 1897 & July 1898
(reproduced by courtesy of the *Kidderminster Shuttle/Times*)

KT 7-8-1897
BEWDLEY.
Elementary Freehand.—First Class—P S Colledge, A.P Vickrage, N L Coldrick, G Barnfield, W H Wooldridge, A D H Wooldridge, W Walker. Second class—K E Newell, E Mountford, M E Britten, F Stone, S E Poole, E B Palmer, H Evans.
Elementary Model.—First Class—A D H Wooldridge. Second Class—M R Dalley, E Mountford, F M Clarke, W Walker, P S Colledge, A P Vickrage, K E Newell, W H Wooldridge.
Elementary Light and Shade.—Second Class—B Hunt.

KS 23-7-1898
BEWDLEY.
MODEL DRAWING.—*Elementary, First Class.*—F. M. Clarke, E. L. Ball, W. H. Wooldridge, W. Walker, A. P. Vickrage, P. S. Colledge. *Second Class.*—H. W. Oakes, E. Mountford, N. L. Coldrick.
FREEHAND.—*Elementary, First Class.*—M. Mackay, W. J. Heydon, H. D. Griffin. *Second Class.*—W. G. Baker, K. E. Newell, E. Mountford, E. G. Aust, F. Stone, E. L. Ball, H. N. Oakes.
LIGHT AND SHADE.—*Elementary, First Class.*—S. F. Dalley. *Second Class.*—M. R. Dalley, F. J. Brunn, W. Walker.
FREEHAND.—*Advanced, First Class.*—W. J. Heydon, P. S. Colledge, F. M. Clarke, W. H. Wooldridge, A. D. H. Wooldridge. *Second Class.*—M. L. Coldrick.

Examination results for 1900
There being no Elementary Examinations in these subjects, a 2nd Class (Advanced) counts as First Class Elementary towards the full Certificate.

Special mention for excellence and works submitted: Percy S. College (sic).[251]

Design (2nd Class): P. S. College (sic).
*Light & Shade from the Cast (1st Class): H. Lees.
Geometrical Drawing (Pass): R. E. Lowe; R. Lawley; R. Oakes; H. Oakes.
*Model Drawing (Advanced Stage): (1st Class): E. Vickrage [was this Mrs. Emily E. Vickrage? *see* Ref. 24 - or Edith M. Vickrage? *see under* Physiology, below].
(2nd Class or 1st Class Elementary): E. Mountford; A. F. Newell; K. E. Newell; E. Palmer.
Freehand Ornament in Outline (Advanced Stage) (2nd Class or 1st Class Elementary): E. Mountford; A. E. Newell; R. Lawley; E. Palmer; E. Reynolds; E. Vickrage.
Physiology (2nd Class Elementary): Norah F. Lawley; Ethel Mountford; Edith E. Ricketts; Charlotte E. Palmer; Ethel M. Hunt; Edith M. Vickrage.

Prizes and Certificates for work during 1903

The Art classes were carried on with their accustomed regularity and success during 1903, and the examinations in connection with the Board of Education were very satisfactory. The following students were awarded local prizes:
Light and Shade: E. Mountford;   Design: P. S. Colledge (sic);
Model Drawing: A. S. Baker;   Freehand: E. M. Vickrage.

The following were awarded prizes for excellent attendance: Hilda Webster; Gladys Webster; Winnifred (sic) Davies and Emily Channin [aged about 17[252]].

Shorthand: All the students passed the examinations in connection with the Midland Counties Association of Institutes. Local prizes and Certificates from this Association were awarded to: Clara Davies; R. E. Lowe; A. J. Green; and C. Pennington.

County E Scholarships were awarded to R. E. Lowe and B. J. Oakes for Building Construction.

Table 1

Chief Items from Financial & Administration Accounts plus Membership Numbers

Year	Notes	Debit/Expenditure Source	Amount	Credit/Income Source	Amount	Members
1875	Mr. Edward Pease of Darlington offered to give numbers 21-23 Load Street as Bewdley Institute, provided certain conditions were met					72 signatories at public meeting
1877	Mr. J. M. Gething, local architect, had prepared plans [to convert part of the building] showing what could be done for £1000.00 + a modified scheme On 31st December Trust Deed & Plans approved & signed by 15 Trustees				By 10th February £300.00+ (of £513.00 promised)	
1878/80	On 14th October 1878 Numbers 21-23 Load Street opened to both sexes as Bewdley Institute Expected Govt. Grant (£432.63) not rec'd. by time of AGM (Jan. 1880)	. Liabilities on Building Fund (approx.) . Rates . Other outstanding liabilities	£100.00 £1.54 £17.30	. Receipts from Billiard Table . **Total receipts** . Balance in hand/at Bank at 31-12-1879	£47.00 **£131.47** £1.30	101 (incl. 3 Vice-Presidents)
1882/83		. Rates, Taxes & Insurance	£3.79			
1883/84		. Outstanding liabilities . Excess of liabilities over assets	£63.00 £28.00	. Balance in Bank	£3.40	
1884/85	Unusually high consumption of gas & coal in Social Room, where there had been a much better attendance than during the previous year – probably because a special Secretary had been appointed to superintend it	. Outstanding liabilities . Balance due to *Hon. Sec.*, (brt. forward from 1883/84) . *Steward's* Salary . Arrears of Salary of former Secretary (T. Peach) . Tradesmen's bills . Gas . Coal . Rates, Taxes & Insurance . Chief Rent, 1882 & 1883 . Expenses of Lectures . Worcs. Union of Clubs & Institutes . Bazaar Expenses . Incidentals . Excess of liabilities over assets	£47.00 £9.44 £10.00 £5.00 £57.04 £15.83 £20.17 £3.79 £1.45 £1.65 £0.50 £2.00 £1.41 £21.00	. Subscriptions received: . Arrears from 1883 . For 1884 . Donations . Rent of Rooms . Hire of Chairs . Proceeds from Lectures, etc. . Fees for Classes (incl. £1.91 donation from Shorthand Class) . Sale of Newspapers . Donation for Prizes . Government Grant . Balance in late *Secretary's* hands . Receipts from Bazaar . Money Boxes . Balance due to *Hon. Sec.* [entered in the Income Column in the Press Report] . Balance in Bewdley Bank	£2.05 £32.60 £4.25 £4.50 £0.63 £3.33 £6.29 £1.40 £3.00 £7.00 £1.40 £38.52 £1.15 £8.91 £1.77	67 (42 hon. paying 53p or more p.a. and 25 ordinary paying 25p p.a.)

Table 1

Year	Notes	Debit/Expenditure Source	Amount	Credit/Income Source	Amount	Members
1885/86	12 new members joined after Mr. T. C. Dalley printed and circulated 'a paragraph drawing attention to the advantages offered by the Institute' Members decided that, for the ensuing year, there should be only two classes of subscriber - namely, the honorary (53p) and the ordinary (25p); that no subscription for less than half a year be received; and that 'both classes of members meet in one common room under such rules and regulations as may be deemed desirable'	. Excess of liabilities over assets	£2.48	. Donations towards Museum . Entertainment	£2.85 £3.88	[79] (incl. 8 Vice-Presidents in 1885 & 9 in 1886)
1887/88		. Property Assessment . Excess of liabilities over assets	£14.00 £21.55			
1888/89		. Property Assessment (increased from last year's £14.00, + a proportionate increase in Rates) . Excess of liabilities over assets	£28.00 £13.40	. Receipts from Coffee Tavern . *Net profit from Coffee Tavern* . *Net profit from Saturday Evening Entertainments* . **Total receipts from Institute**	£201.49 *£6.71* *£4.00+* **£59.09**	
1889/90	Finances such that Institute could only consider buying a Billiard Table & a Piano via special subscriptions from members By 1889 a rule had been passed whereby a subscriber of £1.05 p.a. was entitled to a ticket admitting all members of his family aged under 21 to the privileges of the Institute (except voting), while a subscriber of 53p p.a. was entitled to admit members of his family aged under 21 on payment of 8p p.a. per member. The ordinary fee was [still] 25p p.a.	. 'at considerable extra expense' a substantial sign board was erected near bridge to advertise Coffee Tavern, *therefore Coffee Tavern balance sheet showed an increased debt of* . Coffee Tavern debt to Institute . Rates and Taxes . Billiard Table (poss. 6 years old) purchased . Piano . Excess of liabilities over assets (incl. *an increase of £9.60 on last year's debt*)	£4.36 £6.10 £8.00+ £36.00 £7.50 £26.98			72 (incl. [10] *Vice-Presidents*)

93

Year	Notes	Debit/Expenditure Source	Amount	Credit/Income Source	Amount	Members
1890/91	Increased Adverse Balance partly accounted for by improvements required by the Urban Sanitary Authority	. Coffee Tavern debt to Institute	£5.14			81
	Shares raised to purchase Billiard Table now paid off, but it still needed about £14.00 repair/renovation work, to which several contributions had been received	. Excess of liabilities over assets	£60.30 (reduced to £50.30 by 31-12-1890)			
	Increase in number of members due to purchase of Billiard Table					
	Nevertheless, the *Church Monthly*, February 1891 noted: '... It is to be deeply regretted that more use is not made of this Institute, especially by those who live near the town. The small subscription places its benefits within the reach of every working man.'					
1891/92	Increased Adverse Balance largely due to expense of continuing the Coffee Tavern	. Adverse Balance on Coffee Tavern	£27.64			
	Proposed Sale of Work to help remove debt	. Excess of liabilities over assets	£80.40			
	During the present year the Coffee Tavern was to be continued by the present Manager as a private concern					
1892/93	Institute now debt-free	. Improvements to Chemistry Lab. (incl. accommodation for students)	£20.00+	. Bazaar & Entertainments	£97.00+	92 (incl. 14 Vice-Presidents)
		. Apparatus for Chemistry Lab.	£40.00	. Takings from Billiard Room	£23.05	
1893/94		. Installation of "governor" gas burners	(£12.00+)	. Part of Institute takings for past year given to Billiard Room Committee	£31.82	111
		. Repairs		. Education grant earned for good exam. results	£24.00	
		. Exterior of building painted & cleaned		. Balance in hand/at Bank on 1-1-1894	£25.18	
		. New window inserted in Art School				
		. Increase to *Steward's* annual Salary	£5.00			
		. **Total expenditure**	**£31.55**			
1894/95	Over £6.00 saved on gas by installation of "governor" gas burners and a few other alterations	. Repairs (of this £12.00+ spent on Roof & almost £7.00 on Painting & Colouring Art & Cookery Schools)	£31.25	. Part of Institute takings for past year given to Billiard Room Committee	£36.14	108
	Whole of building, internally & externally, in a very satisfactory state. No further expenditure expected for some years			. Balance in hand/at Bank	£32.26	
1896/97				. Balance in hand/at Bank	£40.00	101 (1895) 112 (1896)

Table 1

Year	Notes	Debit/Expenditure Source	Amount	Credit/Income Source	Amount	Members
1897/98	Project to rebuild the Social Room & fit it up with 2 billiard tables was considered but postponed because estimated cost (£200.00) too expensive Lord Cobham noticed that as Billiards Receipts increased the number of library books issued decreased! Fear that younger members might spend too much time at Billiards Table and not enough in the Classes!			. Receipts from Billiard Room . **Total receipts for year** . Balance of assets over liabilities	£49.67 **£121.16** £58.01	119
1898/99	Decrease in balance of assets over liabilities due to 'falling off in receipts from the Billiard Room' because present room unsuitable Steps being taken to raise funds for rebuilding the large Social Room, which was in an unsafe condition, with a view to its adaptation for the reception of 2 billiard tables Library adapted for use as a Social Room – effected by shutting off the books by means of wire doors From the report of the A.G.M. in 1899 it seems that the Vice-Presidents were each expected to pay the honorary annual subscription of 53p			. Billiard receipts . *Subscriptions received less than* . Balance of assets over expenditure . Balance in hand/at Bank	£34.77 *£30.00* £50.12 £4.45	118
1899/1900	£54.61 due from Kidderminster School(s) of Science & Art for rent of Institute rooms for Classes written off It was believed that the new Billiard Room would attract new members and that an increased income of £60.00 per annum would accrue A bazaar was planned to help pay off the £170.00 loans from members Library used as a Social Room & the Upper Rooms had been used by the Badminton Club	. New Billiard Room (now completed – to be officially opened in May 1900), new Billiard Table, furniture, etc. . Debit on Capital Account . **Total expenditure for year**	(Expected cost about £370.00) £7.05 **£86.20**	. Billiard receipts . *Promised towards cost of New Billiard Room* . Donations received towards cost of New Billiard Room . Loans received from members towards cost of New Billiard Room . Subscriptions received . **Total general income for year** . Balance in hand/at Bank on 1-1-1900	£32.56 *£200.00* £30.00 £170.00 £27.43 **£98.47** £12.27	123

Year	Notes	Debit/Expenditure		Credit/Income		Members
		Source	Amount	Source	Amount	
1900/01	Decrease in Balance in hand due to paying off some of the large liabilities owing at 1-1-1900 Several portraits of the officers at the Front, incl. late Maj. Childe, had been presented by Mr. Dudfield & framed by means of subscriptions from members, & a framed portrait of Mr. Dudfield (*Hon. Sec.*) had been presented by Mr. Tomes. These had been hung in the new Billiard Room Subscriptions had been collected to buy chairs for the Billiard Room, but more still needed Increase in membership numbers due to 3 causes: (1) the energy of Mr. Dudfield, *Secretary*; (2) the completion of the new Billiard Room; and (3) many visitors to the town in the summer months had joined for the time of their stay, rather than for the full year	. Total cost of new Billiard Room, incl. removal of the old one . Debt remaining on cost of New Billiard Room . Excess of liabilities over assets	£395.87 £254.36 £11.10	. Donation from Bazaar Fund towards new Library Books (urgently required) (figure difficult to read) . Receipts from 2-day Bazaar given to Improvement Scheme . **Total income for year** . Balance in hand/at Bank	£10.00 £106.73 **£116.47** £9.70	151
1901/02		. [Enfranchisement] . Billiard Table	£10.50			149
1902/03	Decrease in receipts from Billiard Table due to introduction of Ping-Pong? New gas burners needed in Billiard Room It might be possible for some of the extra cost of gas consumed at the Art Classes to be returned to the Institute by the Kidderminster Schools…. Executive	. Liabilities on Improvement Fund on 1-1-1903 (incl. Bank Overdraft of £18.21) . Excess of liabilities over assets at 1-1-1903	£164.21 £17.20	. *Gross receipts from Billiard Room* . Receipts from Billiard Room . **Total receipts for year** . Balance in hand/at Bank on 1-1-1903	£46.73 £11.68 **£117.38** £3.84	
1903/04	Decrease on balance in hand largely due to less demand for use of Rooms than previously Half gross receipts from Billiard Room (£27.50, incl. 50p entrance fees from billiard handicap) used to reduce debt on Building Fund; & a quarter each (£13.60) given to Institute & towards internal management expenses of the Room Remaining balance in hand (£9.30) to be used to repay shareholders as soon as possible	. Debt remaining for New Billiard Room on 31-12-1903 . Rates & Taxes ('heavy') . Bewdley Water laid on (approx. cost) . Excess of liabilities over assets at 1-1-1904	£126.70 £17.24 £4.00 £34.01	. *Gross receipts from Billiard Room* . Receipts from Billiard Room . Balance in hand/at Bank on 1-1-1904	£54.45 £13.24 £0.32	145
1904/05	Increase in excess of liabilities over assets due, among other causes, to decrease in receipts from Billiard Room & an increase in cost of coal & gas Cost of upkeep of Institute steadily increasing while the income was not doing so Formerly there had been a number of *Vice-Presidents* who had contributed £1.05 p.a. to the funds	. Debt remaining for New Billiard Room	£103.02	. *Gross receipts from Billiard Room* . Subscription List opened towards clearing Building Fund debt . Balance in hand/at Bank on 1-1-1905	£42.49 £5.25 £0.68	143

Table 1

Year	Notes	Debit/Expenditure Source	Amount	Credit/Income Source	Amount	Members
1905/06	Bagatelle Room established in room formerly used by Horticultural Society, with their agreement. Very popular Increased use of gas there + current bill included 5 quarters Introduction of new members largely due to Mr. Smith of the Heath. He suggested establishing an Airgun Range Institute aiming for 200 members As a result of an appeal the previous year, £23.00 had been contributed towards the Improvement Scheme & £27.00 in shares surrendered New books needed for Library	. Bank Account overdrawn at 1-1-1906 by . Debt remaining for New Billiard Room . New Bagatelle Table purchased . Repairs to Old Bagatelle Table . Excess of liabilities over assets at 1-1-1906	£11.36 £51.76 £18.75 £7.75 £40.68	. Receipts from Billiard Room . Receipts in 9 months from Bagatelle Tables in their new room	£48.55 £19.00+	192 (about 25 being for one quarter year only)
1906/07	Possible reasons for large decrease in receipts from Billiard Room: . Reduction in charges made for use of table . Introduction of Airgun Shooting 2 new airguns donated to Institute Outstanding subscriptions £4.13 (much less than in previous years!) About half the Billiard Receipts (£17.00) used to reduce debt on Building Fund; & a quarter each given to Institute & towards internal management expenses of the Room Remaining balance (8p) paid to Improvement Fund Move seconded that all *Vice-Presidents* should pay annual subscription of at least 50p (*cf* 53p in 1899), but whether or not a resolution to this effect was passed is unclear	. Debt remaining for New Billiard Room at 31-12-1906 . Repairs . Excess of liabilities over assets at 1-1-1907	£34.66 £40.01	. Receipts from Billiard Room . Bagatelle Table receipts . Sale of *Old* Bagatelle Table (removed to make room for Airgun Shooting) realized enough to pay debt on the *New* Bagatelle Table . Receipts from Airgun Shooting (no details, but 'profitable') . Balance in hand/at Bank	£34.16 £13.71 £1.75 £0.26	160
1907/08	Gross receipts from Billiard Room the highest sum received from that source during the history of the Institute	. Expenditure on Repairs (larger than usual due to renovating *Steward's House*) . Excess of liabilities over assets	£3.03	. *Gross receipts from Billiard Room* . Receipts from Airgun Shooting 'satisfactory' . Funds raised via an Amateur Dramatic Performance . Funds raised via 2 Whist Drives . **Total receipts for year**	£65.85 £18.04 £6.88 **£137.01**	178

Year	Notes	Debit/Expenditure		Credit/Income		Members
		Source	Amount	Source	Amount	
1908/09	Both Bagatelle & Airgun receipts only half those of previous year The decrease in Bagatelle receipts largely because many of the players had taken to Billiards Members had subscribed to an enlarged framed photograph of the late Mr. Alfred Baldwin who had always been a generous friend to the Institute The framed photograph was placed in the Reading Room			. *Gross receipts from Billiard Room* . Profits from 2 Whist Drives . **Total receipts for year** . Balance of assets over expenditure . Balance in hand/at Bank	£72.75 £5.41 **£174.51** £30.80 £18.74	168
1909/10	Furniture & effects in the Institute valued at £183.65 New books added to Library Bagatelle Room had been better patronised			. Balance in hand/at Bank	£28.10	154 (incl. 12 *Vice-Presidents*)
1910/11	Interest in Airgun Practice 'had evapourated' Subscriptions in arrears: appeal for early payment	. Estimated cost of appointing 4 new *Trustees* (4 vacancies)	£3.00 or £4.00	. Estimated assets at 31-12-1910 after payment of all liabilities . Receipts from Billiard Room . **Total receipts for year** (incl. the balance of £28.10 carried forward from previous year) . Balance in hand/at Bank	£70.07 £62.72 **£115.28** £38.82	151 (incl. 14 *Vice-Presidents*)
1911/12	Balance at Bank achieved after paying all liabilities to date & placing £50.00 in a Sinking Fund for emergencies			. *Gross receipts from Billiard Room* . Receipts from Bagatelle Table . Sinking Fund Account . **Total receipts for year** . Balance of assets over expenditure at 31-12-1911 (excl. furniture, Billiard Tables, etc.) . Balance in hand/at Bank at 31-12-1911	£73.95 £4.52 £50.00 **£194.15** £103.45 £15.30	147 (incl. 15 *Vice-Presidents*)

Table 1

Year	Notes	Debit/Expenditure Source	Amount	Credit/Income Source	Amount	Members
1912/13				· Gross receipts from Billiard Room	£69.85	164 (incl. 17 Vice-Presidents)
				· Receipts from Bagatelle Sinking Fund Account	£5.55	
				· at 1-1-1913	£50.95	
				· at 23-3-1913	£72.59	
				· Balance in General Fund	£28.33	
				· **Total receipts for year**	**£170.42**	
				· Balance of assets over expenditure on 1-1-1913 (incl. General Fund, interest on Sinking Fund Account & outstanding assets, but excl. furniture, tables & effects)	£125.95	
1913/14	Library had been overhauled. Only 2 subscriptions outstanding, but both members non-resident	· Improving Billiard Room heating apparatus (approx.)	£24.00	· Gross receipts from Billiard Room	£60.42	160 (incl. 17 Vice-Presidents)
				· Receipts from Bagatelle	£6.47	
				· Sinking Fund Account	£92.14	
				· Balance in General Fund	£11.53	
				· **Total receipts for year**	**£171.80**	
				· Balance of assets over expenditure	£110.86	
1914/15	25 members had joined H.M. Forces during the latter part of 1914. 1 member killed in action 8 days before 1915 A.G.M.	· New books for Library		· Gross receipts from Billiard Room	£70.53	162 (incl. 11 Vice-Presidents)
				· Receipts from Bagatelle	£5.74	
				· Sinking Fund Account	£97.84	
				· Balance in General Fund	£22.42	
				· **Total receipts for year**	**£134.06**	
				· Balance of assets over expenditure	£122.75	
1915/16	Decrease in Credit Balance largely due to lower Billiards receipts, several of the regular playing members now serving in H. M. Forces. 1 member killed in action in August 1915. By 1915 the County Union of Clubs & Institutes had lost 10 Clubs because of the War	· Purchase of £100.00 War Loan Stock at 4.5% interest	£99.47	· Billiard receipts	£48.19	152 (incl. 11 Vice-Presidents & also hon. members engaged in military work)
				· Bagatelle receipts	£6.38	
				· Airgun Shooting (revived this year)	£2.60	
				· Sinking Fund Account	£5.14	
				· Donations made towards purchase of a few new books		
				· Balance of assets over expenditure (incl. Sinking Fund, War Loan Stock & assets)	£107.51	

Year	Notes	Debit/Expenditure		Credit/Income		Members
		Source	Amount	Source	Amount	
1916/17	£5.14 withdrawn from Sinking Fund Account + Bank overdraft to meet liabilities for 1916 Net loss on year's working about the same as last year's One third of members had joined H. M. Forces. All were honorary members (i.e. they had free membership) 2 had been killed in action during 1916	. Overdraft at Bank . Net loss on year's working	£9.78 £16.17	. Billiard receipts . Bagatelle receipts . War Loan Stock converted into the new rate of 5% interest . Balance in hand/at Bank (after paying all liabilities, & incl. £1.13 for outstanding subs.)	£43.78 £3.48 £105.26 £96.61	(incl. 11 Vice-Presidents)
1917/18	War Savings Association started – 22 members had purchased 159 Certificates by 31-12-1917 Billiard & Bagatelle Tables fairly well patronised Club fortunate in not having to pay rent and in having a Reserve Fund 1 member had been killed in action in 1917	. Overdraft at Bank . Loss on year's working	£30.63 £21.34	. Billiard receipts . Balance of assets over expenditure at 31-12-1917 . Balance in hand/at Bank at 31-12-1917	£34.10 £30.63 £75.27	164 (incl. 13 Vice-Presidents & also 62 hon. members serving in H. M. Forces)
1918/19	War Savings Association - 268 Certificates 3 more members had been killed in action in 1918	. Overdraft at Bank . **Total expenditure**	£21.05 **£128.63**	. Billiard receipts . Bagatelle receipts . Card Table ('a new, valuable source of revenue') . Balance in hand/at Bank	£50.22 £3.80 £11.66 £85.09	175 (incl. 14 Vice-Presidents & also 67 hon. members serving in H. M. Forces)

Table 1

Year	Notes	Debit/Expenditure		Credit/Income		Members
		Source	Amount	Source	Amount	
1919/20	There had been an increase in general expenses, incl. extra outlay in repairs to the buildings and to the Bagatelle and Billiard Tables. The Billiard Tables would soon need a large sum spent on re-covering them Repairs to the premises impending A subscription list was begun for a permanent War Memorial in the Institute, £10.00 being voted from Club funds towards it. Expected cost £32.00+ Not possible to have a Card Room because of coal ration. Club had already exceeded their allowance There were now only 32 Clubs in the Worcs. Union, compared with 78 before the War Subscriptions raised to £0.30 per annum	. Overdraft at Bank	£11.92	. Billiard receipts . Bagatelle receipts . Card receipts . War Loan . **Total receipts** . Balance in hand/at Bank (after paying all liabilities, & incl. 50p outstanding)	£79.84 £4.34 £15.87 £105.00 **£165.34** £93.60	200+
1920/21	Bank overdraft increased due to expenditure on repairs [Ordinary] membership subscriptions increased to £0.50, the previous year's increase to £0.30 being insufficient to help meet cost of urgently needed repairs and refurbishment. The premises, perforce, had been badly neglected during the war years and the Billiard Tables, although sound, needed £50.00 worth of tender loving care! The new subscription was still wonderful value for the advantages which the Institute offered and compared very favourably with annual fees charged at Kidderminster and Stourport, which were believed to be 50p and 63p, respectively. If, in the future, it became possible to reduce the annual subscription rate then this would be done Institute now had support of many members aged 17-21 A Billiard Competition had raised £2.10 for St. Dunstan's War Memorial erected at a cost of £-8.00 [looks like £18.00]	. Excess of liabilities over assets	£51.80	. Billiard receipts . Bagatelle . Card table	£104.19 £6.47 £31.35	231

Year	Notes	Debit/Expenditure		Credit/Income		Members
		Source	Amount	Source	Amount	
1921/22	Need to spend about £150.00 on urgent repairs to buildings + painting & decorating – expenditure having been postponed because of Wartime economy A Billiards & Snooker Competition had raised £1.50 for St. Dunstan's	• Re-covering Billiard Tables	£45.00	• Gross receipts from Billiard Room • Billiard receipts • Whist Drives • Subscriptions received • **Total receipts for year** • Balance of assets over expenditure at 31-12-21 (after paying all liabilities) • Balance in hand/at Bank	£177.82 £149.90 £26.66 £73.45 **£293.16** £110.32 £11.82	175 (incl. 15 Vice-Presidents)
1922/23	Repairs to building still needed, incl. alterations to *Steward's House* No outstanding subscriptions – first time in 12 years!	• Overdraft at Bank • Building Repairs, Painting Billiard Room, etc. (approx.)	£7.63 £100.00	• Gross receipts from Billiard Room	£155.25	152 (incl. 14 Vice-Presidents)
1923/24	Repairs to Billiard Tables (purchased 34 and 21 years ago, respectively) very satisfactory	• Repairs to Billiard Tables, etc. (estimated cost)	£50.00	• Billiard receipts • Bagatelle • *Profit on year's working* • Balance in hand/at Bank	£127.46 £3.30 £23.33 £10.33	141 (incl. 15 Vice-Presidents)
1924/25	Contracts amounting to £50.00 had been placed for necessary repairs to fabric Members' subscriptions just about paid the cost of gas and coal	• New books for Library • District & Poor Rate ('somewhat stiff')	£22.56	• Billiard receipts • Bagatelle ('interest had declined') • **Total receipts for year** • Balance in hand/at Bank	£117.94 **£229.13** £0.33	170 (Kelly's Directory) 136 by time of A.G.M. (incl. 14 Vice-Presidents)
1925/26	Club outlook bright & promising Outstanding subscriptions £10.30 Appeal made to young men 'to take a share of the responsibility in building up the Institute to a strong position'	• Building maintenance & repairs • Overdraft at Bank • **Total Payments for year** • Excess of liabilities over assets	£47.53 £45.08 **£240.98** £36.40	• Billiard receipts 'encouraging' • Sinking Fund Account • Subscriptions received • Balance of assets over expenditure (incl. a balance of £44.35)	£101.00 £63.00 £47.53	150 (incl. 14 Vice-Presidents)
1926/27	Motion to revise whole of the Rules (last done in 1906) defeated by one vote. No alteration found necessary to Rule 12 relating to opening hours of the Institute. 2 rules were agreed: (1) Reading Room hours 8.00a.m. to 9.00p.m. Billiard Room 2.00p.m. to 11.00p.m. (2) Loan period for library books 2 weeks, with power to renew	• Excess of liabilities over assets	£7.96	• Social & Recreational takings had increased by • *Profit on year's working* • Balance in hand/at Bank	£8.28 *£30.00+* £8.48	161 by March 1927 (incl. 14 Vice-Presidents)

Table 1

Year	Notes	Debit/Expenditure Source	Amount	Credit/Income Source	Amount	Members
1927/28	Reduction in number of membership fees received Recommendation for the Committee to explore possibilities of getting a bar licence	. Overdraft at Bank . Rates . Taxes & Insurance	£7.58 £17.60 £10.29	. Social & Recreation Room takings . Receipts from Billiards 'markedly low' . Sinking Fund Account (still at 5% interest) . **Total receipts for year** . Balance of assets over expenditure (excl. furniture, etc. & goodwill of members)	£11.20 £101.69 **£252.62** £18.06	(incl. 15 *Vice-Presidents*)
1928/29	Understandably, Countess of Portsmouth adamant there should be no licence to sell intoxicating liquors Outstanding subscriptions £6.25 Reduction in membership subscriptions received and in Billiard receipts Need for membership campaign. Particular suggestions were that more young men spend their leisure hours in the Institute instead of in the streets and that parents bring their daughters as well as their sons to the Institute. They were fully entitled to membership at the age of 18 years Overdraft increased in order to instal electric lights (see Ref. 70) & to complete the re-decoration of rooms used by the Girl Guides, plus lesser improvements	. Overdraft at Bank . **Total expenditure for year**	£63.51 **£235.83**	. Whist Drives . Reserve Fund . **Total receipts for year** (incl. £8.48 cash in hand) . Balance in hand/at Bank	£100.00 **£203.91** £13.54	(incl. 15 *Vice-Presidents*)
1929/30	Appeal made for prompt payment of subscriptions, although currently there were none outstanding (a rare occasion!) Repairs & improvements still urgently needed to interior & exterior of premises A remarkable achievement to have paid off £70-£80 in little over 5 months	. Billiard Tables re-covered . New Books added to Library . **Total payments for year**	£30.00 **£272.68**	. Social & Recreation Dept. . Whist Drives, etc. . War Loan Stock at 5% interest . Raised by Sports C'ttee . Rent of Rooms . Subscriptions received . **Total receipts for year** (incl. £13.54 cash in hand on 1-1-1930) . *Profit on year's working* . Balance of assets over expenditure (both figures quoted in same report!)	£113.83 £31.40 £100.26 £31.00 £17.65 £76.75 **£283.05** £60.00 £10.38 or £10.28	160 (incl. 16 *Vice-Presidents*)

Year	Notes	Debit/Expenditure		Credit/Income		Members
		Source	Amount	Source	Amount	
1930/31	£110.00 wiped off the Capital Charge in 6 months Mr. S. Hemingway's brother, Mr. E. Hemingway, had deputised for him in opening the new portion of the building No outstanding subscriptions for the 2nd year running! Mayor Ald. Frost suggested that more lady members become associate members, as had the Mayoress and a few other ladies. Since it would necessitate a revision of rules, this idea was referred to the Committee for report to a General Meeting	. Bank Overdraft for Alterations & Improvements . Payment towards Capital Charge . Third Billiard Table purchased	£340.00 £110.00	. Social & Recreation Dept. (incl. £121.00 from Billiards) . *Profit on Current Account* . Raised by Sports C'ttee . Rent of Rooms . Subscriptions received	£135.63 *£102.58* £77.05 £42.93 £84.00	(incl. 19 *Vice-Presidents*)
1931/32	Careful consideration would be given to admission of lady members if/when they had enough accommodation Meanwhile, any ladies who wished might apply for membership. In Canada ladies' institutes were expanding rapidly Assembly Room becoming better known & more popular but lacked proper cloakroom accommodation Extra duties for *Steward* Mr. B. Plevey at County Library, but his work at the Institute had not diminished Agreed to alter Rule 2 to read 'Any person aged 17 years & over may become a member, provided that persons aged between 15 & 17 years proposed by a member and approved by the Committee may also become members, the subscriptions being 50p per annum or 13p per quarter, payable in advance' It was agreed that youths should leave the premises at 9.30p.m.	. Heating Apparatus in Assembly Room . Bagatelle Table re-covered		. Sinking Fund still intact . Raised by Sports C'ttee . Rent of Rooms . *Profit on year's working*	£39.79 £32.00 *£110.42*	(incl. 22 *Vice-Presidents*)

Table 1

Year	Notes	Debit/Expenditure Source	Amount	Credit/Income Source	Amount	Members
1932/33	Admission of younger members very successful. They proved to be an asset to the Institute	Steward's Salary	£40.00	Social & Recreation Dept. (incl. £131.00 from Billiards and £2.20 from Bagatelle)	£145.56	(incl. 24 Vice-Presidents)
	Redemption of War Loan and profit on [previous] year's working had enabled C'ttee to pay off the balance on the old debt and show a handsome balance at bank of £56.87 which, together with outstanding subscriptions of £3.50, gave a total of £60.37	Newspapers, etc.	£15.96	Redemption of War Loan + Interest (Dec. 1932) (at the time it constituted a Sinking Fund)	£105.26	
		Fuel	£36.00			
		Lighting	£32.00			
		Rates	£19.73			
		Cleaning materials	£5.84	Cash paid in to General Account	£2.13	
	This would be used towards the new cloakrooms which it was hoped to start building that year	Accounts	£20.52	Transferred from Current Account to Improvements Account	£61.43	
		Building repairs	£10.83			
	Total expenditure £18.23 more than last year due to extra lighting, heating and minor repairs	Improvement Account:		Raised by Sports C'ttee	£32.44	
		· Balance due to Bank	£107.86	Total Rent of Rooms for year (incl. £19.90 for rent of Assembly Rooms; £14.00 from County Library; & £14.00 from Girl Guides)	£57.28	
		· Bank charges	£5.27			
		· To H. E. Pritchard for Heating, etc.	£51.43	Subscriptions received	£76.00	
				Profit on year's working	£111.08	
				Balance in hand/at Bank	£56.87	
1933/34	Outstanding subscriptions £˚0.28	**Total liabilities at beginning of year**	**£160.08**	Social & Recreation Dept. (mainly Billiards)	£120.99	(incl. 20 Vice-Presidents)
	Apart from the Improvement Fund, the accounts showed a profit of £34.00	Bank Overdraft for Construction of New Cloakrooms, etc. (of which £203.90 went to builders, Messrs. J. Coldrick & Son)	£241.93	Bagatelle takings 'disappointing'	£0.18	
	Membership slightly down on that of 1932 (no figures given) because many people had left the area	*Payment towards overdraft*	*£93.71*	Raised by Sports C'ttee	£25.67	
		Balance due to Bank	*£150.06*	Rent of Rooms	£54.10	
	Sports Committee had raised £175.00 in 4 years	Rates	£18.55	Subscriptions received	£70.40	
		Fuel	£37.70			
	£100.00 received from Rent of Assembly Room in 4 years. Club could not afford to let the Room for nothing, but they charged low fees and Room had become an asset to the town – fulfilling Edward Pease's wishes	Lighting	£32.93			
		Repairs to Billiard Tables (total £20.00, part to be paid in 1934)	£10.00			
	By 1933 the Club Library was practically unused, being overshadowed by the friendly opposition of the more up-to-date County Library	Steward's Salary	£50.00			
		Total expenditure for year	**£468.03**			
		Excess of liabilities over assets (excl. tables & furnishings, etc.)	£149.81			

Year	Notes	Debit/Expenditure		Credit/Income		Members
		Source	Amount	Source	Amount	
1934/35	The Institute one of Bewdley's finest assets	. Bank overdraft at 1-1-1935	£87.25	. Social & Recreation Dept. (mainly Billiards)	£146.63	(incl. 19 or 20 Vice-Presidents)
	Outstanding subscriptions £8.93 (by time of A.G.M. many of these had been paid in)	. Purchase & overhaul of Piano for Assembly Room	£14.35	. Sale of Bagatelle Table (takings over 3 years having amounted to only £2.37)	£7.73	
	List of original members and benefactors framed	. Building repairs	£7.24	. Raised by newly-constituted Sports C'ttee	£23.23	
		. Repairs to Billiard Tables (half paid in 1933) + new balls	£17.75	. Dances		
	Sale of Bagatelle Table didn't appear in last year's accounts			. Rent of Rooms	£63.43	
	They'd acquired a Dance & Assembly Room described as the finest in the district	. Rates (increased due to additional assessment on new cloakrooms)	£24.76	'other items on receipts side similar to last year'		
		. Fuel	£44.00			
		. Excess of liabilities over assets (after taking into account outstanding subs. & sundry credits)	£74.60			
1935/36	Library lacked support but daily papers & periodicals maintained theirs	. Bank Overdraft at 31-12-1935	£8.78	. Social & Recreation Dept.	£141.84	(incl. 19 Vice-Presidents)
		. Building repairs	£15.62	. Sports C'ttee	£32.22	
	Death of Countess of Portsmouth	. *Repairs to Billiard Tables (An error? It's almost the same sum as total spent in previous 2 years!)*	£33.95	. Subscriptions received	£64.68	
	Outstanding subscriptions £8.63			. *Profit for the year*	£40.65	
	More members needed. It was remarked (as it had been as far back as 1905) that "…. the real trouble was a falling-off of *Vice-Presidents*" who, in the past, had been expected to pay an enhanced sum	. Rates	£30.29			
		. Excess of liabilities over assets	£33.96			

Table 1

Year	Notes	Debit/Expenditure		Credit/Income		Members
		Source	Amount	Source	Amount	
1936/37	Payments during the year were £112.00 more than in 1935! Donations had made this possible Redecoration in progress in Entrance Passage, Hall, Lower Rooms & Landing. Urgent need to do the Assembly Room, Billiards Room & that adjoining it. A start would be made as soon as funds permitted Roofing repairs due to gales in August & September Special appeal to raise funds, headed by Lord Cobham, had raised almost £20.00 & was still attracting subscriptions Percentage of deaths and removals from the area during 1936 had been high. Appeal made for new members Adoption of new rules prepared by a sub-committee because old ones were somewhat out of date. One alteration empowered members to elect Life Members when necessary. Another provided that all officers of the Institute should be elected at the Annual Meeting (Formerly, although the *President, Chairman, Auditors,* etc. were elected at the Annual Meeting, names for election to the Committee were only *submitted* at the Annual Meeting, and the ballot to appoint them took place a day or so afterwards) Much discussion regarding a *proposed increased charge from 1d.* (approx. 0.42p) *to 3d.* (1.25p) *for members introducing a friend.* Some members thought this a prohibitive amount which would debar visitors from the Club. Others felt that 1d. was a ridiculous figure for a day's enjoyment. The *Secretary* had enquired what other Clubs charged, but had been unable to find one which provided for its members' friends. It is unclear whether the increased charge was introduced Redemption of Chief Rent would mean an annual saving of £0.73 for all time	. Debit balance on Current Account . Building Repairs (including re-roofing one gable end of Billiard Room & other [smaller] building repairs) . Redemption of Chief Rent . Decorators' work . Rates . Bank charges (£2.00 less than in 1935) . **Total expenditure**	£14.65 £43.45 £12.00 £24.00 £32.49 **£113.40**	. Total receipts from Social & Recreation Dept: . *Billiards & Snooker* . *Cards* . Reserve Fund established to meet the necessary re-decoration . Donations . Sports C'ttee (incl. Dances) . Balance of assets over expenditure	£151.28 *£144.25* *£7.03* £19.73 £23.92 £5.08	(incl. 27 *Vice-Presidents*)

Year	Notes	Debit/Expenditure		Credit/Income		Members
		Source	Amount	Source	Amount	
1937/38	Assembly Hall in need of re-decoration & improvement plus 1 or 2 radiators. Number of applications for use rising Since converted 7 years ago the receipts from it had realized £250.00 Recreation Room re-decorated Another Fan needed in Large Room to eradicate smoky atmosphere completely Almost £700 spent on improvements in last 7 years Re-decoration fund deficit of £1.71 on 31-12-1937 had been paid by time of A.G.M. Trust Deed redeemed A special general meeting to be held to consider appointment of new *Trustees* because number fallen below 6 specified in Deed Some outstanding subscriptions Hoped to do something special next year – Institute's Diamond Jubilee	. Installation of Electric Exhaust Fan in Recreation Room . Re-decoration of Recreation Room (money donated by special appeal)	almost £40.00	. Billiards & Snooker . Cards . *Profit on year's working* . Balance of assets over expenditure	£118.80 £10.96 *£51.50* *£56.63*	(incl. 27 Vice-Presidents)

Table 1

Year	Notes	Debit/Expenditure Source	Amount	Credit/Income Source	Amount	Members
1938/39	Heavy building expenditure imminent			. Billiards & Snooker (similar to last year's)	[£118.25?]	(incl. [27] Vice-Presidents)
	No extra-ordinary meeting held regarding election of *Trustees* because negotiating for purchase of the Reversionary Interest from Countess of Portsmouth's estate Purchase agreed just last week (April 1939) at a probable cost of £25.00			. Other income (sources and amounts unspecified, but probably includes donations of £1.00+)	£11.67	
				. Balance of assets over expenditure	£118.13	
	Distinct possibility of having a licence in near future now that owned premises. It was understood that all *Trustees* approved, but Bar question would have to be decided at an extra-ordinary general meeting of members			. Balance in favour of the Club	£61.50	
	No-one wished to flout Edward Pease's wishes, but there was a constant struggle to pay heavy expenses incurred for maintenance on the old property					
	Times had changed, too, & a licensed bar was all that was needed to bring the Club up to the standards of others in the area. All Mr. Pease's other wishes would be strictly adhered to. At present the Trust Deed was non-existent					
	Decided increase in Rent of Rooms because the Committee Room was on hire to the Ministry of Labour					
	Some outstanding subscriptions. Early payment needed					
1939/40	Agreed to recommend that 8 names be added to *Trustees*	. *Steward's Salary* (increased because of increased workload)	£76.67	. Balance carried forward from 1938 Accounts	£102.35	165 (incl. 27 Vice-Presidents)
	Negotiations for purchase of Reversionary Interest brought to a successful conclusion in August 1939	. Lighting & Heating	£81.29	. Billiards receipts	£89.90	
		. Repairs & Renewals	£24.01	. Cards & Visitors	£8.63	
	Lord Cobham held an important position at the War Office	. Refreshments	£112.63	. Darts	£1.90	
		. Rates & Taxes	£46.68	. Rent of Rooms	£80.90	
	Although subscriptions received showed a further increase, a reduction in the amount received in the immediate future was expected because members serving in H. M. Forces would have free membership	. Purchase of Reversionary Interest	£17.15	. Subscriptions received	£71.93	
		. Re-lighting Assembly Room	£15.63	. Refreshments	£199.19	
	Receipts from Rent of Rooms were considerably less than those from the Assembly Room in 1938			. **Total income for year**	**£566.46**	
				. Balance of assets over liabilities (excl. freehold, furniture & effects)	£213.30	
	Heavy expenses & building repairs were inevitable and costs had gone up with the increased turnover			. Assets of the Club (excl. freehold)	£321.05	

Bewdley Institute

Year	Notes	Debit/Expenditure		Credit/Income		Members
		Source	Amount	Source	Amount	
1940/41	Institute in a sound financial position 1940 was the first complete year since alcoholic refreshments became obtainable on the premises following the acquisition of the freehold from the estate of the Countess of Portsmouth 14 members, including Lord Cobham, serving in the Forces Proposed provision of a Bowling Green was informally discussed at the close of the meeting	· Expenditure for year	£927.38	· Billiards 'showed a slight decrease on last year's takings' · Subscriptions received · Gross profit on Refreshments · **Total income for year** (incl. £111.24 c/f from 1939) · Total assets (excl. freehold) · Balance in hand/at Bank	£88.93 £177.98 **£1034.19** £343.30 £106.82	167 or 168 (incl. 29 Vice-Presidents)
1941/42	Disappointingly, the idea of the Bowling Green could not be carried through, although the *Secretary* thought it a necessity in the summer and a project well worth borrowing money to carry out Brewers' allocations reduced. Shortage of supplies of other beverages £5136.00 in Bonds & Certificates purchased through the Club for War Weapons Week Agreed that same sub-committee should act for Bewdley Warship Week 5 additional *Trustees* appointed Suggestions to be taken to Management C'ttee: (1) that *Steward* Plevey be given a War Bonus (2) that a 2-engine beer pull would help *Steward* & improve beer – estimated cost = £40.00 to £50.00			· Billiards receipts (a small reduction) · Subscriptions · Gross profits on Refreshments · Bar takings (exceeded by £187.70 those taken in 1940) · Profit on year's working (incl. £50.00 War Bonds, which had to appear as a book entry debit as it was paid for out of the Current Account)	£105.00 £231.55 £138.20	176 (incl. 30 Vice-Presidents)
1942/43	20 members serving in H. M. Forces. Each had received a Christmas gift of 100 cigarettes or the equivalent 36 members' subscriptions due on 1-1-1943 were currently outstanding. 78 had been one year overdue at 31-12-1942! Agreed that a typed list of all members should be placed inside the Club and as each paid his subscription his name should be erased	· Salaries · Repairs & Renewals · Travelling expenses	£192.67 £80.24 £75.00	· Billiards, etc. (difficult to read) · Visitors' boxes · Rent of Rooms · Profit on Refreshments · Profit on year's working	£120.17 or £120.42 £1.88 £75.94 £227.83 £173.79	(incl. 30 Vice-Presidents)

Table 1

Year	Notes	Debit/Expenditure		Credit/Income		Members
		Source	Amount	Source	Amount	
1943/44	Some 20 members serving in H. M. Forces had received a Christmas gift of 100 cigarettes or the equivalent Sports C'ttee set up to run a number of special competitions in aid of the 'Salute the Soldier Week' savings campaign in Bewdley Wartime economy prevented circulation of usual printed statements	. Salaries . Light & Heat . Beer Engine & Fittings . Rates & Taxes . Repairs & Renewals . **Expenditure for year**	£187.58 £63.24 £44.40 £64.44 £37.71 **£1273.50**	. Billiards, Cards, etc. . Building Fund Account (balance carried forward from 1942) . Competition (towards Building Fund, etc.) . Rent of Rooms . Subscriptions received . Refreshments . Profit on Refreshments . Profit for year . Balance in hand/at Bank	£108.97 £36.48 £13.00 £78.62 £92.70 £1066.86 £207.23 £32.73 £178.42	(incl. 32 *Vice-Presidents*)
1944/45	Proposal to reduce C'ttee from 18 to 12 members adopted by 24 votes to 7 Formally agreed to pay *Auditor* £2.10 per annum (thought to have been agreed 2 years previously but members could find no trace in Minutes) Building Fund had been almost entirely augmented during year by a 25% allocation from the weekly football sweep Members serving in H. M. Forces had again received a gift of cigarettes at Christmas			. Building Fund Account . Refreshments . Profit on Refreshments . **Total income for year** (incl. £206.52 brought forward from 1943) . Balance at 31-12-1944 (after payment of all liabilities)	£55.65 £955.17 £174.72 **£1451.93** £85.67	(incl. 33 *Vice-Presidents*)

Year	Notes	Debit/Expenditure		Credit/Income		Members
		Source	Amount	Source	Amount	
1945/46	Fund opened for a presentation to Mr. B. Plevey who had recently retired as Steward after 17 years	. Temporary repairs to Steward's Living Quarters		. Balance in Building Fund Account	£77.88	(incl. 34 Vice-Presidents)
	£127.00 from War Dept. would be needed to put the Assembly Room into order	. Repairs to Billiard Tables		. Received from War Dept. for use of Assembly Room	£127.00	
	Club in need of renovation throughout			. Balance in hand/at Bank	£151.64	
	Lighting throughout needed attention					
	Need to build proper living accommodation for Steward					
	New vigour given to Club by returning members of H. M. Forces					
	Shop taken over by returning Serviceman as a hairdressing saloon					
	The Secretary had refused to accept the usual honorarium of £15.00 per annum, but the Committee insisted he *should* have £10.00					
1946/47	Excess of expenditure over income largely due to the necessary extensive renovations which had been executed when the new Steward took over	. Repairs & maintenance (mainly to Steward's Accomm.) (prices had risen)	£221.27	. Receipts from Games	£169.44	185 (an increase on 1945) (incl. 35 Vice-Presidents in 1946 & 30 in 1947)
	It was the Committee's intention to spend as much as allowed by law for the provision of better accommodation &, eventually, a new house for the Steward	. Salaries	£183.00	. Building Fund balance	£84.76	
		. Light & Heat	£120.64	. Hire of Assembly Rooms	£100.53	
	Proposition by Needle Industries Ltd. to take over the Assembly Room had been rejected since the C'ttee not prepared to give up the only recreation room of its kind left in the town	. Rates & Taxes	£79.95	. Subscriptions received	£87.99	
		. Excess of expenditure over income	£79.86	. Refreshments	£1400.00	
	Agreed to erect a Memorial Plaque in honour of members who fell in action between 1939 & 1945			. Profit on Refreshments	£221.21	
1949/50				. *Profit on Refreshments (up to 31-8-1949)*	£116.39	
				. Balance in Building Fund at 31-12-1949	£100.00	
				. Balance in Entertainments Accounts at 31-12-1949	£10.00	

Notes and References

Introduction p.xiii

[1] Mr. Bob Tolley, B.Sc. (Hons.), Dipl.Arch., R.I.B.A.
[2] Tunnicliffe's Directory, 1788.
[3] Institute Annual Report, 1906.
[4] Pevsner, Nikolaus: The buildings of England – Worcestershire. Penguin, 1958.

Chapter 1: Numbers 21-23: Bewdley Institute – The birth pp.1-15

[5] *Kidderminster Shuttle*, 25th December 1875.
Members of the Pease family had already given schools and a Library to Darlington.
(*Source*: D.N.B. Smith, Elder & Co., 1895).
Mechanics' Institutes had been established in, for example, Birmingham, Sheffield, Liverpool and Manchester by this time. Among Worcestershire towns boasting such Institutes were Bromsgrove (established by 1861) and Pershore (established 1849).
(Source: Records and recollections, 1923-1973/edited by Maurice F. Nauta. Worcestershire County Council, Libraries Dept., 1973, pp.1 & 2 - referred to hereafter in this text as 'Nauta').

[6] 471 persons had contributed amounts varying from one farthing (0.104p) to £50.00 towards this sum. Probably most contributors were local residents.
In 1871 the population of the Municipal Borough of Bewdley was 3021, of Wribbenhall 1115, and of Ribbesford Parish 98 (a total of 4234).
Total population for the *Parliamentary Borough* (which included Stourport, 3081 and Upper Mitton hamlet, 299) was 7614. (*Source*: Post Office Directory, 1876).

[7] The hyphenated form *Winnington-Ingram* appears in: Littlebury's Directory of 1879; Kelly's Directories for 1884, 1896, 1904, 1912, 1916, 1924, 1928, 1932 & 1940; and in *The story of the Parish Churches of Bewdley and Ribbesford*:
(a) 7th ed., British Publishing Co., n.d., but between 1956 & 1959; and
(b) Tower Publications, n.d., but probably *c*1972, pp.10 & 21.
• Burton's *History of Bewdley* (1883) does *not* include the hyphen in that name in his list of Rectors of Ribbesford; neither does the Post Office Directory for 1876.
• *Short biographies of the worthies of Worcestershire* (1916) does *not* include it in 'Ingram, Arthur Henry Winnington (1818-1887)' or in 'Ingram, Thomas Onslow Winnington (1816-1858)', but does use it in the name of the former's son (the Rev. A. G. Winnington-Ingram) and in that of the latter's father (the Rev. E. Winnington-Ingram).
(*Source*: *Short biographies of the worthies of Worcestershire*/edited by Edith Ophelia Browne and John Richard Burton. For the authors, E. G. Humphreys and Wilson & Phillips (p.81) - referred to hereafter in this text as '*Worthies of Worcestershire*').

Interestingly, the hyphen does not appear in the name E. H. Winnington Ingram, Archdeacon of Hereford, who wrote the Foreword to Wedley's *Bewdley and its surroundings* in *c*1914, but it is included in the subscription to various photographs of the family therein!

cf Edward Winnington and Edward Ingram, both of whom in *c*1746 leased ground on or near St. Anne's Church to the Bailiff and Bridgewardens of Bewdley. Were they one and the same person? (see Title no. 1 in this series: *'Over agaynst the chappell': 21-23 Load Street, Bewdley - the buildings and occupants from c1632 to c1875).*

[8] Described in Littlebury's Directories of 1873 and 1876 as the Rev. John Fortescue, M.A., living in Wribbenhall. Incumbent at St. Anne's Church.
He had died by 1879, a memorial window being erected to him in that year in St. Anne's Church, where he had become incumbent in 1852.
(*Sources*: Kelly's Directory, 1896, p.23 and *The Story of the Parish Churches of Bewdley & Ribbesford* [*c*1972], p.21, respectively).

[9] Tomkinson, Kenneth & Hall, George: Kidderminster since 1800. 2nd ed., K. Tomkinson, 1985, p.107. (Referred to hereafter in this text as 'Tomkinson & Hall').

[10] Hobson, Joan: 'A short history of the "free grammar school of King James in Bewdley" ' in Essays towards a history of Bewdley/ edited by Lawrence S. Snell. University of Birmingham

113

Department of Extramural Studies, [1972], pp.109 & 112. (Referred to hereafter in this text as *'Essays ...'*).

[11] At the Jubilee Year A.G.M. (1928) the KS quotes from its Opening Ceremony report : 'The "SHUTTLE" proudly refers to the time when Bewdley was an entrepot of commerce, being a depot for Manchester and Birmingham, while Liverpool was but a fishing village...'

The lamplighter (illustration: David Edwards, 2003) p.5

[12] By 1858 there was a gas light outside the *Wheatsheaf* and in 1894 Bewdley Institute was described as a large gas user. (*Source*: Scaplehorn, Alan W: The best in Bewdley. The Author, 1995, pp.32 & 20).

The building p.14

[13] As noted on p.1, Mr. Gething's modified plan said that the 2nd class room would be 27 feet by 16 (approx. 8.3 metres by 4.9).

[14] The Plan attached to the Trust Deed dated 31st December 1877 (p.6) shows a large building in the yard and, beyond it, a smaller one, its not-quite-rectangular shape suggesting that it was the older of the two. The internal measurements of the north and south walls of this smaller building are **18 feet 6 inches** (approx. 5.7 metres), the east **29 feet** (8.9 metres) and the west **30 feet** (9.2 metres). The east wall forms part of the eastern boundary of the property. Perhaps this was the chemical laboratory.

[15] Members paid an additional sum to use individual facilities, e.g. to play cards, to join the educational classes/lectures, to read the newspapers and/or library books, etc.

[16] Littlebury's Directory, 1879. He lived at Areley Court, Stourport.

[17] Directories: Post Office, 1876 and Littlebury's, 1879 (Alderman); and Kelly's, 1884 (Mayor).
He died in 1886, aged 60, and was buried on 18th March at Ribbesford.
(*Source: Bewdley Parish Magazine*).
In 1862 Samuel and Thomas Price were curriers and tanners in Severn Side. I have not checked whether or not they were the Price Brothers who were tanners and curriers there and in Dudley in 1855, nor their relationship to Luke Price, tanner of Severn Side in 1850. By 1873 Samuel and Thomas were tanners in Bewdley and in Dudley. (*Source*: Directories).

[18] *Worthies of Worcestershire*, p.158 and Parker, Mrs. J. F: Two brothers. Reprinted from the *Kidderminster Times*, 11th May 1946. The Tangye family came from Cornwall.
The brothers set up the Cornwall Works in Birmingham in *c*1862 and became well-known for their patented inventions, especially gas-engines and hydraulic jacks - one of which was used for erecting Cleopatra's Needle in 1878. (*Source*: D.N.B.)

[19] Kelly's Directories, 1884 and 1896.

[20] Wedley, I. L: Bewdley and its surroundings. *Kidderminster Shuttle*, 1914, p.51 (referred to hereafter in this text as 'Wedley: Bewdley ...') and Parker, Mrs. J. F. (nee Alice Tangye): Two brothers, p.6.
Mrs. Parker says that the house, built in the style of the Victorian house in which her father had lived at Handsworth,* was constructed in an orchard called the Hern's Nest - once the home of a heron - and on the site of the former royal palace kennels.
*Did Joseph Tangye live in Handsworth at the same time as John Marshall Downing, and if so, then did they know each other before they came to live in Bewdley and Dowles, respectively? Interestingly, both were about the same age. (*see* Ref. 201)

[21] Scaplehorn, Alan: op. cit., p.30.
Mrs. Parker says the gasworks was one of her father's hobbies. (*Source*: Two brothers, p.6).

[22] Littlebury's Directory, 1879.

[23] Alfred Longbottom (*c*1852-1925) lived at the School House, near the *Black Boy* in Wribbenhall in 1881, the Census recording that he was an Elementary Schoolteacher, born in Barkisland, Yorkshire, aged 29, unmarried. Fanny, his unmarried sister and housekeeper aged 30, also lived there.
By 1891, Alfred had married Melena, a schoolmistress aged 41 and born in the same county as her husband. They lived in Kidderminster Road, Wribbenhall (probably still in the School House) and their niece - Ethel Capper, a Yorkshire lass aged 10 - was recorded with them (although she may simply have been visiting on Census night). Alfred was appointed master of the Wribbenhall church schools in 1875 and 'an excellent tone prevailed throughout his mastership'. He died in 1925 'after a long and trying illness'.

Notes & References

He had been 'closely involved with almost every organization in the village' and was a member of Bewdley Rowing Club. His wife died in 1913. (*Sources: Kidderminster Shuttle*, 28th March 1925 and Chesshire, Cecil J: 50th anniversary - All Saints' Church, Wribbenhall. The author, 1929, [pp.10 & 11], respectively).

[24] William Henry Vickrage was the *Master* and Mrs. Emily Elizabeth Vickrage *Mistress* of the National School, Lax Lane from at least 1873 to 1896. Mr. Vickrage was one of 2 auditors to Bewdley Corporation in 1896. (*Source*: Directories). Littlebury's Directory of 1879 lists him at 23 High Street.

The 1881 Census records William H. Vickrage, aged 32, as married to Emily E. Vickrage, aged 34. Both were 'Teachers of Public Elem[entary] Schools'. He was born in Dudley and she in Prestbury, Cheshire. They had 3 sons, William A. (aged 8), Henry L. (aged 3) and Alfred P. Vickrage (aged 1), all born in Bewdley. Their household at 7 Lower Park included House Keeper/Boarder Miss Mary A. Vickrage (aged 25, born in Dudley) and Kidderminster-born Fredrick (sic) D. Pritchard, aged 19, 'Teacher Apprenticed Elem[entary] School'.

Chapter 2: The long-awaited public room/s pp.16-23

[25] Griffith, George: Reminiscences and records. John Randall, 1880, pp.555 & 559.

Membership p.16

[26] Unless indicated otherwise, details have been taken from reports of the Institute's Annual Meetings which appeared in the *Kidderminster Shuttle* (KS) or *Kidderminster Times* (KT):
KS 31st January 1880; KS 31st January 1885; KT 6th February 1886;
KS 2nd February 1889; KS 8th February 1890; KS 31st January 1891;
KS 6th February 1892; KS 25th February 1893; KS 24th February 1894;
KS 23rd March 1895; KS 26th February 1898; KS 4th March 1899; KS 24th March 1900;
KS 23rd February 1901; KS 21st February 1903; KS 2nd April 1904; KS 4th March 1905;
KS 17th March 1906; KS 16th March 1907; KS 14th March 1908; KS 13th March 1909;
KS 26th March 1910; KS 18th March 1911; KS 16th March 1912; KS 23rd March 1913;
KS 21st March 1914; KS 20th March 1915; KS 25th March 1916; KS 24th March 1917;
KS 23rd March 1918; KS 22nd March 1919; KS 27th March 1920; KS 9th April 1921;
KS 1st April 1922; KS 24th March 1923; KS 12th April 1924; KS 4th April 1925;
KS 27th February 1926; KS 12th March 1927; KS 17th March 1928; KS 13th April 1929;
KS 8th April 1930; KS 7th March 1931; KS 12th March 1932; KS 4th March 1933;
KS 10th March 1934; KS 16th March 1935; KS 14th March 1936; KS 20th March 1937;
KS 12th March 1938; KS 22nd April 1939; KS 9th March 1940; KS 15th March 1941;
KS 7th March 1942; KS 6th March 1943; KS 18th March 1944; KS 10th March 1945;
KT 6th April 1946; KS 28th March 1947; KS 7th April 1950.
(Where there are gaps in the sequence I could trace no reports of the Annual Meetings in either the KS or the KT). The Annual Meetings were generally well-attended.

[27] KT, 6th February 1976.

[28] *Soldiers died in the Great War 1914-19. Part 34: The Worcestershire Regiment* (Hayward, 1989, p.11) says: 'Bentley, Thomas b[orn] Rugby, Warwicks., e[nlisted] Worcester, ([residence] Bewdley, Worcs.), 46066, P[riva]te, ...' He was in the 4th Battalion.

[29] *Kidderminster Shuttle*, 20th April 1918, p.7. I could find no reference to him in Soldiers died in the Great War 1914-19. Part 34: *The Worcestershire Regiment*.

[30] *Soldiers died in the Great War 1914-19. Part 11: The Royal Warwickshire Regiment* (H.M.S.O., 1921, p.116) says: 'Coldrick, Herbert b[orn] Bewdley, Worcs., e[nlisted] Birmingham, ([residence] Bewdley, Worcs.), 15/1600, P[riva]te,...' He was in the 16th Battalion.

[31] *Soldiers died in the Great War 1914-19. Part 34: The Worcestershire Regiment*, p.29, says: 'Ewins, Arthur John b[orn] Kidderminster, Worcs., e[nlisted] Worcester, ([residence] Malvern Link, Worcs.), 63527, P[riva]te, ...' He was in the 1/8th Battalion.

[32] Pte. Heath's name is missing from the War Memorial at the east end of St. Anne's Church, Load Street. I was unable to find any mention of his death in the *Kidderminster Times* or *Kidderminster Shuttle* between March 1916 and March 1917. Perhaps he was a temporary, non-resident member.

Could he have been Private *William* Reginald Heath who died on 3rd September 1916 *who was also in the Royal Warks. Regt.* (the 15th Battalion)? He has no known grave and is commemorated on the Thiepval Memorial, Somme, France. (*Source*: Commonwealth War Graves Commission website - http://yard.ccta.gov.uk/cwgc/regi.../).
W. R. Heath was born in Aston, Birmingham, e[nlisted] Birmingham ([residence] Aston), 242, P[riva]te, killed in action, F[rance] & F[landers] (including Italy).
(*Source: Soldiers died in the Great War 1914-19. Part 11: The Royal Warwickshire Regiment,* p.109).

[33] *Soldiers died in the Great War 1914-19. Part 11: The Royal Warwickshire Regiment,* p.119, says: 'Minton, Charles b[orn] St. George's, Kidderminster, Worcs., e[nlisted] Birmingham, ([residence] Kidderminster, Worcs.), 66, L/Cpl., ...' He was in the 16th Battalion. (*see* photograph, p.19).

[34] No known grave. 'Remembered with honour, Helles Memorial, Turkey.' He was in the 7th Battalion, South Staffordshire Regiment. (*Source*: Commonwealth War Graves Commission website - http://yard.ccta.gov.uk/cwgc/regi.../).

[35] *Soldiers died in the Great War 1914-19. Part 34: Worcestershire Regiment,* p.83, says: 'Tolley, Frank b[orn] in Wribbenhall, Worcs., enlist[e]d Bewdley, Worcs., ([residence] Bewdley, Worcs.), 17261, P[riva]te (sic), ...' He was in the 3rd Battalion.

Some of the Life Members p.16

[36] Although Mr. R. H. Whitcombe (jnr.) had died in 1935 *(about 4 years before he was reported as 'still surviving'),* it was probably he who had been the first Life Member, for Mr. R. H. Whitcombe *(snr.)* had died way back in 1909. The appointment is not mentioned in local Press reports of the Annual Meetings for 1910 and 1935, respectively, which record the deaths of the two Mr. Whitcombes and I found no mention of the Award Ceremony in the reports of the Annual Meetings which I could trace! Perhaps the facility to elect Life Members had always existed and the operative words in the New Rules of 1937 (*see* Table 1) were *when necessary.* (*see also* Refs. 181 & 188) In fact, the second of '... *one of only two inaugural members still surviving'* in April 1939 was Mr. Edward Southan ('Uncle Ted'). His death was noted with regret at the A.G.M. in 1940.

Some fundraising events p.20

[37] Not all the fundraising events held at the Institute were in aid of its own funds: e.g. the proceeds of a well-attended concert held there in January 1890 went to the poor. (*Source*: KS 1st February 1890).

[38] Her husband, Miller Corbet, was the deputy coroner of Bewdley in 1878. (*Source*: KS 15th June 1878).

[39] KS, 2nd June 1900 and 8th September 1900.

Chapter 3: Social and recreational facilities pp.24-31

[40] How long the cricket club continued is not known at present. It is not mentioned in local Press reports of the Minutes traced after 1885. Perhaps it was discontinued because of the Boer Wars, followed by World War I and the Depression. It had certainly ceased before the advent of World War II, the *Kidderminster Shuttle* of 16th March 1946 (p.8) reporting on plans to form a new Bewdley club (although not in opposition to a team run by Wribbenhall Social Club on the Maypole Ground).
Interestingly, Captain C. R. F. Threlfall was appointed *Chairman* of the Interim Committee for the Bewdley Cricket Club. Was he related to Richard E. Threlfall, author of *The story of 100 years of phosphorus making, 1851-1951. Albright & Wilson, 1951?* (*see* Title no. 4 in this series: *Bewdley Institute, 21-23 Load Street - founder Edward Pease and some of his associates re* The Sturge family and the Albright & Wilson connection).

[41] At the A.G.M. in 1926 Mr. T. D. Potter recalled that, during its first year (1878/9), receipts from the billiard table were £47.
At the 1927 Annual Meeting he recalled that the original billiard table was purchased in 1883 for £36, remarking that, if the same table was in current use, then it was wearing well! The bill for £36 does not appear until the 1889 Accounts.
Perhaps the 1878 table was hired or borrowed until funds could be raised to purchase it.

[42] Repairs to the billiard table/s figured in the accounts for many years (*see* Table 1).

[43] I am told that there is also a lady ghost with long, flowing robes. She is evidently from a much earlier period (Elizabethan?), for she wears a tall pointed head-dress.

[44] It is not specifically mentioned in the description given in Littlebury's Directory, 1879.

Notes & References

[45] Report of the 1906 A.G.M.

[46] Did the Godsall Cup have any connection with William Godsall, Victualler at the *Wheatsheaf* in 1820? (*Source*: Lewis's Directory).

[47] *cf* the General Strike in 1926 in sympathy with the coal miners.

[48] KS, 21st January 1922, last p. and KS, 28th January 1922, respectively.

[49] KS, 29th March and 5th April 1930.

[50] KS, 29th March 1930, p.8.

Chapter 4: Educational facilities pp.32-49

[51] Noake (writing in *c*1868) says: 'That gentleman [Mr. Charles Sturge] ... is a liberal supporter of the flourishing Working Man's Institute established in Bewdley four or five years ago.' (*Source*: Noake, John: Guide to Worcestershire. Longman & Co., 1868, p.42).

[52] At the 1909 Annual Meeting Mr. Birtwistle recalled, "When the old club was formed in 1859 the late Rev. Fortescue rendered it great assistance. The rooms were on Severn Side, and the interest was continued when the late Mr. Pease gave to the Borough the present Institute premises..."

As noted elsewhere, the Rev. John Fortescue was *President* of the original 'working party'.

[53] Messrs. Jonathan Birtwistle and T. E. Dalley were joint *Secretaries* of Bewdley and Wribbenhall Working Man's Institute, Severn side in 1873. (*Source*: Littlebury's Directory). Prior to 1873, had the Bewdley and Wribbenhall Working Man's Institute ever met in the British School(s) (established in 1859 by Charles Sturge,* future father-in-law of Edward Pease)? (* *Source*: KS, 17th September 1881).

[54] KS, 10th February 1877.

[55] The 55th A.G.M. in 1934 noted: '... When [the Institute] opened in 1878, it amalgamated the old Literary Society and the Working Men's Institution...' - a natural move for the latter, for Workmen's Clubs were the village equivalents of the town Mechanics' Institutes.

[56] Kelly's Directory, 1884 and *Church Monthly* for March 1892 and March 1893. By 1893 the Rev. E. H. W. Ingram (a *Trustee* of Bewdley Institute) was one of the Wribbenhall Club's *Vice-Presidents*. (*Source: Kidderminster Shuttle*, 25th February 1893). A good rapport seems to have existed between the two Clubs by 1910 (and probably from the start). The *Kidderminster Shuttle*, 26th February 1910, recorded that Bewdley Institute members Mr. Edward Southan, Mr. T. D. Potter and Mr. Stanley Hemingway were among those who attended the Wribbenhall Club's A.G.M. - which was chaired by the last-named! At Bewdley Institute Annual Meeting on 27th February 1933 Mr. A. R. Southan, a member of that Institute in the 1920s, was described as 'formerly *Secretary* of the *old* Workmen's Club at Wribbenhall'.

[57] KS, 7th November 1896, p.8, reported: 'Dr. Creighton, the new Bishop of London, will be remembered at Bewdley. When the annual meeting of the Worcestershire Union of Clubs and Institutes was held at Bewdley Dr. Creighton was president and delivered an exceedingly able address on the delights of reading and the useful work that the Union was doing in promoting the circulation of healthy literature in the towns and villages of the county.' Presumably the same man, Dr. Mandell Creighton was formerly the Bishop of Peterborough (*Source*: KS, 20th June 1896, p.6). A *Mr.* & *Mrs.* Crighton (sic) of York attended librarian Eliza Sturge's funeral in 1905. Could this have been *Dr.* Creighton?

[58] KS, 11th October 1879, p.6.

[59] KS, 10th August 1895.

[60] There had been evening classes in the town before the establishment of Bewdley Institute. e.g. In 1878 on each Monday and on three Thursdays in January and on each Monday and Thursday in February there was a 'Night School for Women and Girls at the Park Lane School Room at 7.15p.m;' and on each Tuesday and on three Thursdays in January and each Tuesday and Thursday in February a 'Night School for Men and Lads at the Wyre Hill School Room at 7.30p.m.'

Evidently, some evening classes continued elsewhere for at least a short time after the Institute opened. e.g. In December 1878 on the first three Mondays and Thursdays there was a 'Night School for Young Women in Park Lane School Room at 7.15p.m.' (*Source: Bewdley Parish Magazine* 1878 & 1880. Reprinted by Nigel Knowles, Star & Garter Publishers, 1999, pp.9, 17 & 67).

Park Lane School Room (demolished in *c*1960s) was situated almost opposite Burltons Almshouses. Wyre Hill School Room (1868-1950*) was roughly on the site of today's Barratt's Close. Afterwards occupied by Telford Press, the building was demolished in *c*1970s. (**Sources*:

Kelly's Directory, 1896 and Hobson, Kenneth & Purcell, Charles and Angela: Bewdley's past in pictures. B.H.R.G., 1993, vol. i, p.25, respectively).

[61] KS, 31st January 1885, <u>Presentation of the 6th Annual Report and Accounts</u> at the A.G.M. of Bewdley Institute, held in the Lecture Hall on Monday evening, 26th January.

[62] Was this Joseph Marshall Sturge of Dowles?

[63] As the *Church Monthly* of March 1892 commented: 'Until the Government and the County Council had jointly formed a Scheme to provide Technical Education at almost nominal fees, the real difficulty for the Institute had been the impossibility of supplying more or less advanced teaching, suitable for adults, and young people who have left school, at a price that would be remunerative to the Institute, and at the same time not out of reach of those who might be expected to take advantage of it... We feel that now for the first time the Institute is beginning to fulfil the objects for which it was brought into being. One thing is certain, that, if the Institute buildings had not been in existence, many of the present classes under the Technical Education scheme could not have been held in Bewdley at all, and none of them could have been held at the same convenience to all parties...'

At the 1891 A.G.M., however, Mr. J. M. Sturge had said he found it very unsatisfactory that a large number of Institutes in the country were not self-supporting. Throughout the Midlands and Southern Counties there was scarcely one in ten which was so, yet in Yorkshire, Lancashire and other Northern Counties nearly all the Institutes were self-supporting.

Mr. Birtwistle hoped that the County Council would be able to make increased grants to such Institutes as their own. "It was true that such Institutes and other educational agencies had received much support from the county grants, but while the Government had been giving them help with one hand they had been taking it away with the other, for South Kensington were going to withdraw their grants from the various technical schools to a large extent. In future no grants would be paid for elementary teaching in science, and a good deal of elementary science was needed to enable students to benefit by the advanced technical education given under the County schemes. The advantages gained by the County grants were not as large, therefore, as they seemed upon the surface..." Viscount Cobham promised to do what he could in the direction Mr. Birtwistle had indicated.

After the Technical Instruction Committee was abolished by the Education Act of 1902, agricultural education was overseen by a sub-committee of the new Education Committee. In 1907 grant-aided horticultural work became the responsibility of the Agricultural Sub-Committee, having been for the previous 15 years the work of the *Worcestershire Union of Workmen's Clubs and Institutes*. (*Source*: Gaut, R. C: A history of Worcestershire agriculture and rural evolution. Littlebury, 1939, p.376).

Interestingly, Lord Cobham, *President* of Bewdley Institute from 1890-1922, was also *President* of the *Worcestershire Union of Workmen's Clubs and Institutes* in October 1894 when he and **James Udale** (described as 'gardening instructor') arranged the first Fruit Show and Conference in the Shirehall. (*Source*: Gaut: op. cit., p.428).

James Udale was the chief horticultural instructor for Worcestershire and the first adviser appointed in the County. He opened the Conference on 'Apples and fruit-growing' - one of the subjects discussed during a 5 days' Show organized by the Agricultural Sub-Committee in the Shirehall in October 1900 - and published *Gardening for all* and *Pruning, grafting and budding* in 1897 and 1906, respectively. (*Source*: Gaut: op. cit., pp.410, 429 & 454).

[64] Using older pupils (**monitors**) to teach younger ones had been among ideas of **Joseph Lancaster** (1778-1838). Small classes were each superintended by a monitor and groups of these classes were overseen by a head monitor. This proved a successful experiment which eventually attracted interest abroad.

In 1846 the newly constituted education department decided that monitors should be superseded by **pupil-teachers**, 'all of whom were required before apprenticeship to pass through the elementary course, and afterwards to receive regular instruction and to be trained for the office of teacher.' By 1895, where funds allowed, the pupil-teacher system itself was being replaced by the employment of adult teachers.

Notes & References

Joseph Pease (1799-1872) (father of Edward, the donor of Bewdley Institute and of larger premises for the Wribbenhall & Bewdley *British Schools*) had **aided Joseph Lancaster** in his educational work. The *British and Foreign School Society* had developed from the Lancasterian system of education. (*Source*: D.N.B. Smith, Elder & Co., 1895).

[65] The meeting reported that the Education Department now made grants based on examination results. The grant earned in 1893 was £7-0s-0d. (£7.00) for Art results. 13 students had gained 2nd Class passes during the session January to April 1894. (*Source*: KS, 24th April 1894, p.6).

[66] Although this result was disappointing at the time, could the Bewdley Agricultural Association - which 'supplied produce to refreshment rooms, etc.' in January 1903 - owe its existence to these classes, or to the Bewdley & District Horticultural Society which (established in 1854) met at the Institute by 1900?
(*Source*: KS, 3rd January 1903, p.8 and 18th February 1922, p.6, respectively).

[67] The venue is not given in the newspaper report, but a Debating Society had met in February 1882 and most of the people who attended were members of Bewdley Institute. (*Source*: KS, 18th February 1882, p.8).

[68] Mr. J. Marshall Sturge (1838-1916) had been elected representative of the Institute on the Board of Management of the Kidderminster Schools of Science and Art in 1891. He became partially crippled in mid-life, this perhaps being why he was unable to continue in office. (*Source*: KT, 22nd January 1916, p.10).

[69] KS, 17th January 1903.

[70] A Morse sounder had been installed at Bewdley Post Office in about May 1890, enabling **telegraphic messages** to be 'sent and received with dispatch'. This was 'a considerable advance upon the needle telegraphic instrument which for many years ...had been regarded as good enough for Bewdley'. The [Telegraphic] Department had not yet issued an order for a "Wheatstone". 'It was [also] said that the town would soon be lighted by **electricity**.' (*Source*: KS, 24th May 1890).
By July 1899 there were several subscribers to the **telephone** in Bewdley (*Source*: KS 8th July 1899), but whether the Institute was connected is doubtful, for no mention of payments is made in the Press reports of the Annual Meetings.

[71] KS, 26th February 1927.

[72] The Rev. Solly, a dissenter, was a Chartist representative of Yeovil at the Birmingham conference of 1842, and joint editor of *The Beehive* from 1869-1870. (*Source*: D.N.B.) Curiously, an area near the Summerhouse, Wribbenhall (home of Charles Sturge) was called the Beehive at about that time. (*see* Title no. 4 in this series: *Bewdley Institute: 21-23 Load Street - founder Edward Pease and some of his associates*).

[73] KS, 25th March 1939, p.18.

Chapter 5: Library facilities pp.50-56

[74] Post Office Directory, 1876.

[75] Billing's Directory, 1855. (*see* also Refs. 105 & 175)

[76] Littlebury's Directory, 1876.

The Library and Reading Room p.50

[77] *Official guide of Bewdley*. (sic) T. F. W. Harris, 1927, p.24.

[78] Could the Working Men's Reading Room have developed from the *Reading Room*,* Load Street (recorded in 1862), which in turn perhaps had developed from the *News Room*^ 'at Mr. W[illiam] Tench's, [glass and earthenware dealers] Load Street' in 1855? *Keeper Christopher Pountney. (*Source*: Slater's Directory, 1862). ^Secretary: A. Pardoe, Esq. (*Source*: Billing's Directory, 1855).

[79] KT, 6th February 1886, p.8.
Was the *honorary members' Reading Room* the panelled one at the end of the Hall in the Institute building and was the *Working Men's Reading Room* in their Club Room in the yard at the back - both described in the KT, 19th October 1878?

The Institute Library p.51

[80] Report of 1885 Annual Meeting.

[81] including the following interesting donations: 12 volumes of *The Illustrated London News* from Mr. F. Porter, 2 copies of his own work *Mending men* from Mr. E. Smith, and a copy of *Old Bewdley* presented by a few members.

[82] 255 in **1919**, 306 in **1920**, 620 in **1921**, 480 in **1922**.

Miss Eliza Mary Sturge (1842-1905), *Librarian*
p.53

[83] Report of Eliza Sturge's funeral in KS, 2nd December 1905.
[84] and also for her father, brother, sister, brother-in-law and other members of the family, of course.
[85] Sarah Pease died on 14th June 1877, aged 41. (*Source: Descendants of Isaac and Rachel Wilson*, vol. 1, 1912 (1949 revision), p.170).
[86] Press reports of the Institute A.G.M.s, Kelly's Directory, 1892 and *Church Monthly,* March 1892, severally.
[87] Mary Darby Sturge (nee Dickinson). (*Source:* Eliza Mary Sturge's Birth Certificate). Mary was a Darby of Coalbrookdale. (*Source:* B.H.R.G. File 3, no.18, p.22). Born in Birmingham, Eliza was recorded in the 1851 Census as aged 8, visiting her aunt, Miss Rebecca Sturge (aged 63) at Summer Hill, Wribbenhall (later the home of Charles Sturge).
Interestingly, in 1846 Charles's brother *Joseph Sturge* had married *Hannah Dickinson* (c1817-1896), daughter of Barnard Dickinson of Coalbrookdale. (*Source:* D.N.B). *n.b.* I have not checked whether Hannah and Mary were related.
[88] Report of Eliza Sturge's funeral in KS, 2nd December 1905. A *Street* in Birmingham is named after *John Bright* (who was a Liberal).
[89] Post Office Directory, Birmingham, 1876. (Or could it have been her aunt or her cousin, *Priscilla* Sturge?).
[90] Report of Eliza Sturge's funeral in KS, 2nd December 1905.
[91] Electoral Roll, 1899 (via B.H.R.G.).
[92] Wedley: Bewdley ..., p.45.
[93] Ann Dickinson Sturge (sister of Sarah Pease and Eliza Sturge) had married Mr. Jacob [Hort] Player in Warwick. (*Source:* Lewin, Sylvia Lloyd: Gaunts Earthcott to Frederick Road - an account of the Sturges of Birmingham. Ronald Lewin, 1980, pp.16-17).
In 1881 they were aged 47 and 40, respectively. Mr. Player was a manufacturing chemist, born in Frome, Somerset. The couple had 6 children, all born in Birmingham: Eliza (15), Margaret (14), Grace (11), Ralph (9), Hugh (7) and Gilbert (6) and their household at 31 Calthorpe Road, Edgbaston, Birmingham included a cook, two housemaids (one of whom had been born in 'Pensux', Worcestershire) and 24-year-old Bewdley-born nurse Jane Lambert. (*Source*: 1881 Census).

Mr. J[acob] Hort (sic) ***Player*** of Birmingham evidently purchased 3 copies of the Rev. John R. Burton's *History of Bewdley* (published by William Reeves, 1883), for his name appears on the 'List of Subscribers' therein.
At some time between 1845-1895 Mr. Player was a teacher at the Severn Street First-day School, Birmingham (founded in 1845 by Joseph Sturge - [uncle of Sarah, Eliza and Ann]). (*Source*: White, William: The story of the Severn Street and Priory First-day Adult Schools, Birmingham. George Jones & Son, 1895 - being the Schools' Jubilee Year - p.126).
Interestingly, an ancestor of Sarah, Eliza and Ann Dickinson Sturge - another Joseph Sturge (1722-1779) - had married one Frances Player... (*Source*: Lewin: op. cit., p.5)

The Wigan Library p.54

[94] Morgan, Paul: 'Wigan's library, Bewdley' in *Trans. Worcestershire Archaeological Society,* vol.30, 1958, pp.61-66.
[95] Burton, John R: History of Bewdley. William Reeves, 1883, p.85 gives no dates, but [says] '... after 1749, when the Rev. (blank) (sic) Boraston became the incumbent there...' (*n.b.* This book is referred to hereafter in this text as 'Burton: ... *Bewdley*').
[96] Morgan (op. cit., p.64) says 3,200 items.
[97] Burton: ... *Bewdley*, p.51.
[98] Nauta, p.2.
[99] Morgan: op. cit., p.61.
[100] Griffith, George: Going to markets and grammar schools. William Freeman, 1870, (2 vols.), vol. I, pp.104-105, where he cites the *Further Report of the Commissioners for Inquiry Concerning Charities,* vol. 26, 1835 (228), pp.562-563.
[101] Hobson, Joan: in *Essays* ... , pp.108-109.
[102] Morgan: op. cit., p.62.
[103] Hobson, Joan: in *Essays* ..., p.109.
[104] Whittington Landon was a sidesman at Ribbesford Church for many years, later (from Easter 1883 to Easter 1886) becoming Churchwarden there.
(*Source: Church Monthly*, November 1892).
A former licensee of the *Landon Vaults* (numbers 37 & 38) Load Street, he was a J.P. whose home was in High Street when he died in 1892, aged 59.

(*Source*: KS, 15th October 1892, p.6). The 1881 Census records London-born Alderman Landon, J.P. and Wine Merchant, at 25 High Street, Bewdley.

[105] This reference to the *Old Post Office* is interesting.

The Post Office Directory records Thomas Edward Dalley as Postmaster in 1876 (the year of the meeting about which Morgan writes), and the *Old Post Office* seems to refer to (a building on the site of today's) *number 12* Load Street (i.e. next door to Mr. Dalley's business premises at number 10/11).

Wedley (Bewdley ..., p.25) agrees, saying, '... the house of the police sergeant stood where formerly the post office did. ... after Mr. Farrington finished postal work, Mr. T. C. Dalley [amended to T. *E*. Dalley on an unnumbered Errata Page] added to his many duties by becoming postmaster. He had a doorway leading from his shop into the office.'

The *1871, 1881* and *1891* Censuses record *number 12* as being where the *'police officer'*, *'head constable'* or *'sergeant of police'* and their families were living; while the *1861* Census confirms Wedley, in naming '[illegible] Farrington, Post Mistress, Post Office' at number 12 (probably Mrs. E[llen] or Helen Farrington, according to Cassey's and Pigot's Directories for 1860 and 1862, respectively).

Presumably, it was thought that there was enough room to house the Wigan Library at number 12 without inconveniencing the tenants!

Today *number 14* Load Street is known as the Old Post Office. The 1881 Census lists Thomas Reeve, grocer and postmaster, living at number 14 with his family, and the Post Office seems to have remained at number 14 until *circa* mid-1970s, when it moved to number 11 Load Street and became a Sub-Post Office!

Not until the 1980s did the Sub-Post Office remove to its present accommodation at number 7 Load Street.

[106] Morgan: op. cit., pp.62-63.
[107] Hobson, Joan in *Essays* ..., p.109.
[108] Burton: ... *Bewdley*, p.82.
[109] Jorden, George (1783-1871): Bewdley (manuscript), pp.12 & 49, 69 & 70.
[110] Bewdley Grammar School Trust, via the late Cllr. Mrs. F. S. Pritchard, M.B.E. Edward Pease shows a fine sense of history in donating number 23 and the adjoining premises for educational purposes!

[111] Burton: ... *Bewdley*, pp.51 & xvii.

The pupils at Bewdley's earliest known school were taught by the curate 'in some room adjoining the chapel'. In 1577 the Chapel - and Bridgewardens spent 2s-8d. (13p) 'to put the schoolemaster's chambers in order' and in 1600 they paid *John Monox* (sic) 'iiid. (1.25p) for mending to stope out the boyes in the lofte in the church, and nayles'.

Whether the latter payment referred to a *school* is not clear, but it is interesting to note that *William Monnox* (sic) of Bewdley, tanner, 'by will dated 17th Feb[ruary], 1591, left £6 per annum for a Grammar School, payable out of the Pentrenant estate in Montgomeryshire.' The said Grammar School was built in *c*1599-1606, land and property [in the Park] having been given for it by Gregory, John and Thomas Ballard and Humphrey Hill, respectively. Today the school is a private house.

[112] Although Mr. Baillie, Kidderminster Borough Librarian, refers to the Wigan Library as being at Bewdley Town Hall at that time. (*Source*: KS, 2nd May 1931).
[113] Morgan: op. cit., pp.63-64.
[114] Morgan: op. cit., p.64.
[115] A Birminghan University spokesman.

<u>The County Library p.55</u>

[116] Nauta, p.10 <u>and</u> KS, 3rd January, 7th February and 2nd May 1931 <u>and</u> KT, 2nd May 1931.
[117] Nauta, p.37.
[118] Nauta, p.8.
[119] KS, 2nd May 1931, p.3.
[120] Nauta, p.8.
[121] Probably the Bert Plevey recorded in the 1881 Census as aged 3, living at 41 Load Street with his father (Richard Plevey, *Saddler*), 2 older brothers and a servant. The 1891 Census lists him at 64 Load Street with his parents, an older and a younger brother, a sister and a lodger.

Mr. Bert Plevey was recorded in 1932 as '*saddler*' at 23 Load Street - a nice link back to the *Wheatsheaf's* coaching days - and possibly back even further, to 1734, if the husband of former copyholder (tenant of the Lord of the Manor) Ann(e) Bodenham was Thomas Bodenham *saddler*, rather than the innholder of that name who was listed with his namesake in *Victuallers' Recognizances* of that year!

A Bewdley Institute Billhead dated 10th February 1934 shows 'B. Plevey' as [still being] *Steward* (as mentioned elsewhere, an office he held until *c*1945/1946). Evidently, he also continued as a saddler at number 23 until at least 1940, by which time Arthur Bert Plevey, A.C.A., *accountant* was sharing these premises with him.

Mr. Plevey may have moved to number 23 from 42 Load Street, the location of his premises given in Directories for 1924 and 1928. In 1912 his saddler's business seems to have been at 35 Load Street, although his first name was spelled 'Birt' in the Directory.

[122] KS, 13th September 1957, p.2 (advertisement) and p.3 (report) and Minutes of Worcestershire Education Committee 1957, p.309.

[123] KS, 13th September 1957.

[124] KT, 9th January 1970.
First open to the public on Wednesday, 14th January 1970, the Library was officially opened in 'Spring' 1970.

Chapter 6: Some other occupants of Bewdley Institute premises pp.57-62

The Coffee Tavern p.57

[125] Haydon, Peter: The English pub - a history. Hale, 1994, pp.80-83.

[126] Hobson, Kenneth: A history of the George Hotel, Load Street, Bewdley. Winwood Design & Print Agency/Norman Hills Print, 1994, p.3 and Prattinton, Peter (1771-1840*): Collections for a history of Worcestershire, vol. iv, p.395.
*n.b. *Worthies of Worcestershire* quotes Prattinton's dates as 1776-1845, but these are amended to 1771-1840 by Barnard, E. A. B: Some additional notes concerning the Prattinton collections of Worcestershire history in *Transactions of the Worcestershire Archaeological Society,* vol. viii, 1931, p.68. Mr. Barnard (ibid.) adds that Dr. Prattinton died on 11th July 1840 and that a complete typed transcript of his Will 'is now deposited at Birmingham Reference Library'.

[127] Encyclopaedia of dates and events. 3rd ed., Hodder & Stoughton, 1991.
n.b. Haydon (op. cit., p.80) cites 1650 as the date that coffee was introduced into Britain - i.e. 18 years after the date given by the *Encyclopaedia of dates and events* for the opening of the first London Coffee *Shop!*

Haydon continues, '... and the first Coffee *House* proper at the Sign of My Own Head was opened in 1652... Chocolate was introduced in 1657 and tea... in 1660...'; while George Berry Seventeenth Century England: traders and their tokens. Seaby, 1988, p.25) says: 'The earliest known coffee *house* in England was the Angel in Oxford, which opened in 1650.'

[128] *Bewdley Parish Magazine,* 1886/reproduced by Nigel Knowles. Star & Garter Publishers, 1997, p.91 and *Church Monthly,* April 1887.

[129] Kelly's Directory, 1928.

[130] *Bewdley Parish Magazine,* 1878 & 1880/reproduced by Nigel Knowles. Star & Garter Publishers, 1999, p.57.

[131] op. cit., p.24.

[132] op. cit., pp.57-58 & 141.

[133] op. cit., p.94.

[134] op. cit., p.141.

[135] Although I have found no trace of another Coffee *Tavern* in Bewdley at about that time, there had been tea and coffee *rooms* in Wribbenhall in 1862, ([proprietor] William Devereux); and in 1879 Benjamin Dalloway, tripe dresser, kept a coffee *room* in Wribbenhall.

[136] KS, 11th October 1879, p.6.

[137] KT, 28th February 1880, p.7.
Kelly's Directory of 1884 lists the *County and City of Worcester Coffee Tavern Co. Ltd.* as still being at 53 Load Street, with William Jones as Manager.

[138] Reports in: KT, 5th March 1881, p.3; 3rd April 1882, p.7; 24th February 1883, p.7; and 1st March 1884, p.2.

[139] KS, 11th October 1879, p.6.

[140] KT, 28th February 1880, p.7 & 3rd April 1882, p.7.

[141] *Bewdley Parish Magazine,* 1886, p.91.

[142] Watson Binns was Secretary of the Bewdley and Wribbenhall Temperance Society and Band of Hope* in 1879 and Jonathan Birtwistle had held that office in 1873. (*Source*: Littlebury's Directories).
*Described in the Church Monthly, June 1887, as the Junior Branch of the C.E.T.S., presumably it was so in 1879.

[143] *Bewdley Parish Magazine,* 1878 & 1880, p.58.

[144] *Bewdley Parish Magazine,* 1886, p.124.

[145] The Institute's A.G.M. in February 1892 advised that Mr. Tomes was to run the Coffee Tavern as a private venture.

[146] Kelly's Directory, 1904.

Museum p.62

[147] The report in both the KS and the KT, 25th December 1875, had mentioned that a museum was to be included in the proposed new Institute at Bewdley.

[148] Probably the gift of Mr. J. Tangye and Mrs. Baugh, for such a gift was gratefully acknowledged by the Institute Committee at their Annual General Meeting in 1885.

[149] Burton: ... *Bewdley*, pp.60, 61 & 26.
Mrs. Thomas Baugh was probably Edward Baugh's sister-in-law, for Wedley (Bewdley ...,p.38) says that Mr. Thomas Baugh, [one-time J.P.] the Minister's son, lived at the Redthorne after the Prattintons, while Thomas's brother, Edward, 'a zealous naturalist', lived in Wribbenhall.

[150] Rector of Ribbesford, 1765-*c*1795 and incumbent at St. Anne's, 1780-*c*1814. (*Source: The story of the Parish Churches of Bewdley and Ribbesford*. Tower Publications, n.d., but probably *c*1972, pp.21 & 22).

[151] Burton: ... *Bewdley*, p.61.

[152] Burton: ... *Bewdley*, pp.59, 73 & 41.
Alderman Best had a museum, although whether it was located at his Bewdley home Burton does not indicate.

[153] An original *Trustee* of Bewdley Institute.

[154] Parker, J. F: Tickenhill folk-museum. Repr. from *The Montgomery collections: the Transactions of the Powys Land Club,* vol. 1, no. 1, 1947.

[155] The Kidderminster *Express and Star*, 15th January 1999, says that the Museum at Hartlebury Castle was opened in 1966 to house the collection made by Mr. and Mrs. J. F. Parker.

[156] Relocated – and with a new name - the Birmingham Museum of Science & Discovery opened on 29th September 2001: address Thinktank at Millennium Point, Curzon Street, Digbeth, Birmingham B4 7XG.

Registrar of Births and Deaths for Bewdley sub-district p.62

[157] Directories as follows: Bentley's, 1840; Slater's, 1850; Billing's, 1855; and Kelly's for 1916, 1924, 1928, 1932 & 1940.

Chapter 7: [If only he could speak ...] then what a proud history he could tell! pp.63-67

The Assembly Room p.63

[158] KS, 11th April 1931.

[159] KS, 9th February 1935, p.8.

[160] KS, 2nd March 1946, p.8.

The Institute p.63

[161] e.g. in the Lecture Hall, 1890 and 1903; the large Class Room, 1892; the large Art Room, 1894; the Library, 1906 and 1913; and the Billiard Room, 1921, 1924 and 1926. *n.b.* the actual room was not always noted in the newspaper reports.

[162] KS, 12th March 1881.

[163] Ken Sollom's *Memories of a cox: a personal history of Bewdley Rowing Club 1929-1939* (Bewdley Printing Co., 1998, p.1) notes: 'Bewdley Rowing Club records its foundation in 1877, although there were competitions and organised rowing before this.'

[164] KS, 26th March 1896; 17th March 1906; 27th February 1909; 20th March 1915; 25th March 1916; 10th March 1917; 22nd March 1919; 20th March 1920; 19th March 1921; 23rd March 1924; 14th March 1925; 26th March 1927; 23rd March 1929; 22nd March 1930; and 1st May 1937.

[165] KS, 18th February 1922.

[166] KS, 15th March 1910; 17th January 1920 and 1st March 1924.

[167] KS, 22nd January 1921; 18th February 1922 and 18th March 1939.

[168] KS, 8th March 1919, p.7 & 4th March 1922, last p.

[169] There had been several severe winters during the previous decade or so, e.g.
- The KS, 17th January 1880 recorded that Captain Spencer had given money obtained from a small charge made for skating on the Spring Grove Pool 'during the recent frosty weather':-
- to Mr. Crane, *Treasurer* of the Wribbenhall Relief Coal Fund*, £7-8s-8d. (£7.43); and
- to the Treasurer of the Kidderminster Infirmary, almost £10.
- Also noted: '... hundreds of gallons of soup* have been distributed, about fifty tons of coal* have been doled out, and a large sum of money spent in the purchase of blankets and warm clothing...' by the Bewdley Board of Guardians.

- The KS, 29th January 1881 reported:
'SHEEP ROASTING ON THE SEVERN - For many days the Severn has been frozen for some distance above the bridge. A "Frost Fair" was held on Wednesday, and two sheep were roasted, one of which was cut up and distributed to the

poor. Many hundreds of persons were present, and many disgusting sights were witnessed.'

• Bewdley Parish Magazine May 1886 (p.49) noted: 'The weather this spring has been so unusual as to seem to deserve some record in our Magazine. With ten days' skating up to March 16th, a heavy fall of snow on April 10th, and the Cherry Orchard [today's Hales Park? or Ribbesford?] not in blossom for Easter, though Easter Day has fallen on the latest day possible (April 25th), we may fairly expect that it will be some time before we are again called upon to register such an exceptionally cold season.'

• Susanna Davis's book *Bewdley as it was* (Hendon Publishing Co., 1979, [p.25]) shows a picture of people skating on 'The River Severn frozen over during the winter of 1890-1891'.

* The *Church Monthly*, January 1891, reported that the Mayor proposed to re-open the Soup Kitchen and that of February 1892 recorded that the Wribbenhall Workmen's Club was 'grateful to those kind friends who have helped towards the Coal Fund and Soup Kitchen'.

[170] Members of a Junior branch of the C.E.T.S. (the *Band of Hope*) entertained a large and appreciative audience (venue not given) on 2nd June 1887 with a *Story with Song*, entitled 'For Harry's Sake'.

The *Church Monthly* of November 1892 reported: 'The Band of Hope continues to flourish, with an average weekly attendance of nearly 120.'

Appendix I: Some of the officers, committee members and members pp.69-83

Members of the Working Party & the Original Committee of Management p.69

[171] KS and KT, 25th December 1875.
[172] Conveyance, 12th October 1877.

Trustees p.69

[173] 1861 Census and KS, 11th March 1911, respectively.
[174] KS, 9th January 1937.
[175] The 1871 Census records Thomas C. Dalley as aged 16, Stationer's Assistant, born in Bewdley and living at 10-11 Load Street with his father (Thomas E. Dalley, aged 43, Printer employing 1 man and 2 apprentices), mother, 4 younger brothers and a nurse.

[176] KS, 28th March 1908, p.8.
Dr. Gabb was the senior magistrate in the Borough, a governor of Bewdley Grammar School and Chairman of the Bewdley Gas Company. A popular man, he was a skilled chess player and an acknowledged expert on geological subjects. One of his hobbies was poultry rearing, on which subject he gave 'many an interesting talk at Bewdley Institute and elsewhere'.

[177] KS, 3rd May 1930.
[178] KS, 2nd March 1895.
[179] James Parrott, aged 55, born in Leeds, was an Ironmonger, living at 58 Load Street with his wife (Hannah, aged 60) according to the 1881 Census. Wedley (Bewdley ..., p.30) describes James Parrott, a Methodist local preacher, as a modern-day Sherlock Holmes. He enjoyed drinking his dish of tea from 'the old-fashioned big bowls so rarely seen to-day.' As part of the band who led the singing in the Chapel before the advent of the harmonium there (in *c*1850*), Mr. Parrott 'tried his hand at the' cello, but being very deaf, relied upon someone else to tell him if he was in tune'! (*Source: Dernie, Sue: Inspired by Wesley - two centuries of Methodism in Bewdley. Published in conjunction with the Bicentenary of Bewdley Methodist Church, 1995).

[180] Joseph Tonks, Chemist, 55 Load Street in 1879 and 1884. (*Source*: Directories).
The 1881 Census records him as a chemist, aged 32, born in West Bromwich, Staffs., living with his wife, 2 daughters and a young domestic servant at 55 Load Street. Kelly's Directory, 1896 (p.60) says: 'The living of Dowles is a rectory, in the gift of the Earl of Portsmouth, and held since 1892 by the Rev. Joseph Tonks, of St. Aidan's, who resides at Park House, Bewdley.'

[181] Mr. Robert H. Whitcombe [snr.], Solicitor, was recorded in the 1891 Census as aged 69, born in Cleobury Mortimer and living at 70-71 Load Street with his wife, 3 daughters, son (Robert H. Whitcombe [jnr.], Solicitor, aged 31, born in Bewdley), a cook and a housemaid. (*see also* Refs. 36 & 188)

[182] *n.b.* At the 1912 A.G.M. elections took place for new *Trustees* to fill vacancies 'caused by the deaths of all but 5 and the incapacity of one of the original *Trustees* (sic) appointed in 1879'.

[183] *n.b.* the Annual Report for 1913 names these ten gentlemen as having been elected by a ballot, but

says their names were chosen from *30* nominees and implies that they were elected at some time after the 1912 Annual Meeting, whereas the report of the Annual Meeting in 1912 says that the election *took place at that Meeting* and that the 10 were elected from *20* names submitted. (reported in the KS, 23rd March 1913 and 16th March 1912, respectively).

[184] Was this Enoch A. Bawdon, recorded in the 1891 Census as a Butcher, aged 31, born in Weston-super-Mare, Somerset and living with his wife, daughter aged 8, sister-in-law and a domestic servant at 49 Load Street?

[185] Robert A. Harcombe, Draper's Assistant, was recorded in the 1891 Census as aged 18, born in Chippenham, Wilts. and living at 62 Load Street with his father, Robert R. Harcombe (Draper), mother, sister (a Draper's Assistant), one other Draper's Assistant, a Draper's Apprentice and a domestic servant.

[186] Brother of Robert A. Harcombe, William Harcombe was aged 14, a scholar, born in Chippenham, Wilts. and lived at 62 Load Street according to the 1881 Census.

[187] KT, 21st October 1916, p.4.

[188] KS, 16th March 1935, p.10. (*see also* Refs. 36 & 181)

[189] E. S. Barth, R. L. L. Hemingway, A. G. Humpherson, W. E. James, P. W. Palmer, J. Taylor, T. Wall and B. T. Webster (who was very ill in 1941 and died at some time between March 1942 and March 1943).

Presidents p.70

[190] Debrett's Illustrated Peerage, 1995, p.276.
[191] ibid.
[192] ibid.
[193] ibid.
[194] KS, 5th March 1954, p.10.

Vice-Presidents p.71

[195] KS, 14th March 1925, p.6.
[196] KS, 22nd January 1910, p.6.
[197] KS, 15th February 1908, p.5.
[198] *Who was who, 1897-1980.* Black, 1981.
[199] KS, 29th May 1915, p.5.
[200] Was there any connection with today's Frank Chapman Centre at Ribbesford, ([on the site of] the former Smethwick School Camp)?
[201] KS, 24th April 1897, p.8. Farmer Downing is described as 'Possessed of a knowledge of science, especially meteorology. Gentle, benevolent, unassuming.'

Mr. John Marshall Downing appears on the 1871 Census at Dowles Hill Farm, aged 44, single, a farmer of 160 acres who employed 30 men and 1 boy. He and his sister, Hannah Downing, Housekeeper, aged 39, had been born in Handsworth,* Staffordshire. They had a servant, Loisa (sic) Smith, aged 18, unmarried, born in Bewdley.

John Marshall Downing was recorded in Kelly's Shropshire Directories for 1879 and 1891 as 'farmer, churchwarden, waywarden, guardian & overseer, Dowles hill.'

*Did John Marshall Downing live in Handsworth at the same time as Joseph Tangye, and if so, then did they know each other before they came to live in Dowles and Bewdley, respectively? Interestingly, both were about the same age. (*see* Ref. 20)

[202] Bewdley Town Clerk. (*Source*: KS, 10th December 1932, p.6).
[203] KS, 6th March 1943.
[204] KS, 19th May 1888.
[205] *Church Monthly,* March 1893.
[206] KS, 25th February 1949, p.8.
[207] KS, 15th January 1910 and Tombstone, Quaker burial ground, Lower Park, Bewdley.
[208] Grazebrook, H. Sydney: The heraldry of Worcestershire. John Russell Smith, 1873, p.691.
[209] Talisbase catalogue at Kidderminster Library.
[210] KS, 12th February 1954, p.10.
[211] KT, 17th January 1948, p.5.
[212] KS, 19th November 1932, pp.7 & 10.
[213] KS, 20th March 1886.
[214] KT, 10th March 1950.
[215] KT, 22nd June 1912.
[216] KS, 3rd April 1959.
[217] KS, 22nd July 1916.
[218] KT, 22nd January 1916, p.10.
[219] Lewin: op. cit., pp.16-17.

Chairmen of Committee, Hon. Secretaries, Auditors & Librarians pp.72-74

[220] KS, 25th January & 1st February 1902.

Mr. Dudfield was recorded in the 1891 Census as an Ironmonger, aged 32, born in Spetchley and living at 58 Load Street with his wife, 2 daughters (aged 7 and 4) and a domestic servant.

[221] KS, 9th January 1915.

Dr. Thomas Pennington lived at Ivy Cottage, Wribbenhall between at least 1896 and 1912. (*Source*: Directories).

There had been a *Police-Constable* Thomas Pennington of Wribbenhall, but he died in March 1888. P.C. Pennington probably lived at Prospect Cottage, Wribbenhall from c1879 until at least 1884. (*Source*: Directories).

[222] The 1891 Census records William S. MacKay, carpet designer, aged 15, born in Kidderminster. He lived at 15 Load Street with his parents, Scottish born manager of a carpet factory, Mr. Daniel Mackay (aged 48), and Elizabeth (aged 44) and his sister Eleanor M. (scholar, aged 13) and brothers Daniel R. (assistant manager of carpet factory, 19), Edward F. (assistant to carpet merchant, 17) and 2 servants.
By 1897 Mr. Daniel Mackay lived at Lower Park House (*Source*: KS, 14th August 1897).

[223] Although the KS report of the 1923 Annual Meeting described Mr. T. D. Potter as a former *Secretary* of the Institute this was probably an error.

[224] Was this the Joseph Haydon (sic) listed in the 1891 Census as printer's compositor, aged 32, living with his wife, 4 young children, widowed mother-in-law (Jane Shepherd, baker) and a domestic servant at 42 Load Street?

Members, Friends and/or Subscribers p.74

[225] KS, 4th February 1911.
[226] *The story of the Parish Churches of Bewdley and Ribbesford,* [c1972], pp.21 & 22.
[227] KS, 9th January 1937.
[228] Was this Mr. H. M. Elliott, of Bewdley Bank, who was appointed manager of a new branch of the Birmingham & Midland Bank Ltd. in Sheffield? (*Source*: KS, 7th June 1890).
[229] Marshall, E: All Saints' Church, Wribbenhall, Centenary 1879-1979.
[230] Henry G. Harradine was aged 32 and lived with his wife and 2 small children at 65 Load Street at the time of the 1881 Census.
[231] Was this Frank Heydon, baker, 1 High Street? (*Source*: Kelly's Directory, 1916).
[232] *The story of the Parish Churches of Bewdley and Ribbesford,* [c1972], p.21.
[233] ibid., pp.20 & 21.
[234] Was this Mr. C. Jacquiss (sic), headteacher of the National School [Wribbenhall?] in 1925? (*Source*: KS, 28th March 1925, funeral of Mr. Alfred Longbottom).
[235] Was this Mr. Matthew Johnston, M.R.C.S., whose marriage was reported in the KS, 11th November 1893?

[236] KT, 17th March 1906, p.5.
[237] A Miss Lloyd Davis (sic), with others, revived a drowning man at Bewdley. (*Source*: KS, 11th November 1893, last p.)
[238] KT, 25th February 1933, p.9.
[239] ibid.
[240] *The story of the Parish Churches of Bewdley and Ribbesford,* [c1972], pp.20 & 21.
[241] ibid.
[242] KS, 28th September 1915, p.6.
[243] *The story of the Parish Churches of Bewdley and Ribbesford,* [c1972], pp.20 & 22.
[244] Hobson, Joan: in *Essays* ..., p.113.
[245] KS, 9th April 1932, p.7.
[246] It was probably this Mrs. Stairmand whose death was reported in the KS, 29th March 1924. Was she Mrs. Deborah Stairmand (aged 40, Boot and Shoe assistant) daughter of Mrs. Charlotte Jones (Boot and Shoe Manufacturer, aged 81 or 84) and wife of Henry Stairmand (Manager, Boot and Shoe Warehouse, aged 36), recorded at 59 Load Street in the 1891 Census?
[247] Tombstone, Quaker burial ground, Lower Park, Bewdley.
[248] A reporter in the KS, 25th November 1898, wrote: 'Dr. Webster was thrown from his horse while visiting his patients in November 1898. He was found unconscious near Park Farm. No bones were broken, but he was confined to his room for some time.'

Appendix II: Some of the examination results and free studentships, prizes and certificates gained by students at Bewdley Institute pp.84-91

[249] KS/KT, various dates.
[250] Were Thomas - and Mary (*see Technical Education, Bewdley,* October 1891 (p.36)) - related to *William* Wrather, 'gardener to Giles Shaw, Esq. of Winterdine' (sic) in 1896? (*Source*: Kelly's Directory).
[251] Was P. S. Colle(d)ge a relative of John Colledge, a retired dairy farmer of Patchetts Hill, Dowles, who had been Surveyor at Bewdley for several years and who built the quay wall on Severn Side North? (*Source*: KS, 12th March 1921, last p.)
[252] According to the 1891 Census, Emily was aged 5 and living at 45-46 Load Street with her father, William J. Channin (aged 31?), Messenger/Postman, mother, Mary A. Channin (30) and her two brothers (aged 9 & 8).